THE LAST RESORT

a Zimbabwe memoir

DOUGLAS ROGERS

"This vibrant, tragic and surprisingly funny book is the best account yet of ordinary life — for blacks and whites — under Mugabe's dictatorship."
New York Times

"So do we really need another memoir by a white Zimbabwean? The surprising answer is yes, if it's as good as Douglas Rogers' *The Last Resort*. A ripping yarn, for sure. But it is in the nuance Rogers brings to Zimbabwe that he truly excels. It moves beyond memoir to become a chronicle of a nation. There is black and white, yes, but much more in the shades and tones of their mix — and it is in exploring them that Rogers, too, finds his art." *Time Magazine*

"A gorgeous, open-hearted book. Rogers manages to do the vital work of taking race out of Zimbabwe's story and putting the heart and humanity back into it. A must read for anyone who really wants to understand the extraordinary decency of ordinary Zimbabweans." Alexandra Fuller, author of *Don't Let's Go to the Dogs Tonight*.

"Zimbabwe in vertiginous decline is the backdrop for Douglas Rogers's corrosively funny *The Last Resort: A Memoir of Zimbabwe* in which Rogers's parents, among the country's last remaining white farmers, attract everyone from prostitutes and diamond dealers to their backpacker lodge." *Vogue*

The Last Resort was first published by Harmony Books,
an imprint of The Crown Publishing Group, a
Division of Random House, Inc. in 2009

This edition published by Short Books in 2010
3A Exmouth House
Pine Street
EC1R 0JH

10 9 8 7 6 5 4 3

A CIP catalogue record for this book is available from the British Library.

ISBN 978-1-906021-91-7

Every effort has been made to obtain permission
for material in this book. If any errors have unwittingly occurred,
we will be happy to correct them in future editions.

For my parents

It is one of the strange discoveries a man makes that life,
however you lead it, contains moments of exhilaration;
there are always comparisons which can be made with
worse times: even in danger and misery the pendulum swings.
GRAHAM GREENE *The Power and the Glory*

CONTENTS

ONE
Phoning Home

I WAS EIGHT thousand kilometres away, drunk and happily unaware at a friend's birthday party in Berlin, when I learned that the first white farmer had been murdered. Someone had left a television on in the corner of the apartment. I knew, even with the sound off, that it was a news report on Zimbabwe.

There's something about rich, red earth the colour of blood that you can never wash away, no matter how far you've travelled, or how long you've been running. It was a Sunday afternoon, 16 April 2000.

For the previous month back in Zimbabwe the government of President Robert Mugabe had been threatening to take away land from the country's 4,500 white farmers. Gangs of armed men – said to be veterans of the liberation war that had ended white rule twenty years earlier – had begun invading white-owned land, assaulting black farmworkers, looting homes, burning tobacco barns and stoning dogs, pigs and cattle to death. Still, it was a shock to discover that a farmer had now been murdered. His name was David Stevens. He had been savagely beaten, and then shot in the face and back at point-blank range with a

13

shotgun, after a mob abducted him from his farm in the district of Macheke.

I had been out of Zimbabwe for seven years, travelling, writing, drinking away my late twenties and early thirties in the rootlessness of London, but I knew that Macheke was only an hour's drive from my parents' game farm and backpacker lodge in the eastern mountains of the country, and that they were in terrible danger. If they didn't leave fast, they would surely be murdered as well, and it would be a brutal, bloody, all-too-African end. They would die like this man Stevens.

I frantically dialled their number and waited for what seemed like hours to get a connection. My mother finally answered.

She sounded on edge, her voice high-pitched through the static.

'Hello, yes, who's this?'

'Mom, it's me, Douglas. Jesus, what's happening? Are you guys all right?'

'It's terrible,' she said.

I pictured her and my father barricaded in the house, a mob rattling their gates.

'What's happening? Mom, what's happening?'

'We've already lost four wickets.'

'Four what?'

'Four wickets, darling. Not going very well at all. It's ninety-one for four ...'

Christ. She and my father were watching a cricket match. I could hear the crackle of the commentary on the TV in the background. I wasn't sure whether to be relieved or horrified.

'Jeez, Ma. Not the cricket. The *farm*. Have you any idea what's going on? This guy has been murdered up the road from you. Are you sure you're okay?'

There was a long pause, as if I had sucked the air out of a balloon. I heard her take a drag of her cigarette. She would have a drink nearby. Bols brandy on the rocks. She'd switched from Gordon's gin years ago. Said it gave her headaches.

I could picture my father clearly now, too, down the passage-way, around the corner in the living room, feet up in his leather recliner. The remote would be in one hand, a mug of Coke in the other, and he would be cursing at the new batsman for playing a loose shot: 'Move your bloody feet! Get into line! Ag, hit the ball, for Chrissake!' Dappled late-afternoon sunlight would be streaming through the arches of the veranda, illuminating the purple crests of the mountains behind and setting on the wheat fields of the farms in the valley below.

Those farms could have been on fire for all my parents knew.

'Oh, that,' my mother finally said, her voice fading through the static. 'Yes, well, it doesn't look very good, does it? I guess we're just going to have to wait and see.'

Wait and see didn't seem a wise option to me.

I told her I thought it best they pack up fast and lie low, whether in Mutare, the closest town, in another valley over the mountain pass nineteen kilometres away, or, even better, across the border in Mozambique. Mozambique. It sounded absurd just suggesting it. Mozambique had been at war for most of my child-hood. People fled Mozambique for our side of the border. But like the seasons, in Africa the state of nations turns and occa-sionally comes full circle. Yes, Mozambique. Anywhere would be safer than Zimbabwe.

But my parents, I discovered on that phone call, were not go-ing anywhere.

'Darling,' my mother said, 'don't be ridiculous. We are Zim-babweans. This is *our* land.'

And then I heard steel in her voice, fury rise in her throat.

'*Over my dead body will they take this place. Over my dead body.*'

By the time I put down the phone my mother was asking me

how I was, and when I was going to come and visit again. She had the stoic, breezy air of someone who had lived through a lot and expected to live through this, too. She had seen worse.

'How are they?' my friend asked when I returned to the party.

'They're watching cricket,' I said. 'They have no idea what's going on.'

TWO

If We Build It, They Will Come

THE PLANE DROPPED out of a cloud and arrowed in on a black strip bordered by wilted maize fields. A midmorning glare rippled the wings and glinted off the few modest skyscrapers of Harare, the capital city. Exiting the aircraft, I was smacked square in the face by the bright fist of an African sun. My pasty skin, from another English winter, told me I was a foreigner in my own country. My travel document said the same thing. After nine years in London I had finally qualified for a British passport and put my useless Zimbabwean one – the old green mamba – back in my desk drawer. At last: no more interminable queues for visas in the second-rate consulates of the First World countries I really wanted to be visiting at that time – yet I couldn't help feeling a slight flush of embarrassment as I handed it to the immigration official. You lose something of yourself when you return to the country of your birth under the convenience of another.

The officer thumbed through it with exaggerated indifference.

'Occupation?'

I could have said *journalist*, the title I usually gave myself as a struggling freelance writer in London, and I was here on an assignment from a British newspaper to write about the upcoming presidential elections. But it wasn't a good time to be coming into Zimbabwe as a journalist. The Mugabe government was detaining reporters, expelling foreign correspondents, rejecting media visas. It had recently firebombed the offices of a local newspaper.

'Cocktail bar critic,' I said, repeating what I had written on the form.

It sounded ludicrous, but it wasn't even a lie. I had found a rewarding sideline over the past three years reviewing fashionable cocktail bars around the world for the website of an Irish whiskey company. I had a slick, laminated business card. I could even give him the Web address if he needed it. Besides, I was much more of a travel writer anyway, a leisure and lifestyle guy, not the fearless kind of foreign correspondent Zimbabwe clearly needed right now.

'You're not coming to write anything on our elections?' he inquired.

'No, *shamwari*, I'm a Zimbabwean. Just visiting my parents in Mutare.'

He looked me up and down, weighing my threat to national security. Then he laughed.

'Mutare. A beautiful town. Have a good holiday.'

Outside the terminal the familiar scent of diesel, wood smoke and ripe fruit floated on the hot, dusty air. Already the grimy chill of London, which I had left only twenty-four hours earlier, seemed a lifetime and a world away. I didn't have money for a hired car, so I woke a taxi driver I found asleep on the hood of his clapped-out Datsun 120Y and got him to drop me sixteen kilometres down the Harare–Mutare road, from where I would hitchhike the 290 kilometres to my parents' farm.

I loved hitching in Zimbabwe. I had thumbed all over the

country in my late teens and early twenties. It was always so safe and easy, as if the country's very geography, landlocked in southern Africa between the great currents of the Zambezi and Limpopo rivers and the towering Rift Valley mountains, had somehow preserved some of the old-fashioned manners and courtesies that you can no longer count on in Europe, America or the rest of Africa.

At least it used to be that way. It took me two hours now to get a ride. There were few cars. A fuel shortage had severed the country's transport arteries. The vehicles that did pass seemed to speed up when they saw me. Buses belched black fumes in my face. An old black man in a straw hat driving a rusted jalopy weighed down with a harvest of ripe tomatoes pulled over to explain why he wasn't *able* to give me a lift.

'It is dangerous for me to be seen with a white man in this area,' he said.

'Dangerous? Why's that, *sekuru*?'

'There are militia here. Sorry, young man, I cannot pick you.'

Butterflies danced in my stomach.

It was March 2002 and the elections were only four days away. Everyone was jittery.

I read the *Daily News*, one of the few independent newspapers left in the country. The front-page picture showed a black man whose back and buttocks had been whipped raw. 'Militia Attack Opposition Activists in Ruwa', read the headline. Ruwa lay sixteen kilometres ahead. The butterflies fluttered. The sky seemed to darken and rumble, as if acknowledging my anxiety. The land invasions had continued with a brutal efficiency in the two years since the murder of the first white farmer, David Stevens, and that frantic Berlin phone call I'd made home to my parents. Nine white farmers had been murdered now, and two thousand had fled their lands.

President Mugabe and his ruling Zimbabwe African National Union – Patriotic Front (ZANU-PF), in power since liberation from white rule in 1980 – maintained that the farm invasions were intended to return land to black peasants who had been dispossessed by whites in colonial times, as far back as the 1890s. Living in England, I had found it easy to believe that a violent race war had been launched in Zimbabwe against the last thirty thousand whites left in the country, a fraction of its thirteen million people. But it was apparent to many within Zimbabwe that the real reason for the violence had less to do with race than with the rapid rise of a popular new opposition political party, the Movement for Democratic Change (MDC), which for the first time in 22 years posed a serious threat to Mugabe's long rule.

The deaths and evictions of white farmers had made front-page news around the world, but hundreds of thousands of black farmworkers and their families were being beaten and driven off the land at the same time, accused of supporting the MDC, and across the country black activists of the opposition party were routinely tortured, disappeared, killed. A government militia – olive-uniformed youths, dubbed 'Green Bombers' after a poisonous fly – had joined the war veterans on drunken, drugged-up rampages through farms and townships. Now, two years after the start of the violence, a country that once had been known as the Breadbasket of Africa, able to feed itself and its neighbours, a model of tolerance and development, was turning to bush, its economy in free fall.

Eventually a white farmer in a diesel bakkie pulled over.

'Where you going?' he asked.

'Outside Mutare, a place called Drifters,' I told him.

'Drifters? The backpacker lodge that had the pizza night?'

I did a double take.

'Ja, the lodge with the pizzas. It's my parents' place. You know it?'

He laughed. 'Everyone knows it. We used to drink there all the time. Hop in.'

He was stocky, ruddy-faced, with a thick black moustache and skin tanned to the colour of stained oak. He made my doughy northern flesh look white as an albino's. As we drove he chain-smoked throat-searing toasted Madisons and ground the gears of his bakkie as if it was a tractor.

We headed east, away from the sun.

'Are your folks still on their place?' he asked with a hint of surprise.

'Ja, so far. It's not really agricultural land. Accommodation mostly, a tourism business, the backpacker lodge. They should be all right.'

He looked at me like I was deluded, touched by the sun.

'I wouldn't be so sure about that, my friend.'

After two hours, rolling blonde savanna gave way to tumbling hills of granite and grassy woodland, and in the distance a giant barrier of purple cloud-topped peaks rose like a tidal wave out of the geological jumble: Manicaland, the Eastern Highlands, the Mozambique frontier, the area I was born and raised in and which, when all was said and done, I had been in a hurry to leave.

The farmer dropped me at the bottom of my parents' drive, and I walked five hundred metres up the dirt track toward their house in the hills, the late-afternoon sun pressing through the leaves of sycamores and mango trees shading the road, bright-winged loeries and weaverbirds plucking at the ripe, low-hanging fruit. I was surprised to find the rusty gates to the house flung open to the world, but then when had my parents last locked their gates? Not since the liberation war twenty-two years earlier, when we'd lived – under siege, grenade shields on our windows and a loaded automatic rifle by the bed – on a grape farm in the northern part of the valley, and before that on a chicken farm farther east. 'If you lock things up, people will think you have something to steal,' my mother always said, and although I now thought this philosophy utterly foolish, I was impressed they still stuck to it, given the current situation. Tello, my father's springer spaniel, ran out to lick my legs, and I walked up moss-covered brick steps onto the high front lawn.

It wasn't one of the two farmhouses I had grown up in, and so it had none of the emotional pull a childhood home has on an adult. But it was easy to see why my parents had bought it a dozen years ago, soon after my father, a lawyer, retired and Helen, the youngest of my three sisters and the last of us four children, left home.

A rambling 1950s ranch house, it was flanked on its east and west sides by giant fig trees and a pair of ghostly baobabs – knobbly, stout-trunked trees more suited to arid lowlands, and strangely out of place among the lush explosion of dahlias, vlei lilies, roses and geraniums that made up my mother's garden. Its red corrugated-iron roof was common to many colonial Rhodesian farmhouses, while a handsome arched veranda was draped with twisted grapevines and fuchsia puffs of bougainvillea. Most spectacular of all was the view. From its high promontory you could watch the sun rise over Mozambique thirty-two kilometres to the east, see it set somewhere above the blue haze toward Harare in the west, and follow its arc in the day over the fields of rich and fertile farmland that carpeted the Mutare River valley below.

And what farmland! If Zimbabwe was the Breadbasket of Africa, then this valley was a bakery, a fruit bowl, a dairy and a butchery. Maize, the nation's staple crop, grew like a weed; ripe fields of wheat and barley stretched to the river bank; tobacco leaves the size of elephant ears spread to the foothills; and dairy and beef herds grew fat on the rich loamy pastures.

I paused for a moment and looked down on the panorama.

The Harare road I had just travelled snaked beyond the line of sycamores and acacias that marked the southern border of my parents' land. But beyond it, I instantly saw something was wrong, out of place. Instead of the usual luminous green fields, all I could make out was delinquent bush and a few listless crops on rough, unploughed ground. Dozens of mud huts had sprung up where maize and tobacco once grew, and wood smoke wafted out of the thatch, like kettles steaming on bush fires.

I knew then that the valley had been hit hard.

I dumped my bags by the Adirondack chairs on the veranda and padded into the house. For a moment I thought my parents were out on their ritual afternoon walk – past the residential cottages they had built at the back of the land and down to the backpacker lodge. But then I surprised my mother in the kitchen. She was stirring a stew pot on the Dover woodstove and looked up at me with an excited shriek.

'God, you gave me a fright!' she squealed, and ran over. 'Hello, my darling, it's so good to have you home.'

Then she added with a wry chuckle: 'Welcome to the front lines.'

My mother always laughed when she was anxious. It was her shield. Laughter and cigarettes protected her.

I noticed she was thinner than ever, slender as a fence pole, and I could feel the crenellated ridges of her spine as I held her close. But she was strong, too: sinewy, coiled. The deep lines on her tanned face told the story of thirty years spent on African farms, and yet she was still strikingly beautiful. She had grey eyes, an aristocratic nose, and an almost theatrically English accent. She had been an artist, actress and drama teacher before she was a farmer. Although she had been born in Mutare, our hometown over the hills, in 1941 and could trace her ancestry in Africa as far back as the 1820s, her elegant, stagey manner would not have been out of place in a Home Counties village or on a West End stage.

My father heard the commotion from his study and came bar-relling through with the force of a rhinoceros.

'Aha – so you made it, did you!' he bellowed, and we hugged awkwardly for a moment, uncertain of this show of affection.

A stocky, broad-shouldered man with enormous, rough, calloused hands, his grey hair had turned almost white in the three years since I had last seen him – was that age or stress? – but he still had a healthy thick mop, and his pale blue eyes were lively behind his wire-rimmed glasses. My father was sixty-six years old. He could have passed for fifty.

'We were expecting you at lunchtime,' said Mom. 'Put your bags away, have a shower, and we'll fix you a drink. We've got so much to catch up on.' Then she added with another flourish: 'My God, the stories we've got to tell you.'

I carried my bags through the living room, past the oak book-shelves, antique stinkwood chest and upright Carl Ecke piano now layered with a thin film of dust, and into the second spare bedroom on the east side of the house. The room had two nar-row beds, the same beds Helen and I had slept in as children, and after a cold shower I lay on one of them and stared up at the ceiling as a column of ants moved inexorably toward a hornets' nest in the corner.

I cleared my head.

They had bought the house and the land, 729 acres, in the winter of 1990, ten years after Zimbabwe's independence from Britain, not so much as a business – although my father was al-ways scheming up new ways to spin a buck, to make that elusive fortune – but to occupy the time on their hands now that he had retired and my three sisters and I had all left home.

I was in my second year at university in South Africa at the time, continuing a litany of disappointments to my father by giv-ing up playing cricket (or at least giving up playing it well; he'd once dreamed I would become an international) and by choosing to study what he considered the most unreliable of professions: journalism. 'Get your foot on the first rung of the corporate ladder, my boy,' he had told me, intending for me to pursue a business degree. I had switched courses as soon as he was out of sight.

Back in 1990 there was nothing on this land but bush, stone and the rambling farmhouse owned by an octogenarian Afrikaner and his born-again Bible-thumping wife. My parents signed the title deed in the dark living room one Sunday afternoon as the old Boer's scrawny herd of Afrikander cattle, bells tinkling around bony necks, chewed up the frosted remains of the front lawn, and his wife thumped on her Bible from a corner rocking chair in the gloom, warning my parents not of floods or drought or – and this might have been useful, I now realised – the next war that would one day come, but of a lack of television coverage.

'No reception at all,' the woman wailed. 'None. Can't get a bleddy thing out here.'

The old couple sold up for better TV, and my parents were glad to buy. But what to do with it? It was a farm, but it wasn't farmland. You couldn't grow crops or raise livestock on those rugged hills, as the old man's emaciated herd indicated.

'Backpackers,' Dad said to my mother as they tramped through the dense bush at the bottom of the property one summer afternoon in 1991.

'What?' Mom replied, incredulous, as a bus backfired like a machine gun on the main road.

'Backpackers!' he said excitedly. 'Tourism. Everyone's coming to Zimbabwe these days. We can turn this into a budget game lodge. Clear all this crappy bush, build a camp, some chalets, a restaurant and a bar. Bring in some antelope and zebra for foreign tourists to look at. You know they *love* that kind of thing.'

My mother's heart sank.

On one hand, he was right. Back in 1991 Zimbabwe's economy was starting to grow; tourism was booming, and although Robert Mugabe was already entrenched as an autocratic ruler of a one-party state, he was regarded, even in the West, as a model postcolonial African leader. The country was seen as a success story, a good place to invest in, and the currency was strong: one Zimbabwe dollar could buy you fifty US cents.

But my mother knew enough about my father's schemes and dreams to know that this sounded like more stress and hard work, and frankly, she wasn't up for it.

It had always been *his* idea to live on farms, even during the war.

She thought of chickens, the 1970s, our first farm in the valley, on a twelve-hectare plot overlooking Mozambique, from where Mugabe's Zimbabwe African National Liberation Army (ZANLA) insurgents would infiltrate to attack farms. She, the starry-eyed actress, the wannabe Liz Taylor, had been reduced to twisting the heads off poultry, an Uzi sub-machine gun over her shoulder, with four kids at her feet covered in blood and feathers and rooster shit, while he tended to his clients in town and his short game at Hillside Golf Club.

And she thought of grapes – or the wine farm, as they called it. But the wine they made turned out to be less like the fine Pinotage they drank on our annual holidays at my grandmother's island home in Knysna and more like a potent, lumpy red moonshine: wildly popular with black farmworkers in the valley, but against the law to sell to them without a licence. Which was the other humiliation: as a lawyer, my father specialised in obtaining liquor licences, mostly for hundreds of black clients who owned beer halls, bottle stores and bars in the townships and rural areas of the Manicaland district. For some reason he had failed to get a licence for himself.

And now tourism? *Christ, no!* She would put her foot down.

Wasn't this *new* property supposed to be the beginning of a leisurely, bucolic retirement? He could consult part-time as a lawyer and play golf; she would start painting again and play bridge. They would host dinner parties for their friends and, in between, travel the world, visiting their children, who for some unknown reason had not chosen to live a rural life in a remote corner of Africa.

But my father's mind was set. He had a stubborn lawyer's knack for never losing an argument, and the fierce pioneering streak of his own people. His mother, Gertruida Johanna Gauche, was an Afrikaner of Dutch and Huguenot descent whose ancestors arrived in the Cape in the mid– and late 1600s. He had *roots* here, blood in this soil.

He also had a way with words. 'If we build it, they will come,' he told her, a line she found rather convincing at first, until she discovered he'd stolen it from *Field of Dreams*, which he watched time and time again on the VCR.

Inevitably, backpackers it was, and within three years they had built it. They erected an electric game fence around the perimeter and stocked the land with those zebra and antelope: sable, kudu, impala, bushbuck, a dozen eland. They drew the design for the lodge on a napkin up at the house, and broke ground just back from the Harare road in 1992. A handsome two-storey timber-and-brick structure with a cathedral spire of a thatched roof, it had an open-plan restaurant and bar on the top floor and sweeping saligna wood decks out front and back. The front deck overlooked a ceiling of acacia trees and the lush farms in the valley below. On the ground floor were a kitchen, rows of bunk beds for backpackers and an art gallery; on newly planted lawns surrounding the lodge was a camp site and a dozen thatched chalets modelled on African huts, all set around a gleaming swimming pool that glowed luminous blue at night under the valley moon.

In a nod to the adventurous young travellers they hoped to attract, they named it Drifters, and after hiring a wizened old *n'anga* from a neighbouring farm to bless and protect the place, they opened in 1993.

And blow my mother down if they didn't come!

By the mid-1990s Drifters was attracting hikers, backpackers and overland travellers from South Africa, Australia, New Zealand, America and Europe, here for cheap food, cheap lodgings and game walks. Lonely Planet gave it a glowing two-hundred-word review, raving about the game trails and Friday-night pizza bake. Townies – residents of Mutare, among them many of my parents' friends – would regularly drive nineteen kilometres over the mountain pass for late nights of beer and brandy and pizza, and soon the tight-knit community of white farmers whose crops and livestock grew so well in the valley made it their watering hole, too. It was known for miles around as the best backpacker lodge and bar in the country.

At the back of the land, meanwhile, on the slopes of two rugged camel-humped hills and on a grassy vlei in the saddle between, my father built the second wing of his empire: sixteen simple two-bedroom brick cottages with sweeping valley views, which he planned to sell or rent out as holiday and retirement homes. Much to my mother's horror, he cashed in his entire pension to do so – a Z$40 000 fortune supposed to see them through rough times – and then sold the beautiful home in Knysna that he'd inherited in 1990. She panicked: *What will we live on if this fails?* But the gamble paid off. The cottages were soon all snapped up, so by 1999 my parents had not only an itinerant crowd of international tourists and white locals drinking at their lodge bar but also a permanent residential community on the land behind it. By the turn of the millennium business was booming. My parents had taken a barren range of hills in Africa with nothing on it but bush and stone and turned it into a thriving resort.

They had staked a claim on the land in Africa and were sitting pretty.

And now?

Now the backpackers were long gone. The restaurant-bar was deserted. The cottage residents were eyeing the exits. Except for dwindling savings in South Africa left over from the sale of the Knysna house, my parents' only source of income was drying up.

I woke with a start. Mom was calling me from the veranda.

I heard a hornet screech and looked up. The ants had reached the nest.

I had the distinct impression my parents were trying to hold back a tide.

'It's like holding tickets to an execution,' my mother said grimly, sipping her Bols, the ice tinkling in the glass. 'You're never sure who's next or when it's your turn, but you know it's going to happen – and soon.'

I had joined them on the garden chairs on the front lawn. It was dusk. The sun threw a brilliant blood-red veil over the bruised sky, and the wood fires in front of the mud huts in the valley below began to glow brighter as night fell, as though a constellation had crashed to earth. The view was one of the reasons they had fallen in love with the house.

The valley *had* been hit hard by the land invasions: the white commercial farms were being plucked off one by one. From their high vantage point in the hills my parents had a grandstand view of the chaos, spectators at the Colosseum.

'It's not exactly what we bargained for when we bought the bloody place,' my father grinned wryly, his feet up on the lawn table.

Out of 50 white farmers in their part of the valley, almost half had lost their homes now, and I was shocked to discover how close my parents had come to the violence.

'See that place down there, through the tree line?' Dad said, pointing to a run-down farmhouse across the road, a kilometre or so from where we sat.

I nodded.

'That was Frank Bekker's place. He was one of the first. He was a regular in the bar at Drifters. An interesting bloke. His grandfather was a bloody tracker for Cecil Rhodes when the first whites came here. Jeez, that got a bit nasty.'

My mother gritted her teeth and whistled softly.

'Nasty,' she echoed.

'What happened?'

'About thirty war vets moved in and started staking out plots in his vegetable fields,' my father explained. 'We could see it happening from up here, but there was nothing we could do. They call themselves 'war veterans' or 'settlers' or 'new farmers,' but really they're squatters, too young to have been in the war at all, just sent in by the government to cause shit.'

I flinched a little at the word *squatter*.

For eight years now I'd lived in a famous street of squats near the Oval Cricket Ground in South London, a tumbledown row of Victorian mansions built in the 1800s for the servants of Buckingham Palace and abandoned in the 1970s. The house was an embarrassment, right next to a scrapyard, but it was free, and paying no rent in London had given me freedom to become a travel writer, to visit all the exotic countries I'd dreamed of visiting as a child bored out of my mind on remote farms in Africa. For a second I wished I was back in London, and I wondered what Grace, my girlfriend, was doing. She hadn't been impressed by my squat. 'Hard to know where the house ends and the scrapyard begins,' she had said. *She should see Frank's place…*

Dad continued: 'Frank called the police, who did nothing, of course. In many cases the police escort war vets onto farms. One night he and his wife were attacked in their house. We didn't hear a thing from up here, but he was cut in the head with an axe. Somehow he fought them off. He speaks fluent Shona, and he heard the leader shout at the others: 'What's wrong with you – you can't kill one white person?' The police accused *him* of attempted murder at one point. He tried to keep farming, but in the end it got too dangerous and they left.'

I looked down at the house again. It was alarmingly close. You could practically throw a rock at it. A fire burned in the dusty front yard, and a dozen people, little dots from this vantage points, milled around. Were they war vets? New farmers? Settlers? Squatters? Could they see us up here? Somewhere in the giant fig tree an owl hooted.

'After that it just became a roll call,' Mom said. 'Now we go into town and hear about a friend losing their home in the same way we used to talk about a flick we'd seen at the Rainbow or a rugby match: "So the Bennetts were booted last week." "Did you hear about Truscott?" "Brian and Sheelagh James have lost their chicken farm."'

She paused, whistled again. 'Really, it's like waiting for an execution.'

'The Truscotts lost their farm?' I asked.

'Oh, ja,' said Dad. 'You won't believe what happened to them.'

The Truscotts were old friends of my parents' who'd farmed eight kilometres to the east. My father used to take me guinea fowl hunting on their estate as a boy, and their son Ivan, who ran it with his father, Rob, had been a school friend of mine.

'They lost it a few months after Rob finished paying off the fifteen-year loan he took to buy it. But get this. Just before he was finally booted he held an auction of all the farm equipment – tractors, pumps, irrigation pipes – just to try to salvage some money. Guess who turns up to bid? Simba Makoni, the bloody finance minister. Anyway, the same war vets who took the farm raid the auction and drive off with his equipment. Rob pleads with the minister to stop them, and Makoni just says to him: "Don't look at me. I'm Finance, not Law and Order."'

My mouth fell open.

'The finance minister? He sat and watched?'

'Of course. This is the kind of thing that happens here. That's our Alan Greenspan.'

My mother laughed again, her bewildered, defensive laugh.

'I did say welcome to the front lines.'

Not all farmers went quietly. A man named Blondie Bezuidenhout, whose farm was a few kilometres to the west, hit and killed a settler with his vehicle and was sentenced to fifteen years in prison. He escaped the death penalty by pleading that it had been an accident – he'd panicked after being set upon in his car by war veterans who were allocating themselves plots on his farm, and the victim had leapt in front of his car as he tried to escape. Blondie, the farmer, turned out to have a black common-law wife, and the dead settler – who wore a suit to the invasion – turned out to be a thirty-one-year-old CEO of a corporation. Was this really a Ku Klux Klan-style, premeditated murder of a landless peasant, as the state-owned media claimed, or a fatal accident in the wake of a violent land grab? Regardless, the war veterans went on a rampage through the valley after the killing. Yet somehow, despite the chaos around them, my parents were still on their land, untouched. They had received no eviction notice yet from the Ministry of Lands, Land Reform and Resettlement, and no visit from the war veterans or the youth militia. What they had received was a scribbled note from the settlers who now occupied Frank's place across the road.

'You must see this,' said Mom, and she trotted into the house and returned a minute later with a crumpled piece of paper torn from a school textbook.

Scrawled in pencil across the page were these words: *Open your gates, we come in peace.*

'When did you get this?'

'A couple months ago. They dropped it off with John Muranda. He's the old guy who now runs the bar down at the camp. I mean, we never lock our gates anyway, but I'm not sure old Frank Bekker thought that they came in peace.'

It was dark now. The moon had ducked behind the hills.

When the mosquitoes started up we moved inside for supper.

My mother had made oxtail stew, my favourite dish, and Dad opened a bottle of Pinotage. We sat at the antique yellowwood table in the dining room and talked late into the night. Or rather, they talked, I listened. They were letting go, a catharsis; they needed someone who would listen.

In the background the television was on, tuned to some international news channel, and occasionally it would broadcast a report on Zimbabwe. My parents would fall silent for a moment and listen to what was being said. Usually it would be accompanied by a speech from the president. You could see their faces drop when they heard what Mugabe had to say.

My parents seemed to be holding up well, though, and I knew the reason why. They had one thing to cling to, the reason I was here: the elections.

The poll was to take place over the two days of the coming weekend, and for the first time in any presidential election in Zimbabwe there was a tangible feeling that this actually might be the end of Robert Mugabe, that the people were going to vote him out.

It wasn't going to be easy. State-run newspapers and the national television station, ZTV, kept up a constant stream of vitriol aimed at whites and the opposition party, which it considered a puppet of Britain, Tony Blair and the West. 'We will not go back to being a colony,' Mugabe railed on the news. The state security minister, head of the notorious Central Intelligence Organisation (CIO), or secret police, warned there would be another war if the Movement for Democratic Change won. Meanwhile, Western election observers had all left the country, unable to move around freely since they had arrived. The only observers allowed in were friendly to the regime, mostly those from neighbouring African countries.

And yet despite the violence and intimidation, the MDC was campaigning strongly. The party was led by a fifty-year-old trade unionist named Morgan Tsvangirai, who was drawing huge crowds at rallies in Harare and elsewhere – bigger crowds than Mugabe. Across the country MDC supporters were bravely waving the MDC's open-hand salute.

I knew my parents were praying for an MDC win and would vote MDC, yet it was still a shock when, putting down his wine glass during dinner, my father calmly announced to me that he had become a member of the opposition. He pulled out a card from his pocket and tossed it to me across the table, like he was throwing down chips at a casino. It had his name on it and the letters MDC in block capitals.-

'You did what?' I spluttered.

'I joined the MDC.'

I was stunned. David Stevens had been an active MDC member, and look at what had happened to him. Many white farmers who had lost their land had funded the MDC. To me it seemed fine to support the party, but to join them? My father was making a target of himself and my mother.

'Jeez, Dad, are you sure that's wise?'

He didn't seem too bothered about their security. It was as if not losing the farm these two years had filled him with a sense of invulnerability and bravado.

'The way I see it, it's our last chance,' he said. 'If we don't get this government out, they're definitely going to come for this place. Then what? Either we die defending it or we leave. It's no time to be sitting on the fence. Anyway, on Saturday I have to drive around to some of the polling stations, check if our polling agents are okay. There are no proper observers here. It's up to us. Quite a lot of whites are getting involved. Come with me if you want.'

It still sounded too strange to me. This wasn't like joining the Labour Party in Britain, or becoming a Republican in the United States. This was Zimbabwe; politics was life and death. More than a hundred MDC members had been murdered in the past two years. But my father, at the age of sixty-six, had become a political volunteer.

We had argued a lot about politics these past twelve years. It was another thing that had come between us. Since going to university I had come to see my parents as typical white land-owners in Africa: businesspeople who worked hard, made money and paid taxes but, despite being Zimbabweans, lived a life apart, a privileged minority behind the high walls of their sprawling homes and sports clubs. Few whites ever got involved in politics in Zimbabwe. It was safer to stay out of it, and the government wanted it that way. Yet here was my father, risking his home, and possibly his life, in a campaign against the president.

And suddenly I felt something else. It was hard to place at first, but then I got it: a pang of envy. Wasn't I supposed to be the idealist? It was what had made me want to become a journalist. To be part of events. To make a difference. But it occurred to me now that I had never joined a political party or voted in an election in my life. I was a sojourner, a global traveller: at the age of thirty-four I had already lived in three countries – Zimbabwe, South Africa, the UK – and held two passports. I barely felt Zimbabwean anymore. Where did I belong?

I was envious, but I was nervous, too.

I wasn't sure I wanted to join my father driving around to polling stations on election weekend, meeting MDC agents, making a target of myself. But I could hardly tell him that.

'Ja, that sounds great.' I gulped. 'Of course I'll go with you.'

He grinned. 'Who knows – it might get *interesting*.'

I looked at my mother. She calmly sipped her wine, saying nothing.

'So, Ma, what do you think? Do you think Tsvangirai can win?'

She smiled at me.

'Do you really want to know what I think?' she said softly.

'Ja, tell me.'

And then she burst the bubble.

'*Never*. I'm sorry, but it's just not going to happen. Mark my words: the result of this election is already decided. And don't think this government doesn't know what we're up to. Whom we support. They have long memories. They know who did what in the war, and they know who is doing what now. They're watching us as we speak, and if we're not careful, they will come for us.'

I could see my father physically deflate as she spoke.

'Oh, come on, Rosalind, have a bit of faith here,' he snapped.

'Faith!' she spluttered. 'Faith? I can't believe how naive you're being! They have rigged this election already! Just watch. You'll see.'

And here were their personalities in perfect profile: he the romantic dreamer, she the rooted realist. One of them was in for a surprise.

Outside the owl kept up its maudlin call, and down in the valley shadows huddled around flickering wood fires.

I woke early the following morning, set up my laptop in Dad's study off the back patio, and made some phone calls – interviews for my article.

A momentous election was three days away, but life seemed to carry on as normal for my parents. In the afternoon my father went to play golf in town – he was a former club champion at Hillside and still shot off a six – and Mom hosted her weekly bridge four up at the house.

A more surreal scene you could not hope to see: down in the valley a land war was simmering, while up here four middle-aged white ladies sat around a table on a sun-kissed veranda bidding 'two no trump' over tea, coffee and chocolate cake served by Philip Pangara, my parents' elderly Mozambican housekeeper of five years, a magnificent giant of a man – nearly two metres tall when he stooped. As the afternoon wore on, the ladies broke out gin and brandy from the cabinet and got more reckless in their bids.

'So this is what it's like on the front lines, hey, Ma?' I chuckled, helping myself to a fat slice of cake.

'Darling, civilization would fall apart if we couldn't play bridge,' she said.

Later I took a walk down to the camp. Not so much for the exercise – I was never one for farm walks – but to get some sun on my skin and perhaps a beer in the bar.

The lodge was in a grassy clearing just back from the Harare road, but I took the long way round to get to it, walking past the sixteen cottages on the back of the farm, which were linked to the camp by a dirt road my dad and a dozen black workers had carved into the hillside ten years ago.

As far removed as I felt from this farm and my parents' lives, it was impossible not to be impressed by what they had built here. From the high point of the road I gazed down on the rooftops of the cottages, the lodge, the chalets. The electric game fence surged up the spine of one hill, along the ridge behind, and down the other side. A tenant watered a garden; another drove up and parked in a garage beside his cottage. It was incredibly quiet, the air crisp as cut glass, the only sound the low hum of the electric fence and the weaverbirds in the trees. Time seemed to have been suspended. I had the feeling everyone was waiting.

I reached the lodge as a dazzle of zebras trotted across the dirt road into thorny scrub by the game fence, and a lone kudu gazed up at me from the short grass near the swimming pool. Usually Drifters would be busy at this time of year: backpackers would be around the pool sipping beers, writing in diaries, lounging in front of the chalets or on the lawns of the tent site.

But it was quiet. Two cars with local plates were parked in the drive: travelling salesmen passing through, the only guests. A few lodge staff – a uniformed cleaning woman, two kitchen workers – sat at the cement picnic tables by the swimming pool with nothing to do.

I walked up the creaking pine steps, past the brick pizza oven my father had built in lieu of a trip to Florence he had promised my mother, and into the bar. It was empty, too, except for an old black man in a floppy blue hat and denim overalls stooped over an open cooler, counting beer stock behind the counter. I pulled up a stool and he turned round. He was about sixty, with an absurdly long face and a cartoonish mouth that seemed to droop way below his chin. He had yellow teeth and bloodshot eyes, and if I hadn't known better, I would have said he was stoned. I did know better. My parents ran a tight ship; they wouldn't tolerate drinking on the job by their black staff, let alone smoking *dagga*. My father hated the fact that my mother smoked *cigarettes*.

'Hello, Douglas,' the old man said drowsily, with a crooked grin.

I was taken aback that he knew my name. I didn't recall meeting him before. The voice was even more surprising. He spoke in a deep gurgled baritone that seemed to come less from his larynx than from his belly. He sounded like a saxophone.

'Hello, um ... er ... sorry, man, I've forgotten your name.'

He smiled droopily again.

'I am John. John Muranda. I was cooking for you pizza last time.'

Ah ... last time.

I hadn't exactly made a habit of coming out. I'd visited my parents four times in the twelve years since they'd moved here. But the last time had been at the millennium, a family reunion, two and a half years before. We'd had a dinner here the first Friday of the New Year – Friday was pizza night – and John must have made the pies. I recalled that night. The bar had been packed. We'd all gotten drunk, and Mom and Dad had danced to Neil Diamond's 'Cracklin' Rosie' between the tables. I remember thinking, *They look so happy.*

'Yes, John,' I lied. 'Good to see you again. So you are barman now?'

'Chef and barman,' he said. 'It is quiet these days. Little customers.'

My parents had employed a dozen staff at the camp in 2000. Now they had been forced to let half of them go. For some reason they'd kept this old man on, though. I ordered a Zambezi beer, which he poured with a priestlike sense of devotion, tilting the glass on a bar coaster and wiping away some spilled foam with a napkin. Then he lit a Madison and went back to work.

I looked around. The lodge smelled of straw and wood smoke. A dozen pine tables were dotted across the floor. A red-brick fireplace stood smack in the centre. In winter it was always lit, and the smoke had blackened part of the thatch and the ceiling beams. The windows looked out on the tops of acacia trees, but the reed curtains were down and it was gloomy inside.

The bar was handsomely stocked, though. Neat rows of Beefeater gin, Mainstay cane spirit, Bols brandy, and Johnnie Walker Red lined the shelves next to packets of Willards chips, cartons of Madison, Kingsgate and Everest cigarettes and boxes of Lion matches.

There was an old radio on the shelf, too, and I recognised it instantly. It was my father's Barlow-Wadley shortwave, the one we'd had on the chicken farm in the 1970s during the war. We'd never had a television growing up – one of the reasons my sisters and I hated living on farms – and that radio had been our only connection to the outside world. We'd listened to Wimbledon, the Olympic Games, Currie Cup rugby matches and news of trouble in faraway places – Berlin, Belfast, Beirut – but mostly news about us, our war. And suddenly I remembered it: the helicopters, forty of them flying low in formation through the valley directly in front of our house, coming from Mozambique, so low that I could see the helmeted pilots, the boots of the soldiers, the barrels of their machine guns. My father yelled at me: 'Douglas! Go get the radio! Hurry!' We tuned in to all the stations with their unique view of the conflict: 'Twelve hundred refugees massacred in air raid,' 'Twelve hundred guerrillas killed in Rhodesian attack,' 'Twelve hundred terrorists dead in Mozambique.' Terrorists, that was it – that was the one.

I thanked John, took the beer out to the front deck, and tried to call Grace on my cell.

A beautiful, straight-talking New Jersey girl, half Irish, half Armenian, we'd met at a party in London four months earlier. She had been a television news producer in Hong Kong and was now studying at the London School of Economics. My mother had been trying to get me to visit them these past two years – 'There are lots of stories out here, darling, lots of stories,' she would say enticingly – but it was Grace who'd finally persuaded me to come.

'I suppose I could write about the elections,' I said.

'Don't go because of that. Go for your parents. You should see them.'

'But it's so boring there,' I told her. Zimbabwe seemed like a regression to me. I had left it behind, moved on.

'No, it isn't. It's on the news every night.'

Now I was glad she'd made me come, and I wanted to describe the farm to her, the view from where I was sitting: the acacias, the kudu bull grazing on the grass by the swimming pool and looking up at me with sad eyes. The signal was poor, though, and I couldn't get through.

The kudu was soon joined by an eland, and I found myself thinking of my sisters. When my parents had first introduced animals to the property they'd named three of the eland does Stephanie, Sandra and Helen. Apparently, when they released them from the holding pens, the three young antelope had run helter-skelter straight for the hills. 'We'll probably never see them again,' Mom muttered sadly, 'just like the girls.' I wondered if this was one of them.

I finished my beer and went back into the bar.

John had been joined by another employee, who sat on a stool under the dartboard. He was about forty years old, not much more than four foot nine, with a perfectly shaved head, a long, glossy black beard, and a dazzling white-toothed smile. He had on orange overalls, which lit up his handsome face, and sandals made of car-tyre rubber. He looked like a prophet.

'Hello, Douglas,' he grinned at me, his teeth beaming like headlamps.

He knew my name, too? What was it with these guys?

'Hi. And you are ... ?'

'I am John, Douglas. John Agoneka. I am the tour guide here. I met you last time.'

'Yes, I remember,' I lied again. 'Another John. You are the two Johns?'

'Yes, we are the two Johns,' the younger one laughed. 'Sometimes your parents are calling me John Orange for my overalls. And Mr Muranda they are calling John Old.'

The older John muttered something in Shona under his breath from behind the counter. He seemed to take it as an insult. He was trying to tune in a station on the radio, but all he was getting was static. It was annoying the hell out of him. My father used to be the same way.

'Have you got any tourists to take on game walks?'

'Not right now, Douglas,' said John Orange. 'Actually, I can say the political climate in our country is not conducive to the tourism business at this point in time.'

He had a beautiful way of speaking. Words flowed like water. I now recalled my dad telling me about this John. He'd been hired as a gardener many years ago but spoke such good English that my dad had trained him to be the tour guide. 'He doesn't know an antelope from an elephant, but he speaks very well, and the fact that he's black means foreign tourists think he knows what he's talking about,' Dad had told me.

I chuckled as I remembered the story.

'Can I buy you a beer, John Orange?' I asked.

'I do not drink beer, Douglas. I am Apostolic.'

I should have known. The Apostolic Church had several charismatic sects in Zimbabwe, and their members – the men known for their shaved heads and long beards – didn't drink. More beer for everyone else.

'What about you, Mr Muranda?'

The old man grinned that dopey yellow grin and shook his head.

'If I am drinking, your mummy getting very cross,' he said.

'My mother's not around, John.'

He shook his head again. 'Very cross.'

After a while he found the station he was looking for and his face lit up, as did the other John's. They huddled round, listening intently through the static. They told me it was a talk radio station called SW Radio Africa, and it broadcast from London because its staff were not allowed to operate freely in Zimbabwe. I felt embarrassed. I lived in London, but I'd never heard of it. A phone-in show was on. Callers from Zimbabwe were telling listeners how the militia and war veterans were terrorising their villages. They spoke in whispers, terrified of being heard. The two Johns huddled closer. One caller wasn't afraid. He said he was a commercial farmer who had lost his land in the invasions. 'There is no way Mugabe can win this election,' he bellowed. 'I swear, if he does, I will run through the streets of Harare naked!' I was surprised. Not because of his threat to streak through the capital, but because he wasn't a white farmer but a black one. Black farmers who supported the opposition party were losing their lands, too.

I sat with them awhile longer, paid for my beers, and then walked back to the house, taking the narrow path through the bush on the eastern edge of the camp and over a wooden footbridge that spanned the creek that ran down the saddle of the hills.

I'd just reached the front gate when an enormous mechanical roar rolled in from the hills, scattering the crows from the tops of the baobabs and shaking the branches of the fig tree. I looked up and saw a helicopter, lithe and green as a snake, skimming low over the roof of the house and racing west down the valley, toward Harare, following the course of the road.

I ran up and saw Mom standing with Philip Pangara on the front lawn, their eyes wide as saucers, staring after it.

'Jeez, that was bloody low. Who the hell was that?'

Philip was grinning madly. He had a mouthful of yellow teeth that speared off dangerously in all directions when he smiled, which was most of the time.

'That was the president,' he said.

'Mugabe?'

'Mugabe,' he nodded. 'Today there was ZANU-PF rally in Mutare.'

My mother and I looked at each other nervously.

'I told you they were watching us,' she smiled. 'I just didn't know they were *that* close.'

THREE

Where Is Your Identity?

SATURDAY, THE FIRST day of the election, arrived with all the excitement of a big match.

The MDC's fear was that the election would be stolen, the ballot boxes stuffed with illegal votes at remote rural polling booths, if the MDC could not get their polling agents out to monitor them. MDC volunteers like my father – those with motorcars and cellphones – would drive around, checking in with polling agents and phoning in any signs of irregularities.

I drove to Mutare with Dad early that morning to attend a meeting where he would get instructions on the areas he was to check up on. The meeting was at a local sports club.

Mom stayed at the house. 'Good luck,' she said, waving to us from the back door, as if we were going on a fishing trip.

The police had set up roadblocks across the country to harass and intimidate opposition supporters, and the first checkpoint loomed five minutes after we left home, at the foot of Christmas Pass, the dramatic mountain road that traverses the northern barrier range before Mutare. There had been a roadblock here for as long as I could remember: four policemen usually manned it, a chatty, bored bunch, pestering drivers for licences or IDs, and occasionally dismantling the heaped luggage on the roof of a bus to check for smuggled contraband.

It had never held any threat for me before, but now it seemed to gleam with menace. I wanted to turn round and drive back to the house, where Mom would be pacing up and down the veranda, smoking. I wanted to be back in London with Grace. I didn't want to be here. But I wasn't driving. My father, grim-faced, pressed on until we fell into line behind a dozen cars. Soon it was our turn. A surly plainclothesman with a Kalashnikov over his shoulder – an officer from the Central Intelligence Organisation – came to my father's window and asked for his ID.

Dad gave it to him, staring straight ahead as he did so. I knew that once my father would have chatted amiably with this man, made small talk. Now he didn't look at him, greet him, acknowledge him, say a word to him. He stared straight ahead, silent, seething.

From the passenger seat I did my best to stay friendly. I had with me, under the seat, my notebook and a tape recorder, and I didn't want the police to search the car and find them. They would know I was a journalist.

'*Kanjani*, comrade,' I said. 'How are things? Today's a big day, my friend.'

My father gave me a withering look from the driver's seat.

The officer came to my side of the car now, holding his weapon in his hand like a club.

'*You*. Where is your identity?'

I no longer had a Zimbabwean ID. All I had was the British passport. I handed it to the officer and felt a hole burn in the back of my head: it seemed a betrayal of my father right then, right in front of him, to produce this foreign document, my ticket out of there. I had an escape route, a safe haven. What did he and my mother have? Local passports. They were stuck here.

The officer paged through the document with a lot more concern than the immigration official had shown at the airport a few days earlier. It suddenly occurred to me that it might not be any safer here on a British passport. The president often seemed to be campaigning more against Tony Blair and the British government than against Tsvangirai and the MDC. Mugabe was obsessed with the former colonial power; he believed the British were the power behind the MDC and white farmers. My heart pounded against my shirt. Was the officer going to ask me to step outside? Search the car?

Suddenly there was a commotion behind us. I looked in the rearview mirror.

A goat had escaped from the back of a truck a few cars away, and three male passengers had leapt out of the vehicle and were chasing it, shouting wildly, as it ran toward a stand of trees. They hauled it in while it was still in the long grass and carried it kicking and bleating back to the vehicle.

The officer, briefly distracted, returned my passport and waved us through.

We drove on in silence for a while, but I could tell my father was annoyed.

Then he turned to me and said: 'Douglas, why are you polite to these people? The police in this country are criminals. They stand by while these thugs beat people, burn down farms, run the country into the ground. If our place was invaded, they would never help us. They would stand by or join in. I refuse to be civil to them.'

I was taken aback.

'Come on, Dad, it's best not to annoy them, either. You need to stay out of trouble, keep your head down.' I was afraid he would end up in a Zimbabwean jail.

'What do you mean, stay out of trouble? We are in trouble! We're in deep shit here, and these are the fucking people who are causing it. I refuse to treat them with any civility.'

There was no point arguing with him. My father appeared to believe in his right to be there as much as the black man with the gun. For him it was inalienable, almost tangible. For me it was something to question.

Soon we crested the pass, and there it lay below us: Mutare, a blanket of tree-lined streets set in the green bed of a valley, with giant cloud-reaching peaks that towered behind. Perhaps the stress of the roadblock and my father's angry mood had heightened my senses, for I was surprised now by how the sight of my former hometown, the city where I was born in 1968, took my breath away, as if I was seeing it for the first time.

Mutare is easily the most beautiful city in Zimbabwe, although to call it a city – and it is the country's third largest – is not quite right, for it's more a state of mind: quiet, secluded, hidden in its valley. It is a place, my mother informed my father when they first moved here in 1961, 'for newlyweds and nearly deads.'

We motored down the pass, hugging the edge of the cliffs. A pair of hawks surfed the thermals above us. We drove past Chancellor, my old junior school, its lawns now overgrown, and turned onto the main street, Herbert Chitepo Road, where my father had had his legal practice for thirty years. The street unveiled its first pothole opposite the faded red umbrellas of the Dairy Den ice cream parlour. The central square, where once a year Luna Park and its Big Wheel would come to town, and to which Mom and Dad would drive my sisters and me for a night of roller-coaster rides and cotton candy, was now a shambling open-air market of makeshift canvas stalls. Mutare reminded me of my parents' house: still beautiful, but fraying at the edges, coated in a film of dust. Nearing the Mozambique customs post, we turned right.

'Remember this?' said Dad.

It was the Mutare Sports Club, the cricket ground where I

had played so many games up until my early twenties. I hadn't seen it in twelve years. I had been a good player back then. My dad had coached me from the age of five, and built me a cricket net on the grape farm, where I spent every school holiday hitting balls thrown at me for a dollar an hour by the teenage son of one of the farmworkers. When I finished boarding school in 1986, I played semi-professionally for two summers in England. One of those summers I flew over with a friend who was a good left-handed batsman and wicketkeeper, although, in truth, I considered myself much better than him. But what do I know? His name was Andy Flower, and by the end of the 1990s he was rated the best batsman in the world. It had got a little annoying on a recent travel writing assignment I did in India when, on telling the Indians I met that I came from Zimbabwe, all they could do was jump up and down and shout excitedly: 'Andy Flower! Andy Flower!'

We parked by the clubhouse. I remembered how nervous I used to be arriving here on the morning of a big game; I was nervous now for a different reason. There were about thirty MDC volunteers, several white farmers and some local businessmen, white and black. Dad got his instructions. I ran into the clubhouse before we left. I needed a whisky to calm my nerves, but the bar wasn't open yet. An old grey-haired white man, scarlet-faced, still drunk from the previous night's session, was already inside, waiting his turn at his stool. I vaguely recognised him from my cricket-playing days.

'Have you been sick?' he asked me.

'No, why?'

'I haven't seen you for a while.'

'I haven't been here for twelve years.'

'Oh. That must be it, then.'

We spent the morning driving around Sakubva, a black township my father had supplied most of the liquor licences to in his legal days, and where I once coached cricket at a local high school. And there we came across an incredible sight: outside a polling station was a queue of voters a kilometre long. Some of them must have been waiting in line since sunrise. The MDC had overwhelming support in urban areas like this, where a young, educated black population had watched jobs disappear and prices rise, yet it was still inspiring to see that despite the intimidation they were turning out to vote.

It was the same scene in Dangamvura, a township eight kilometres south. It reminded me instantly of South Africa in 1994. The only serious news reporting I have ever done was in South Africa, where I worked on a city newspaper and at a radio station in Johannesburg, and reported on the first democratic elections in 1994. Millions of black South Africans lined up to vote for the first time. This had a similar feeling, the same sense of pent-up euphoria, as if we were on the verge of something momentous.

I walked down a dusty road past the school and was summoned into an empty beer hall by the tavern owner, a burly black man who wanted to shake my hand and show me his bar.

'The Red,' he said excitedly under his breath, 'the Red.'

'What's the Red?'

'MDC,' he whispered, and then he showed me his membership card. Red is the MDC colour.

'Are you going to win?' I asked.

'Of course! Now is the time!'

He sounded as optimistic as my father.

In the afternoon we drove to a rural area back over the pass, not far from my parents' home. There were no queues here – there seemed to be a lot more polling stations – but all was quiet. We visited several of them, Dad bounding in confidently to ask the agents how things were going. They seemed confident, pleased. I made sure to stand back. I didn't want to be noticed.

At around 5 pm Dad drove me home; I needed to file my story for the *Sunday Times* in London. Dad was joining another white farmer to go and check on an area called the Honde Valley, up in the mountains much farther to the north.

He dropped me off and raced away, so determined to be doing his bit.

I found my mother calmly sipping tea on the lawn. 'Hello, my boy. How's it going?' she asked.

I couldn't contain my excitement. 'It's incredible. There are so many voters. It reminds me of South Africa in ninety-four.'

'Well, don't get too excited,' she counselled.

'Really, it's amazing how many people are turning out.'

'Why do you think the lines are so long?' she asked.

'Because so many people are voting.'

'No, darling. It's because the government has cut the number of polling stations in the cities.'

We had heard this would happen. The government was trying to stop the urban vote. But what difference would it make? There were two days to vote, and people were determined.

My mother shook her head.

'You are as naive as your father. In Harare the lines are much longer. They can wait for days and days – they will never let them vote.'

I turned on the television and saw that she was right. The queues in Harare were extraordinary, but the lines weren't moving. The opposition was literally being stopped from voting in the areas where they had overwhelming support.

'Just watch,' said my mother. 'They know exactly what they're doing.'

And slowly the mood changed. The government machine swung into action as my mother believed it would: methodical, ruthless and, in its way, quite brilliant.

My father called just before I filed my article. He was up in the Honde Valley. The police had arrested dozens of polling agents as well as two white farmer volunteers and their wives, one an American from Texas. A third farmer had been severely beaten and was in jail.

I made a call to a civic rights group. The man I spoke to was in a rage.

'They are arresting hundreds across the country! Hundreds of agents!'

I phoned a senior MDC official named Tendai Biti. Someone had given me his number but I knew little about him then, although later he would become a household name in the opposition, along with Morgan Tsvangirai.

'They are not allowing us to vote,' he shouted down the line. 'They are trying to steal this election.'

It was apparent by now that two days would not be enough for all the people in Harare still waiting to vote. The number of polling stations in the cities had been halved from previous elections, even though the urban population had virtually doubled since the farm invasions.

By 9 pm there was no more news from my father. Mom was getting nervous.

'I'm sure he's all right,' she said, smoking furiously.

Another hour passed. Mom and I drank brandy and smoked her Kingsgates.

Finally, just before midnight, his car lights appeared in the driveway and the familiar sound of his diesel engine came up the hill. I saw my mother exhale with relief.

He walked in, exhausted, his grey hair a mess. Now he did look his age, very much 66. He filled a mug with Coke and gulped it in one go while Mom made him a sandwich.

He said he had spent the past four hours at a police station trying to secure the release of the polling agents and the white farmers and their wives, but they were in jail for the night. Then he turned on the television to find out what had happened elsewhere. It was a big mistake. It appeared that every news station in the world was running a greatest-hits version of Mugabe's speeches.

Mugabe, 78 at that time, was a short, wiry man with outsized glasses that gave him an almost comic, froglike look. But he was an impressive orator, and when he spoke he waved a bony fist – the symbol of the ruling party – defiantly in the air, which induced paroxysms of joy in his legions of supporters. And it would be churlish to deny he had millions of them. Born in rural Zvimba, east of Harare (then Salisbury), in 1924, the son of a carpenter, he was educated at the elite black Roman Catholic mission school, Kutama, and trained as a schoolteacher before forging an interest in Marxism and nationalist politics at the University of Fort Hare in the 1950s. In 1963 he helped form the Zimbabwe African National Union (ZANU), and was the party's secretary general in 1964 when he was arrested by the Rhodesians for 'subversive speech.' He spent the next eleven years in jail. Studious, bookish, socially aloof, he attained three university degrees in prison. On his release in 1975 he crossed the border to Mozambique to join the liberation struggle, and by the end of the war in late 1979 he was the outright leader of ZANU, a hero to millions in Zimbabwe and across the continent. In his first two decades in power Mugabe did indeed do many great things, helping turn Zimbabwe into one of the most literate and productive nations in Africa. But now, three decades on, that legacy was crumbling and he was lashing out at those he claimed were to blame – chiefly Britain, whites and their 'puppets' in the MDC.

But it was when my father heard him say of white farmers, 'To them we say, they have become our enemies. Go back to Britain, go back to Blair,' that Dad exploded. One minute he was sitting in his leather recliner, shaking his head, muttering to himself. The next he was on his feet bellowing at the television.

'Fuck me! Listen to this. Just listen. *Go back to Britain?* I am not British! My people have been on this continent for three hundred and fifty years! I never set foot out of Africa until I was fifty years old. My own mother never left it once. My father only left twice – to fight fascists in Europe. Go back to Britain? My grandfather fought against the British in the fucking Boer War, for Christ's sake. Who the fuck does he think he is? I am not British. I am not British.'

I sat there, stunned. Not by the fact that my father was in a rage – I had seen this before – but by the words *three hundred and fifty years*. Three hundred and fifty years in Africa? It was true, and yet it sounded absurd. His ancestors – my ancestors – had arrived here in the time of Cromwell and William of Orange. They were here a century *before* America's War of Independence, longer than most Americans, including Grace's ancestors, had been in the United States. Were *they* ever told they weren't American? And yet here was my father having to defend his right to be Zimbabwean – to be an African.

Mom went over to him and tried to calm him down. She seemed strangely relaxed now, more relaxed than I had seen her since I arrived. It was odd how quickly their roles had reversed. She didn't say it to my father, but she had known: Mugabe was never going to give up power in this election, or any other one, come to that. She had been prepared for this disappointment and seen it coming; he had to deal with the fact that he didn't understand the country he was living in.

'It's only Saturday, darling, there's another day to go,' Mom tried to encourage him, as if his cricket team had to come from an innings behind, but I think he knew then. We all knew.

When the results were announced three days later I watched them from the safety of a London pub. One hundred MDC activists had been murdered in the buildup to the 2002 election;

fourteen hundred polling agents were arrested over the election weekend, held without charges and only released days after the results. With no one from the opposition at those stations, government agents were free to do with the ballots as they wished. The ruling party won in a tight contest, and every one of the invited observer teams, the South African delegation leading the way, lauded the process and announced it free and fair.

But all I could think of when I listened to the results was my parents on a range of hills overlooking a ravaged valley. My father was sixty-six years old. My mother was sixty-one.

It was time they started thinking about their future.

FOUR

Frogs and Spiders

IN JANUARY 2003 Grace moved to New York, and I followed her in the spring. She had taken a good look at my living conditions – the tumbledown dump next to the scrapyard – and decided it wasn't for her.

I came in on a media visa sponsored by my travel editor at the *Daily Telegraph* in London, a fellow Zimbabwean named Graham Boynton, who had spent years working on glossy magazines in Manhattan.

'New York?' he said. 'Watch out – it's much bigger than Mutare.'

Grace found us an apartment in Harlem, the only place we could afford two rooms. I wanted to replicate the large space I'd had in London, where I'd had a study overlooking a park.

From 141st and Broadway, above the bodegas and pineapple stands of Little Dominica, I now communicated with my parents via intermittent e-mails. My father had installed a secondhand computer in his office off the back patio. The e-mail worked when Zimbabwe's phone lines worked, which wasn't very often or for very long, but at least I could keep in touch.

My mother, although bewildered by 'this Internet thingy,' wrote occasionally, too. I learned that Tello, the dog, had died after being caught in a poacher's trap set on their land, the wire for the trap made from my parents' game fence by the settlers across the road.

So much for coming in peace.

'We're now finding zebra and antelope carcasses in the hills,' she wrote. 'It's awful. The fence we erected to keep the animals in is now being used to throttle them.' They would not be getting another dog, she wrote, 'because dog food has become too expensive.'

I couldn't imagine my parents without a dog. We'd always had dogs on the other farms: Flossy, a beautiful springer spaniel who would dig out cricket balls I hit into hedges; Sally, a gun-shy pointer with the spots of a Dalmatian. But most of all there was Ruff, a huge German shepherd with the mane and temperament of a lion. Ruff was almost handsome, but his right ear had flopped down after a vaccination one year, and it never went up again. It gave him a slightly docile look, but he was thoroughly vicious. Ruff snarled at everyone except my father. When my dad was away on compulsory Rhodesian Army call-ups during the war and we were home alone with Mom, the first thing he would ask when he called was, 'How's Ruff?' We had the grenade shields on the windows and Mom had the Uzi automatic by the big bed in case of an attack, but my father was convinced it was Ruff who really protected us.

I remembered when Ruff had died. It was at the grape farm, and Dad found his lifeless body by the back door, still facing the gate he'd always guarded. Ruff had snarled at most of the black workers on that farm, but when he died they went into mourning. Neighbouring farmworkers who had always navigated the stretch past our house in terror in case Ruff charged out, now came to offer my father condolences, as if one of us had died.

The workers who insisted on burying him laid him to rest like a chief beside the gate, piling a high mound of rocks on top of his grave 'to protect his spirit'. My mother said she had only ever seen my father cry once in his life, when his uncle Norman Melville died, but he had tears in his eyes that morning: grieving the loss of his dog, yet humbled by the respect black farmworkers had shown for him. He had assumed they hated Ruff.

I wondered who would guard the house now that Tello was gone.

Far worse than losing their last dog, though, was that they were also losing many of their friends (including their doctor), who were emigrating to the United Kingdom, New Zealand and Australia. And so it was happening again. You could mark the political convulsions in the country by its exoduses. In the early 1970s the white population of Rhodesia numbered 270 000 – five per cent of the total – but when the guerrilla war intensified, 50 000 left for South Africa. Then came 1980, when Mugabe won power in a shocking election landslide, ushering in majority rule. One hundred and fifty thousand whites would leave that decade – two thirds of the white population. I recall, as a twelve-year-old, the many drunken arguments and late-night fallings-out my parents had with friends who were going, unable to live under a black government, or what they assumed would be a Marxist one.

In truth, my parents briefly considered leaving themselves when Mugabe won that election, but a speech he made on national television – Dad had finally rented us a black-and-white set from Look and Listen – eased their nerves. They sat down to watch it, terrified of what he was going to say about us whites; they listened with a growing sense of astonishment.

'If yesterday I fought you as an enemy, today you have become a friend and an ally,' Mugabe said at one point. 'If yesterday you hated me, today you cannot avoid the love that binds you to me and me to you. Is it not folly, therefore, that in these circumstances anybody should seek to revive the wounds and grievances of the past? The wrongs of the past must now stand forgiven and forgotten.'

My parents looked at each other.

'He speaks rather well,' said Mom.

'Yes, he does, better than Smith,' said Dad.

Smith was Ian Smith, whose Unilateral Declaration of Independence (UDI) from Britain on 11 November 1965 – rather than accede to black majority rule – had ushered in the start of the violent, fifteen-year-long liberation war. My parents, part of a small coterie of liberal white Rhodesians, had always despised the man they called Smithy.

Weeks passed, then months. We waited for the backlash. Nothing happened. My parents shrugged and decided to stay.

'We're Zimbabweans now, better get used to it,' they finally told my sisters and me, and they meant it. Of the whites who remained in the country, many began to send their children to exclusive, predominantly white private schools. My parents kept us in state schools – 'I refuse to isolate you from reality in elite institutions,' my mother said – and in 1983 sent me to Prince Edward, a government boys' boarding school in Harare, which, by the time I graduated in 1986, was eighty per cent black. One day we were fighting a race war; the next we were sitting in classes sharing notes on Jane Austen with the sons of black men our fathers had fought against. 'You're no better or worse than any black person,' Mom told me when she packed me off to Prince Edward. Still, I suspected my father had really sent me there because they were good at cricket.

In 2002, my mother wasn't faulting anyone for leaving anymore. She put a brave face on it, though, playing up her stoic colonial image.

'The loss of Dr Walker I can handle,' she wrote, in that

blasé, offhand manner she had. 'But some of my ladies are going now, too, and soon I won't have a bridge four. Whatever is this country coming to?'

It was in June 2003 that I got the news I had been dreading. My father told me in an e-mail that they had just received their Section Five. He made it sound as if a Section Five was a special commendation, a prestigious award. It was in fact a government notice that arrived in an ominous brown envelope and read like something out of Orwell's *Nineteen Eighty-Four*: *You are hereby notified that it is intended to compulsorily acquire the land described above … for the purpose of resettlement.*

My parents had somehow survived the initial invasions, but here was confirmation that the government really did intend to take their farm.

I called them in a panic and got my father.

'Ag, well, ja,' he said, 'we got our letter.'

'And what now?'

He paused.

'Well, it looks like we're in the shit.'

I knew that this was the end of the line. You could appeal a Section Five (a Section Eight was the final marching order), but the state had now marked them out. It would be pointless to hold on much longer. For what? To be violently evicted? And so I decided to fly home to tell my parents it was time to leave. I even had a plan.

My younger sister, Helen, worked in London as a marketing manager for a property company, and she had recently bought a plot of land in Pemba, on the north coast of Mozambique, over the Internet. After years of civil war and Marxist misrule, Mozambique was now becoming an unlikely tourist destination, just as Zimbabwe was going in the opposite direction. My parents refused to leave their farm, but Helen and I reckoned that perhaps they would consider temporarily relocating across the border.

They could help build a house on her beachfront plot, run it as a guesthouse, just as they had Drifters, and wait to see if things turned around back home.

I thought the plan would have a pleasing symmetry to it.

My parents had honeymooned in Mozambique in its 1960s tourist heyday; Stephanie, my eldest sister, was convinced she had been conceived on Paradise Island in the Bazaruto Archipelago, nine hundred kilometres south of Pemba. But my mother also had roots in Mozambique, blood in its soil. Her maternal grandfather, Edgar Eggleston, the son of a railway clerk from Derbyshire, had moved to Mozambique in the early 1900s and became a stationmaster in Gondola, a no-horse town on the just-completed Beira Corridor railway that still links landlocked Zimbabwe to the Indian Ocean via Mozambique. My mother's mother, Evelyn Eggleston, likely would have been born in Mozambique had it not been for the fact that one Eggleston daughter had already died of malaria there, and another almost succumbed to blackwater fever contracted on its tsetse-fly-infested plains. Instead, Edgar sent his wife, Sarah, back to England to give birth to my maternal grandmother.

On second thought, perhaps there wasn't such a *pleasing* symmetry.

In September 2003 I flew back to Zimbabwe to tell my parents it was time to go. I had a mission this time, unlike my previous visit, when I'd felt out of my depth. *The Daily Telegraph* had assigned me to write about my parents, these *bittereinders*, the last of a dying breed. There were now fewer than a thousand white farmers left on their lands, and twelve had been murdered. The invasions had only intensified since the 2002 election.

I rented a car this time, and when I drove through their front gate at sunset and saw them standing there, waiting expectantly, as if for rescue, I knew instantly that they had aged a decade. My dad had lost so much weight that he wore his trousers halfway up his belly, tied tightly with an old leather belt. He seemed to have lost a few inches of height, too, as if it was not only his game fence that was being chopped away by the settlers but also his very stature.

He had grown a thick grey beard and was starting to resemble some of the rugged armed men in the sepia-tinted photograph of his Afrikaner grandfather's commando unit in the Second Boer War that he had hung in his study. Taken in 1902, two months before the end of that bloody conflict, the photograph shows my great-grandfather, the dashing Gerrit Gauche, in his veld hat and khaki uniform, rifle at his side and a bandolier of bullets across his chest, standing directly behind the white-bearded leader of the commandos, Jan Smuts, the legendary Boer general who later would become prime minister of South Africa.

I wondered aloud: Was the beard his own last stand, a sign of atavistic Boer resistance?

He looked at me like I was an idiot.

'No,' he said. 'There's a shortage of razor blades.'

My mother was so thin that I imagined a strong wind could blow her over. Her hair had greyed rapidly in the past eighteen months, and the lines on her face were now deep grooves.

Still, my parents seemed in good spirits. They had just returned from a boozy farewell party for another friend.

'Soon we'll be the only ones left,' Mom smiled, hugging me tightly, her eyes welling with tears, as they always did whenever I arrived or left home.

The shock of their appearance helped soften the blow when I saw the house. I had spent the night in Harare with my eldest sister, Stephanie, the only one of my siblings to still live in Zimbabwe, and she had warned me what to expect. 'Jeez, Doz, I swear, you could shoot a *National Geographic* documentary in there. They let in all the animals, hey. It's like an ark.'

The house had been nudging into genteel shabbiness eighteen months before, but now it was in full decline. Cobwebs had gathered in the corner of my room, and the ants still roamed the ceiling. Hornets had somehow made a nest of packed sand on the side of my mattress. The rest of the house was no better.

I dumped my bags and joined my parents in the living room for tea just in time to see an albino frog – pale white, with bulging eyes – hop directly into the middle of the living room floor from the veranda. I leapt out of my chair in fright.

'My God. Look at that thing. How can we get rid of it?'

'Oh, don't mind him,' Mom smiled. 'He's just passing through.'

The frog stared at me, unblinking, its translucence utterly out of place on the dark tan of the carpet. Then, sure enough, it hopped steadily on through to the back porch.

It was a good time to bring up the cobwebs.

'Ma, um, listen, shouldn't we remove the spiders in my room?'

She shrugged. 'Remove them yourself, my boy. And besides, why should we keep this place tidy when these bastards could take it away from us any day now?'

In the clear light of the following morning I could see why so many creatures had colonised the place. The land below the front lawn that ran down to the main road used to be cut clear. Now it had grown wild, a breeding ground for insects. You couldn't see Frank's house through the trees anymore.

'Dad, why don't you clear all the bush out by the road?' I said as we sat on the lawn chairs sipping coffee. 'That's why you're getting all these bugs and things flying around.'

I thought it helped make my case that a swarm of gnats, black as a cloud, hovered over my head as I spoke. The gnats didn't seem to go near my parents; they always targeted me.

'No,' he snapped. 'I *want* to grow it like this.'

'Why on earth would you want to be closed in by bush?'

'So that people can't see the house.'

'What do you mean?'

'Douglas, do you have any idea of what's happening here? These people drive down a road, spot a house they like, and just take it. That's how they do it. I don't want them to see us up here.'

It was clear by now that the war veterans and settlers had been used by the Mugabe regime. They were the shock troops, sent in to do the dirty work. They were never given title deeds to the land they occupied, and they never qualified for bank loans to get funding to farm; although the government gave them free seeds, fertiliser and even fuel, they would often sell this to pay for the bus fare to town, where they would buy food. It somewhat defeated the supposed point of the exercise.

Instead, the best farms were being picked off by the chefs: ministers, generals, brigadiers, senior party officials. Few chefs – the term comes from the Portuguese *Chefe*, 'chief' – actually farmed. They lived in the cities, but they used farmhouses as weekend retreats, like Soviet dachas, and often chose the best ones by simply driving around and picking whichever they liked the most. They became known as 'telephone farmers': they would phone in farm instructions from their houses in town.

'So it's like camouflage?' I said, suddenly intrigued.

'Exactly,' he grinned. 'We're in hiding.'

There was a perverse genius to it. The history of development in Africa is one of clearing bush. My father had to clear the bush to build Drifters. That was progress. But now he had come to the conclusion that to survive out here they had to do the exact opposite. They had to go back to bush, let the earth grow wild again, return it to its natural state so they could hide.

Of course they weren't off the radar to people who knew the area, and I was alarmed to hear that a few months earlier a senior official had driven around the farm. Not just any senior official, it turned out.

My parents were in the house one Sunday afternoon when a
black Jeep Cherokee turned off the main road into their driveway. They'd looked down at the vehicle, then at each other. Eight
of the twelve cottage occupants from 2002 had by now left the
country, but none of the remaining four had a shiny black Jeep
Cherokee. Who could afford such a car? A chef could. A Jeep
Cherokee was *exactly* the kind of car chefs drove, and a Sunday
afternoon was exactly the kind of time they arrived to claim a
farm.

'Shit,' said Dad. 'I don't like the look of this.'

My mother hummed to herself and bit her lip. Her heart was
pounding.

They ran into the kitchen and stood at a curtained window
from which they could get a view of their front gate. The car
pulled alongside the gate and idled, but no one got out. They
waited. It was quiet. They could hear a tap dripping.

'Can you see who it is?' whispered Mom.

'No, the windows are tinted,' Dad shot back.

They waited. The car waited. Then, menacing as a crocodile,
it slowly oozed its way into the back of the land. For a second
they were relieved, but then my father remembered something.
'Shit,' he said. 'He's going to see the dam!'

Since receiving their Section Five they had appealed the designation and had lands inspectors come to check the farm – not
once but three times. My father had protested that Drifters was
a tourist business, and hotels were supposed to be exempt from
resettlement. It was also on hilly ground, totally unsuitable for
agriculture, and there was no water to irrigate crops. The inspectors, to his relief, had agreed. But since then it had rained heavily and the low area where the dirt road crossed the creek in the
saddle of the hills had dammed up in the last few days.

Right then the property *did* have water.

'Oh, God,' said Mom. 'That's all we need.'

They waited, and after half an hour, when the car still hadn't emerged, they walked out to the back of the land. And there they saw something incredible. The day before, the saddle below the road had been full of water. Now it was empty. The water had drained away in twenty-four hours.

They looked at each other, bemused.

'That's weird. How did that happen?' said Mom.

My father shook his head.

'I have absolutely no idea,' he said.

But the danger wasn't over. The Jeep was still out there. They walked down to the lodge and found it parked outside Chalet 7. There was no sign of the driver. Dad walked up into the bar. And there, sitting at a stool, calmly sipping a Coke, was a short, plump black man in a smart blue suit and wire-rimmed glasses. Dad didn't recognise him.

Mr Muranda was behind the counter. He nodded at my father but said nothing.

'Hello. Can I help you?' Dad asked the visitor.

'No, thank you,' he said politely. 'I am just looking around.'

Just looking around... That was what Dad was worried about.

The man spoke English with an accent that sounded like he might have gone to Oxford.

'Sure you don't need a room for the night?' my father asked.

'No, thank you. Just looking.'

Dad gulped. There was an awkward silence. The man sat perfectly still, sipping his drink.

'Okay, then,' my father said eventually. 'Have a good night.'

He walked out. He had barely reached the bottom of the steps, though, when Muranda was suddenly at his side, calmly staring straight ahead and whispering under his breath: 'Sa, that is the minister, sa.'

66

'The minister?'

'*The* minister, sa.'

Dad's heart was racing. They kept walking, talking under their breath.

'You mean the Top Man, John?'

'Yes, sa, that is *the* minister. That is the Top Man.'

My father heard a deafening silence: the sound of the world collapsing around him.

Christ. The Top Man.

'Top Man' was the code name he and Mom had given to the most senior government minister in their area, a chef who was in charge not only of the Central Intelligence Organisation, the secret police, but also of the land reform programme. It was said by many that after the president, the Top Man was the most powerful man in the country. He had claimed several farms already, and he was ruthless.

'What's he doing here, John?'

'He was looking at the chalets, sa,' Muranda said, pronouncing the t on the word so it sounded like 'shallots.' 'He is not wanting a room at this time.'

'Okay, thank you, John. Let me know what he does and when he leaves, all right?'

'Yes, sa, goodnight sa.'

He joined Mom by the swimming pool and they walked in silence up to the house.

Now, they told me, they wondered whether the miracle of the empty dam had somehow saved them. It had been four months since the visit from the Top Man, and they hadn't seen him since.

But they weren't going to rely on miracles. I was shocked at dinner on my second night to discover they were taking steps for a return visit: they were locking the front gate at night for the first time, and locking the door to my father's study off the back patio, where he kept his computer. Plus they'd hauled out the shotgun, a vintage double-barrelled 12-bore, mothballed since the end of the bush war twenty-three years earlier. I saw it leaning against the dresser in their bedroom and recalled my mother's words: *Over my dead body will they take this place*. I realised it might come to that. They were prepared to go down fighting.

Next to his tools and Mizuno golf clubs, the shotgun was my father's favourite possession in the world. It was a vintage Hollis and Son side-by-side with beautiful engraving on its barrels. He had bought it from the estate of a deceased client in the early 1970s, and although it was a great hunting gun, it was hardly the best weapon to have in the circumstances.

That would have been the FN, the Belgian-made police-issue automatic we'd had on the other two farms during the war. Now *there* was a gun. Dad would ride shotgun with it as Mom drove us to school in the morning: Stof, Zaan, Hel and me in the back seat of the Chevrolet, eyes peeled in the bush for 'terrs', terrorists – ZANLA guerrillas – who would attack the farms. At night he would sleep with it next to the bed in case of an attack. Then, in the morning, Mom would unload it, check that the barrel was clear, and load it again while Dad was in the shower. Except, of course, for the time she unloaded it into the roof instead. A single shot, it made a noise like a sledgehammer, so loud the house shook and we all thought we were under attack. Somewhere outside, a peacock shrieked. Dad ran out of the shower naked, bellowing: 'Jesus Christ, Rosalind! What the fuck are you doing?'

He took the weapon from her as she stood there shaking in her pink lace nightgown. He picked up the spent cartridge, which had been discharged onto the parquet floor. We gathered round with our coffee, looking up at the small hole in the ceiling. 'Good shot, Ma!' said Stof when our ears had stopped ringing.

We went out onto the lawn to inspect the damage. About fifty tiles had been blown off the roof, and a whole section of it was twisted outward like a tin can. There were feathers everywhere. Debris from the roof had shaved the tail of one of Mom's prize green peacocks. The bird was all right, but it was sprinting around the lawn in circles, bewildered.

'Wow, really good shot, Ma!' said Zaan.

'Can we have the day off school?' squeaked Helen.

'No, you certainly cannot,' said Mom, who had composed herself by now.

They never let us have a day off from school. We had a war to win.

Of course, when the war ended, my parents had to turn over the FN to the police, as well as the smaller, lighter Uzi submachine gun Mom used to sport around the farm during the day. How could they have known, twenty-three years ago, they might need them one day for another war? Now the shotgun was the only weapon they had left, and it would have to do. It didn't make me feel any safer, though. Dad loaded it every evening and stood it against the dresser in their bedroom or behind the curtain close to their bed when they slept, but when a branch snapped in the bush outside one evening while we read in the living room, I flinched.

'See that, Rosalind?' Dad chuckled. 'City boy just got scared by a twig.'

Mom looked up from her weekly *Telegraph* crossword.

'Yes, I noticed,' she chuckled. 'He's been out of the country too long. He was complaining about a spiderweb in his room the other day, a tiny little spiderweb!'

And they laughed their heads off.

The house was in terrible condition – and I say that having lived in pretty basic places in my time – but Philip the housekeeper looked worse. He had been in such good spirits on my last visit. I remembered practising Portuguese phrases on him that I had learned on a travel-writing assignment in Brazil. Philip's eyes lit up when he heard his old language. Yet now, when I saw him, he had become a ghost. Gaunt and frail, he shuffled around looking like the burnt branch of a gum tree. Mostly he didn't come to work at all.

'Jesus, Philip, are you okay?' I asked when I first saw him.

He was sweeping the back patio, bent double, and had to lean against the freezer to rest. That toothy grin was long gone.

'Douglas, I have a malaria,' he said.

'Have you taken medicine?'

'I have Disprin,' he told me. I knew that was just aspirin.

'Philip, you need proper medicine.'

'I only have Disprin, Douglas.'

I ran to tell my mother, but she shook her head. He didn't have malaria, apparently.

'The staff down at the camp say he's been bewitched,' she said.

'Jesus, by whom?'

She rolled her eyes. I was always looking for the exotic in Africa.

'Of course he hasn't been bewitched. He has HIV. We've told the staff about AIDS, but they don't believe in it. If someone falls ill, people just say he's been bewitched. They say if someone gets ill, he's slept with someone's wife and the husband has put a curse on him.'

Zimbabwe had one of the highest HIV infection rates in the world at this time – two thousand people were dying of AIDS a week – and an entire industry had built up around it. Michael Russell, an old school friend I'd met up with briefly on my last visit, had gotten into making headstones.

'Used to be a good business,' he told me.

'Why *used* to be?'

'Because now everyone is bloody making them.'

A few days later, when Philip looked no better, my mother

gave me a wad of cash and told me to drive him to the Methodist mission clinic in the valley. Philip sat in the passenger seat of her battered truck on the way over, eyes closed, mumbling through his yellow teeth.

'I am dying, Douglas. ... I am dying.'

'No, Philip, you're fine. The clinic will give you proper medicine. You'll be okay.'

The clinic gave him more headache tablets. They told me to take him to the General Hospital in Mutare. I drove over the pass, passing the roadblock, where the four police officers were back in cheery mode again. I checked Philip in and returned home.

'The General Hospital?' my mother said when I told her, tears welling in her eyes. 'Shit. That's where they send people to die. Mark my words, he'll be dead in a week.'

Philip actually died two weeks later, soon after I returned to New York. John Muranda tracked down his family in the Burma Valley on the Mozambique border, and Dad drove out to hand them Philip's pension. Then he drove them to the Green Market in Mutare to purchase a coffin and to collect the body from the hospital. My parents didn't attend the funeral. Philip was the fifth member of their staff to die of AIDS, and they were getting used to it. It was just another thing that happened out there.

Down at the camp, meanwhile, things were desperate. Apart from the occasional lost-looking salesman who still checked in, there were no guests to cook for, and tourists had long since stopped coming to Zimbabwe.

There were only three staff left now: John Muranda; his wife, Naomi; and John Agoneka.

John Muranda looked after the bar and booked any surprise guests into the chalets, Naomi cleaned the rooms, and John Agoneka, without tourists to take on game walks, now tended the lawns and gardens of the property, a job my parents said he was hopeless at, though it suited their needs at the front of the land, where they wanted the bush to grow wild.

After dinner at the house, I started spending time down at the camp bar at night with the two Johns. I went partly because I was freaked out by all the bugs and spiders in the house. I wanted to get out. I would walk down through the Rhodes grass with my dad's flashlight, then run through the thicker bush, terrified I would step on a puff adder or python or bump into one of the poachers who came to lay traps on the land under cover of darkness. As a child I used to love it out in the bush at night. I had lost that. Now the bush scared me.

But I enjoyed being down at the lodge, chatting with the two Johns.

This time when I offered Muranda a beer he immediately said yes. My mother didn't come down here at night anymore, since there were no guests to check up on.

As with the big house, the past year hadn't been kind to the lodge. Cobwebs colonised the corners, and a cockroach stared at me from the top of a Gordon's gin bottle. The tables were scattered haphazardly across the floor, as if a hurricane had come through. The old radio was still there, but when I asked Muranda to find us a station he shook his head.

'Radio broken,' he said, 'just like business.'

I had hardly spoken to the two Johns on my previous visit, but now I got to know them around the deserted bar. We would prop up the counter while Naomi – Mrs John, we called her, an old, shy, birdlike Malawian woman who always wore a neat red headscarf – shuffled in, head down, with bowls of warm *sadza*, the country's staple maize dish. She cooked it on a wood fire outside their house, which was behind a fence just past the swimming pool.

Seeing my parents up at the house with a loaded gun had

reminded me of the war, and I wondered what the two Johns had done back then, and what their politics were now. Perhaps they were with the ruling party? Perhaps they wanted to claim my parents' place?

Muranda was born in 1942 and was kraal headman – like a subchief – in his village up in the Honde Valley, a mountain-ous area 128 kilometres to the north that nudges the Mozambique border. The Honde Valley had been one of the most dangerous parts of the country during the war, but John had left it in 1963 for Mazoe, a citrus-farming area north of Harare, in central Zim-babwe, to train as a cook. He got a job as a chef at a hotel called Rylands. And not just any chef.

'I am baker at Rylands Hotel,' he said in that deep, gurgled baritone as we sipped our beers. 'I baking best bread, Douglas. I win first prize at agricultural show. First prize.'

He met and married Naomi in Mazoe, and they had six children, two of whom had since died. He returned to work in the Mutare area in the 1980s and got a job at Drifters in 1998 as a cleaner. But John was ambitious. He didn't want to be a cleaner, he wanted to be a cook. The problem was, my parents already had enough chefs.

One day a British tourist checked into Drifters and ordered fish and chips.

'He want fish and chips, this British, but kitchen here not make fish and chips. But at Rylands Hotel I make the best fish and chips. So I tell this British, "I make you fish and chips."'

That afternoon he took his fishing rod across the road and caught a bream in the Mutare River. He brought it back and fried it in a pan at his house, along with some diced potatoes from the lodge kitchen. He presented it to the guest.

'This British say, "This is best fish and chips I am ever tast-ing." I tell him: "You tell madam this, that way she makes me chef."'

Muranda grinned from under the shade of his big blue floppy hat.

'Then I am becoming chef,' he said.

During the war Agoneka, twenty years younger than Muranda, had been a teenager in a village near Rusape, in the west of the valley, an area almost as dangerous as the Honde Valley.

I wasn't surprised when he told me he had been a *mujiba*. *Mujibas* were young collaborators, village boys, who passed information to ZANLA guerrillas about Rhodesian troop movements, transported weapons and committed small acts of sabotage on white farms: setting cattle loose, slashing maize. They were recruited and trained at pungwes – all-night political education rallies the guerrillas held in rural villages to educate people about the reasons for going to war, the history of colonial rule and the need to overthrow the whites.

One afternoon, in 1978, Agoneka's village was raided by Rhodesian soldiers.

'The helicopters came and my friend started running. But I had learned at *pungwes*, if the whites come, do not run. Stay in your home. But my friend was running. That time I saw he was killed.'

I lit one of Muranda's Madisons and felt the burn in my throat.

'Did you ever have to carry weapons, John?' I asked Agoneka after a while.

'Actually, Douglas, I think so, but I could not tell.'

'What do you mean, you could not tell?'

'Many times the guerrillas put a satchel on my back. A heavy satchel. My task was to transport it on a bus and take it to another location. They asked me, "Is it too heavy?" or "Is it fine?" and I say no or I say yes. But I never looked inside this satchel. I was too scared.'

'Maybe grenades or bullets,' I said, suddenly excited.

But Agoneka didn't seem to think it funny or exciting.

'At that time, Douglas, all I wanted was to return to school. I was fishing once with my friend in a river and I would say to him, 'When can this war be over so we can just go back to school?' I was fourteen years of age and all the schools were closed because of the war.'

Then Agoneka laughed.

'That was 1978. And in two years the war was over and we were back at school.'

I asked Agoneka what he thought of the land invasions, the resettlement programme, and he summed it up in his brilliantly wordy way.

'Actually, Douglas, I can say the government failed to ascertain whether these new farmers were of sufficient quality to produce high yields on such lands.'

When I asked Muranda the same question, though, he told me a story about his father during the war – not the liberation war, but the Second World War.

'He go to fight Hitler in second war. He fighting there in Egypt for British. Many African soldiers fighting Hitler for British. When he come back he get medal. Only medal. But when white soldier come back, he getting land.'

Four hundred thousand black Africans from Britain's colonies fought with heroism and distinction in Egypt, Burma and Malaya during the Second World War, a service largely forgotten today in Africa and Britain. Whites who fought in the same theatre were not given free land as John suggested, but they were given cheap land. Burma Valley south of Mutare, where Philip Pangara came from, was supposedly named because British expatriates who settled there had fought in Burma.

I wondered for a moment whether Muranda approved of the land invasions, saw it as redress for this historic wound. But he didn't think that, either.

'Me, I am not farmer,' he told me. 'I am cook. What I'm going to do with land?' He nodded vaguely in the direction of Frank's place. 'All that is growing there now is snakes.'

It was only later that I learned the two Johns were fervent MDC supporters and had been for years. It was one of the reasons my father kept them both on. He enjoyed speaking to them about politics, and it was why he had given them his old short-wave radio: so that they could tune in to SW Radio Africa, that pro-democracy station I had heard on my last visit that broadcast out of London. But they were MDC not out of obedience to him, a white man, as the government often tried to portray the strong support for the opposition party among Zimbabwe's six hundred thousand black farmworkers and their extended families. They were their own men, with their own minds, and a far more sophisticated reading of history and current events than anyone gave them credit for.

They would make their decisions accordingly.

During these nights I started to think of the few times I had grudgingly visited my parents, and I wondered why I hadn't ventured back more often. It wasn't so bad out here. I could have written about it. I was a travel writer, after all, and my parents ran a tourism business. But it had never interested me. And now? Now it was too late.

I remembered some of the characters I had met on those few trips. There was Mac the mercenary, a rugged former Rhodesian soldier with a thick white beard who carried a hunting knife in his crocodile-skin briefcase and kept a Magnum .45 under the front seat of the Land Rover he drove. During the war he'd been a Selous Scout, one of the elite Rhodesian troops who went on incursions deep into Mozambique to attack ZANLA base camps. Later, he fought as a mercenary in the Congo.

Eventually he'd given up on war and, just as many Vietnam

veterans are drawn back to Southeast Asia, he had moved to Mozambique, where he worked as a timber trader. He lived in a tree house he had built in a teak forest, and I visited him there once with an English girlfriend, Emma. We hitched across the border with a shopping order from Mac: a bottle of Bols brandy, a pack of ice cubes, a frozen chicken. He smoked the chicken on a wood fire, downed the brandy on the rocks and then let us fire his Magnum at a tree trunk. Emma, a published poet, said: 'I don't care what anyone says, this is fucking *cool*.' I'd felt safe in the bush with Mac.

When I asked my father what had happened to Mac, Dad said he'd died of a heart attack. Even the mercenaries couldn't survive.

Muranda would get drunk with me; Agoneka didn't drink and would usually fall asleep on the pine counter, exhausted. Between beers I started to page through the camp guest book, filled over the years with names and comments of hundreds of tourists from around the world. It now gathered dust on one of the tables, a document from a lost age.

I was surprised that I could mark my few visits by names in the book.

'Underarm darts; the best barman in the world,' Dave and Stan, two English travellers I had met on one trip back in 1994, had written. I was that barman. I remembered we'd gotten drunk and hurled darts at the board from the other side of the bar while dancing to a demo tape some friends of Dave's in Oxford had made.

'"We are young, we are free, keep our teeth nice and clean, see our friends, see the sights, feel all right,"' we sang as we threw darts.

'These guys are going to be big,' Dave reckoned.

A few months later I was buying a pair of trainers in Top Shop in London and a song came on the radio: 'We are young, we are free, keep our teeth nice and clean ...' The band was called Supergrass, and they were suddenly very big. Soon Dave, with whom I'd become good friends in London, was backstage at their concerts meeting supermodels.

Not all of the comments in the guest book were complimentary.

One Dutch tourist had written in disgust that he'd watched 'the white owner of the lodge' shout at one of his black employees and threaten to assault him. That sounded about right. My dad frequently bellowed at his staff for some minor misdemeanour in a way that reminded me of my upbringing. At least he had been honest enough not to delete the review.

As I read those words, in my mind I could hear that bellow all the way from the grape farm: '*Douglas!*' he would shout from his workshop. 'Douglas!' I was being summoned to help him lay drainage pipes, mend fence posts or fix the spark plugs on a tractor. But I would cower in the house. I was hopeless at farm work. My father could make a canoe out of a crocodile; I could just about paddle a canoe.

One night after Muranda and I closed up, I took the comments book up to the main house to go through it with my parents, and for a while I regretted it. They had no interest in a nostalgic trip down memory lane. 'We didn't run it as a business,' said Dad. 'We ran it as an extension of our home. It was like a living room. Hell, we had some fun nights. Who knows. One day it might come back.'

I doubted it.

Then my mother, a few brandies to the good, said: 'We never made much money from the place. But that wasn't the point. It made up for the gap left in our lives when all you children left home and never came back.'

She wasn't looking for sympathy, but her words twisted in my gut.

What would fill that gap now?

A night or two later, though, a strange thing happened. Mom started paging through the book, which I had left on the dining table, and came across some names she recognised – a Dutch couple from Utrecht. 'Look, Lyn,' she said, showing him the entry. 'Remember them?'

Dad's eyes lit up. 'Yes! My God! They were the two university lecturers who earned their travel money from their marijuana window box. Hey, give me that book.'

And suddenly they were off: The Swiss banker who bicycled all the way through Africa from Geneva and stayed with them for two months. The English family with nine children who took up six chalets. The travelling Irish fiddlers who paid for their stay with free concerts on pizza night. The hippie from San Francisco who barely said a word for three weeks and then set fire to his tent when a money transfer he was waiting for never come through. Emma Sadler, an English girl from Southampton who helped run Drifters for two years, became a surrogate daughter to them, and broke the heart of every white farmer in the valley when she left to study fruit bats in Papua New Guinea.

I watched my parents reminisce and wondered again: *Why* hadn't I come out more often?

Strangely, though, while things around them were falling apart, my parents had an incredible ability to laugh at the absurdity of their situation.

We took a shopping trip into town one morning, and Dad took his bakkie to be serviced at a garage in the industrial estates. He was always looking for cheap deals, and he told me a mechanic he knew named Gavin le Grange had agreed to do all his vehicle repairs for free.

'How come?'

'Well, you see, Gavin's divorced and there are no eligible

women left in this town. They've all buggered off. He doesn't know about computers, but I have the Internet, so I've agreed to look for a mail-order bride for him if he fixes my car.'

'Heh-heh – excellent. Found anyone yet?'

There was a piece of paper on the front seat. He showed it to me. It was a page of Russian brides.

'Well, I'm giving him this. The thing is, I'm worried that if I *do* find him someone, he's going to bugger off out of the country and that'll be the end of my free garage service.'

I could see why that would be a problem.

When we got to the garage Gavin was looking morose, sitting in his office. He had apparently just returned from South Africa to vet some candidates at a dating service.

'Who's the lucky girl?' Dad muttered, worried his friend was about to leave town.

'No, Lyn, it's not going to work. I couldn't bring a nice South African girl here. What do I have to offer them? Everything's much better down there.'

'What, so the intention is to bring someone to live with you *here*?'

'Ja, well, that's the idea.'

Dad's eyes lit up. 'In that case, Gavin, take a look at these Russian brides.'

I had the feeling his free service was safe for a while longer.

While their house had so far been safe from the thieves and bandits who roamed the area, the empty cottages were routinely burgled, entire living room suites and fridges dragged away through the bush at night. They suspected the settlers across the road.

Mom told me of the time she'd phoned the police about one robbery. 'I called them up, and the officer in charge barely stirred. 'Madam,' he said, 'I have no car. Can you come pick me up?' Then a few days later I found a stray goat in the garden down at the camp. It must have belonged to one of the bloody settlers. Anyway, I called the same station, spoke to the same policeman to tell him someone's goat was missing. I swear, he drove around here in minutes. Of course I refused to hand over the goat. He obviously wanted to *eat* it.'

That was their life: one minute Orwellian nightmare, the next Evelyn Waugh farce.

One afternoon, though, when Dad was back in town visiting Miss Moneypenny – the name he'd given to his black-market money dealer, who got him the best rate for those dwindling South African rands he had (it was foreign money and exchange that was keeping them alive), my mother told me something that made me realise how bad things really were.

We were smoking her Kingsgates on the lawn chairs between sips of wine, gazing down on the valley. The main road below was empty, quiet, the only sound the hum of the wind in the grass. We joked about which of the settlers, whose huts we could see over on Frank's place, would one day move into my bedroom. Then tears started rolling down her face.

I hated it when my mother cried.

Thin and frail as she looked, her appearance was deceptive. She was still strong, and I knew that she was as proud and fiercely determined to stay on the land as my father, so when her grey eyes welled with tears I felt a sudden helplessness, as much for myself as for her. Typically, though, she wasn't concerned about herself.

'I'm really worried about your dad,' she said.

'What, Ma? Tell me.'

'He doesn't show it to you – he's so happy when you're around – but when you're not here, he gets in these terrible moods. I'm scared he's going to do something stupid.'

'Like what?' I asked, though I thought I knew what she meant.

They had told me about the night they'd been woken by screaming from one of the cottages: a burglar had attacked Chris Anthony, an English tenant of my parents', with a crowbar. Dad had run over to Chris's cottage with the shotgun and saved him by blasting the weapon in the air, and then firing again as the burglar fled. 'Did you shoot to chase him away?' I had asked my dad. 'No,' he'd told me. 'I shot at him as he ran. I was pissed off that I missed.'

'Do you really think he might kill someone?' I asked my mother now.

'He might,' she said, grim-faced, taking a long sip of wine. 'But I reckon I would shoot anyone who came for this place, too. No, I'm more worried that he's going to shoot *himself*.'

I heard her words in slow motion, disbelieving them. 'Jeez, Mom. C'mon. Don't joke about something like that.'

'I'm not joking,' she said. 'He goes up into the hills behind the house some nights and sits there on a rock with the gun. I followed him once. He just sat there for hours in the moonlight. He's so furious about what's happening. I swear, if things don't get better he might do it.'

I imagine we were both thinking the same thing: my dad's family had a history of suicide. It was a poorly kept secret that his father, my grandfather, Roland Kitchener Rogers, 83 years old, half blind, sick with diabetes and barely able to walk, had shot himself in the head in the garden of the Knysna house in January 1983. We had spent a wonderful Christmas there and had just arrived home after a two-day drive when we got the news, Gran frantically calling from Knysna.

I was fourteen at the time, and all my parents told us was that Grandpa had died. But Stephanie, who'd stayed in South Africa after that holiday to begin a year at university in Cape Town, had heard the shot and seen Gran cover Gramps's lifeless body with a white sheet. He had apparently filed down the bullet from his

Second World War-issue revolver, wrapped a newspaper around his head and lain down in the front garden to do it. Gran said later that he had bathed himself that morning for the first time in years. He had dressed himself, too, and when she asked him where he was going, he'd replied simply: 'I'm going to kill myself.' She'd thought he was joking, but he walked perfectly upright and without a cane for the first time in ages, and made his way to the garden to do it. She heard the shot a minute later.

My grandfather was born in 1900, at the height of the Second Boer War. He lied about his age to fight in the trenches in the First World War, and fought in Egypt and Italy in the Second World War. He was mayor of his hometown, Kuruman, in the hot, dusty Northern Cape, before moving to Knysna for the clean sea air in 1960, when his eldest son, Donald, the first of two sons to die before he did, fell ill with mesothelioma, asbestos cancer. In the end my grandfather killed himself.

Would my father do the same?

What signs would I have to look for? And what would my mother do if he committed suicide?

Blam!

I was woken by a shotgun blast. Crows squawked in the baobab tree.

What time was it?

Blam!

Another shot. I leapt out of bed and ran to the kitchen.

My mother was in her nightgown, stirring a pot. She didn't seem too bothered.

'Where's Dad?' I asked frantically.

In the distance I could hear howling.

'Not this time,' she said. 'He's shooting at the poachers' dogs.'

'The poachers' dogs?'

'Yes the poachers come in from across the road with their bloody mongrels to hunt down a zebra or an antelope. The dogs catch the animal and the poachers start hacking at it with pangas and sticks. It's happening a lot, but your dad has caught on and he's chasing after them, shooting at their dogs.'

Apparently my father was in the habit of using his gun now. Often he would shoot at the crows in the trees, or the baboons on the back of the land. He didn't need to kill crows or baboons, but he did need people to know that he had a gun. He wanted word to get around that the old white man at Drifters was armed.

My mother made me swear not to mention to my father any of her fears about his shooting himself, and I promised her I would not. But after hearing those gunshots I took it as my cue to tell them about Helen's plot on the far north coast of Mozambique.

At dinner that night I told them how they could go live on the plot and help build a house there, and if things ever got better back home, they could always return. I felt terrible telling them this, as if I was passing a vote of no-confidence on their lives, on their ability to survive out here much longer, but to be honest, their world was collapsing anyway.

My father weighed my words. My mother did the same. But, in the end, they did as I expected.

'We're not stupid,' said Dad. 'We're not going to kill ourselves over a piece of land. But neither are we going to give up. This is our land, and we'll fight to fucking keep it.'

Mom sipped her brandy and gritted her teeth.

'Over my dead body,' was all she said.

There used to be a joke whites told in postcolonial Africa. *When the Jews leave, it's time to go. When the Portuguese leave, it's too late.* My sisters and I had been with the Jews on this one, and most of the Portuguese were already long gone from Zimbabwe. But my parents were like rabbits in the headlights.

From London, Helen called them 'the last of the white Mohicans'. Sandra, a fashion designer in Johannesburg who hated farm life more than any of the rest of us did, always said their life was a long episode of *Little House on the Prairie*; now she reckoned it was a movie being directed by Sam Peckinpah. Back in Harare, Stephanie tried to remain diplomatic. After all, she was still in Zimbabwe. What could she say? But we were all in agreement that my father had made a huge mistake selling Gran's house on Leisure Isle in Knysna. Leisure Isle was now some of the most valuable real estate in the world. If he had kept hold of that house, they could be living there now.

When I said goodbye to my parents in the last week of September 2003, I wasn't sure I would see them at Drifters again. I wasn't sure I would even see them alive again. I hugged my father awkwardly for a moment before pulling away. But Mom held me tight for well over a minute, and I felt such strength in her fragile frame, her racing heart pounding through her bird-cage chest, as she tried desperately not to cry.

Once at the bottom of the drive I looked in the rear-view mirror. Mom had already run back into the house, but my father was standing there watching me go, dead still except for his right hand rubbing the back of his head, messing up the thinning mop of grey hair, as he always did when he was deep in thought.

And an image came to me. I saw an old man lying down in a garden with a newspaper wrapped around his head. I saw another old man sitting on a rock under moonlight with a gun pointed at his head. The men were one and the same. The image would not leave me.

FIVE
Prostitutes Demand Payment in Diesel

IN 2004 GRACE and I got engaged and moved from Harlem to a brownstone garden apartment in Carroll Gardens, Brooklyn, trading bodegas and merengue music for prams and vintage Italian bakeries. After nine years in a dingy squat in London and a year in a tenement in Harlem, I felt I was finally joining the middle class. My parents would have been pleased. Sadly, they were hurtling in the opposite direction.

I dreaded the phone call I was certain would come: *They've lost the farm... They've gone down in a hail of bullets and buckshot defending the farm... Dad has shot himself in the head with the 12-bore.*

The Mugabe regime was now so oppressive that the US Secretary of State, Colin Powell, regularly denounced it. The *New York Times* ran frequent articles on Zimbabwe's economic collapse. European Union countries and the United States imposed a travel ban on the top members of the regime, although the president was still welcomed at the United Nations. Just before I moved to New York an African-American Brooklyn council member named Charles Barron hosted a gala reception for Mugabe at City Hall, where he was given a standing ovation for his struggle on behalf of oppressed Zimbabweans against Western imperialism. It wasn't the first such occasion – or the last. At the UN World Conference Against Racism in Durban in 2001, hundreds of delegates and journalists – *journalists* – leapt to their feet to applaud Mugabe. Years later, when Zimbabwe was experiencing mass famine, Mugabe would be fêted at a UN conference on global hunger in Rome.

When I mentioned to Americans I met that I was from Zimbabwe and that my parents still lived there, they were flabbergasted. I, in turn, was surprised by how much Americans knew about Zimbabwe. Once, on a travel-writing assignment in Nashville, I was speaking to a country singer in a ten-gallon hat and steel-tipped boots who was drinking in Tootsie's, the famous downtown honky-tonk.

'Your folks live in Zimbabwe? They not farmers, are they?'

'Yes, they live on a farm.'

'That ain't safe.'

'They sleep with a shotgun by the bed.'

'Hell, yeah, I would, too.'

Late-night phone calls made me nervous. And yet my father didn't seem suicidal. Indeed, the e-mails I was receiving began to take on an almost jaunty tone. He would send me quotes from President Mugabe's latest speeches: 'Western nations are meddling in Zimbabwean affairs. What do they want here? Do they want to take away our wives?'

'You got to hand it to him,' Dad would say. 'He's quite the statesman.'

When Zimbabwe was mentioned by George Bush or Colin Powell in a speech, my father would cheer up markedly. 'Does that mean we're part of the axis of evil?' he wrote. 'Any chance of an intervention?'

I even felt a sharp surge of envy – if not sheer panic – when my father informed me that he'd bought a brand-new computer (I wasn't sure how he could afford it) and was now writing a book about his experiences. Wasn't I supposed to be the writer? What if he published a book before me?

By 2005, though, not only were my parents still on their land, but my father had still not got around to shooting himself in the head.

Grace and I would be getting married on 30 April 2005. We booked the Church of the Guardian Angel on the corner of Tenth Avenue and Twenty-first Street for the service, and rented a Chelsea loft with a beautiful rooftop view of the city for the reception. It would be a very New York wedding, and my parents would be coming, the first time either of them had been to America.

In February, two months before the wedding, I visited them again.

And here's the thing: I have to confess that I was worried about how my parents might behave in a sophisticated First World setting. What child is not embarrassed by his old people? What child, even at the age of thirty-six, doesn't in some way cringe at his parents' eccentricities? I was concerned that their growing isolation, their life in the bush, had cut them off from the norms of the real world.

I thought of Grace's parents in suburban New Jersey. Her father, Ed, now retired, day-traded in the stock market and attended garage sales. Her mother, Barbara, had season tickets to the opera, read *The New Yorker*, and went to church on Sundays. They took cruises in the Caribbean, river trips in Europe down the Danube. They barely drank.

My parents? Mom now travelled with a bottle of Bols and cartons of cheap Kingsgates in her suitcase to save money. She was known, even in polite company, to tell people: 'If these bastards come for my land, I swear I'll shoot them.' My father could be tactless at the best of times. And now? Would he tease my future mother-in-law about her Catholicism? Ask Grace if she had enough money to support his son? Did he even have a suit?

The bush was not only closing in on their farm and their home, but also, in some ways, colonising their minds, claiming their personalities. On the flight over it occurred to me I would have to gauge how they were doing, and subtly suggest to them that they avoid doing or saying anything that might embarrass me.

My sister Stephanie and her husband, Rob, lent me a car to drive out east this time. It was evening, a twilight dusk, when I neared the farm, but I missed the turnoff altogether. The bush along the road had grown much wilder. It had the desired effect. You had to look hard to see that there was a house up there at all, and when I drove up, the home was dark.

Other things were different. An electric security fence had gone up around the perimeter of the house, and a uniformed armed guard patrolled the road that wound up to the cottages. They never used to have this protection before, and I wondered how they afforded it.

I walked onto the lawn and saw them waiting there watching the sunset, as relaxed as if they were at a mountain spa resort.

'Look who,' said my mother with a smile, walking over to hug me. 'Welcome back, my darling.'

'So you made it, did you,' chuckled Dad, patting me on the back.

They looked very well, much healthier than the year before. My father had put some weight back on, and I saw that he was drinking fresh lemonade, not Coke.

I was surprised by how attractive the house looked, too. The carpets were clean; the antique chairs, piano and oak bookshelves all were polished and gleaming. The walls of the passage, bare last time, had now been given over to framed pictures of my sisters and me and old relatives, many long since dead.

Other signs of depression and decline I had seen a year ago were gone. Dad not only had a new computer but also a fancy new television set. He showed it off to me before dinner, flashing his remote control.

'Jeez, it's better than our TV,' I had to admit.

'Got it down south. Ja, it's pretty good. The dish is working well.'

Grace and I had given up cable to save for the wedding; my parents had a hundred channels at their fingertips.

Of course, they couldn't hold back the tide. There was still a lot of wildlife. House geckoes clung to the walls and ceilings, and I discovered that the albino frog had now become a permanent fixture in the kitchen, making its home on the rim of the copper coffeepot that hung next to the egg rack. I still found the creature disturbing, but my mother had grown rather fond of it. 'He disappeared for a while but then he came back,' she smiled. 'He's so determined.'

There were dietary improvements, too. The fridge, once dirty and filled with mouldy cheese and curdled milk, was now stocked with jugs of fresh lemonade and mounds of ripe fruit, vegetables and herbs. Flower beds my mother had dug up a year ago were now bearing tomatoes, lettuce, aubergine, basil, rosemary and coriander.

There were food shortages across the country, but Mom roasted chicken for dinner, and Dad hauled out a bottle of prize Meerendal Pinotage from the cellar to toast my return.

And then a thought came to me: perhaps all these changes, these improvements, were all just coating. Perhaps my parents were simply facing their own mortality, reaching out to the tangible and the familiar as they neared the end of their lives, trying to bow out with dignity.

'How are the cottages?' I asked at dinner.

'Well, we have a few new tenants at last,' Mom said cheerily.

I was surprised. Was she just putting on a brave face?

'Really? What about the camp?'

I thought I heard Dad stifle a chuckle, which was a little odd.

'You better have some more wine,' he said, changing the subject and filling up my glass.

They clearly didn't want to speak about it, and I feared the worst.

I went to bed early but was woken at eleven that night by the distant thud of music drifting through my window. For a second I thought I was back in Brooklyn and panicked that Grace had turned on our iPod speakers and was about to wake our landlord, who lived two floors above us. Then I smelled the mangos on the trees outside and felt the lumps in the mattress. I was very much at home.

The music was indistinct at first, a faraway muffled sound with a repetitive bass line. But soon my ears, like eyes getting used to the dark, began to make out the sound. It became clearer as I lay there: the unmistakable, low-down dance beats of New York rapper 50 Cent's hit song 'In da Club.'

Very strange, I thought. Had my mother traded in her Neil Diamond records for *Get Rich or Die Tryin'*?

I got out of bed, put on jeans and walked out onto the polished cement veranda. A full moon hovered over the valley. Bougainvillea dripped down the Mediterranean arches of the veranda, silhouetting the tall acacia trees that ran along the main road below. Through wide-open French doors to the right, Mom and Dad were fast asleep in their bedroom, the 12-gauge leaning against Dad's bedside table.

It still shocked me that they slept with everything wide open. Despite their new security – the guard and the electric fence – the only door to the house that was locked was the one into the study. The front of the house had no doors. It seemed to me an open invitation to come get us. It wouldn't have been hard. You could bribe the guard, and while there was the electric fence to climb, all you would have to do would be to wait for one of the numerous power cuts. And since Tello was no longer around, there would be no barked alarm to warn of intruders.

Question was, could my dad get to the gun before they got to him?

At the same time, my parents' old philosophy – 'If you lock things up, people will think you have something to steal' – appeared to be working. They had been left alone. It did them no harm, either, that everyone in the valley knew by now that Dad had a gun on him and wasn't afraid to use it. The squatters had found that out when he blasted away at their hounds.

50 Cent had given way by now to R Kelly's soaring ballad 'I Believe I Can Fly,' a popular hit in New York, and apparently here. The music was coming from the backpacker camp.

I got a flashlight and keys to the front gate from the milk pail in the kitchen next to the copper coffeepot, from where the albino frog, all-seeing, stared at me reproachfully. Then I wandered on down, through the Rhodes grass, under the avocado trees, and across the wooden footbridge.

When I had started going down to the camp at night on my last visit, this walk made me nervous. There were snakes in the grass, bats in the branches. What if I bumped into those bandits coming to steal from the cottages? But now I found myself enjoying it: the full moon, the sound of crickets, the long grass already wet from the evening dew. Best of all, there would be a cold beer at the other end, cigarettes and music. Music! What was happening down there? Had tourists returned to the valley? By now the hip-hop had given way to traditional beats, the jangling guitars of an Oliver Mtukudzi song.

The lodge appeared in its clearing, silhouetted in the moonlight. The last time I had seen Drifters it was empty, abandoned. Now, though, I saw something remarkable: it was close to midnight on a Thursday, and a dozen vehicles were parked on the lawn outside – SUVs, a white Pajero, a Land Rover with government plates. I watched a black couple emerge silently from one of the thatched chalets by the pool and amble up the wooden exterior stairwell toward the bar. The woman seemed drunk, a pair of platform shoes in her hand. The man walked ahead. I emerged from the leaves and followed.

Inside, I was blown away by the sight of about twenty black men and women drinking beer around the bar or slowly dancing to the music blaring from a sleek new hi-fi system behind the counter. No one showed any interest in my arrival, nor did I recognise anyone. I ordered a beer from the barman, a dashing kid in his early twenties with a shaved head. Where was John Muranda, who would normally be serving drinks if guests were around at this hour?

The barman introduced himself to me as Sydney.

'Hi,' I said, 'I'm Douglas.'

'Douglas?' he boomed. 'Mr Rogers's son? I know of you. Welcome!'

I had no idea who the hell he was.

'You are the one who lives in America,' he said. 'How is it there?'

'It's good,' I told him.

'How is Puff Daddy?'

I laughed.

'Not sure,' I said. 'But 50 Cent is fine.'

I wasn't that familiar with the hip-hop pantheon, but I had recently seen 50 Cent and Eminem play in Detroit when I was there on a travel-writing assignment for the London *Times*, which was how I knew the lyrics to 'In da Club.'

'Jay-Z?' he asked.

'I have no idea, man. I never meet these guys.'

He wasn't giving up.

'Snoop Dogg?'

'He's still a gangster.'

'Aish,' said Sydney, 'tight!'

He slapped my hand with his and snapped his fingers.

I asked where Muranda was.

'Muranda? John Old? The *sekuru*? He is sleeping. John Agoneka, he is sleeping, too.'

He looked at the swaying patrons before him.

'These people – they are not sleeping. They are drinking! Haha!'

I ordered a Zambezi and a box of Madisons. I had given up smoking in New York, but something about being out here made me pick up my old habit. They tasted stale.

I was surprised to find the bar in such good condition. A secondhand television had been attached to the wall of the chimney in the middle of the floor, and it was tuned to ZTV, although the sound was off. The president was attending a ceremony in some village. Women wearing his face on their skirts were ululating. He waved his little fist.

The only people not drinking were two downcast youths, no more than twenty years old, sitting on stools in the corner, arms crossed, watching the TV. One wore a Hawaiian-style shirt, except instead of palm trees it bore the many faces of Saddam Hussein. The other had on a soccer shirt emblazoned with the face of David Beckham. In contrast to the other customers, a couple of whom were in suits with wives in high heels and glamorous dresses, they wore mud-stained rubber sandals. If this were a Harare nightclub, these kids would be gate-crashers.

I drank my beer and smoked the cigarettes. A moth singed itself on the overhead fluorescent.

At the far end of the bar a slightly overweight woman in a

tight denim miniskirt that barely constrained her bulging thighs smiled and winked at me. I laughed and gave her a thumbs-up, felt stupid for doing so, and sipped my beer. Then, from my left, a tall, beautiful girl, graceful as a gazelle in skintight jeans and high heels, slinked over to me.

She said sulkily: 'Buy me beer.'

I bought her a beer. She pressed her legs against the bar. Then, in one slick move, she took a swig from the beer in her left hand and slid the long-fingered nails of her other hand between my legs and started stroking my crotch. I choked and spat out the sip, the liquid dribbling down my chin.

'Sixty thousand,' she said, staring straight ahead. 'Let's go.'

I tried to gather my formerly smooth composure. What was the black-market exchange rate these days? Since I was paying three thousand for the beers, I worked out that sixty thousand must have been about US$20.

The girl was stroking my leg now.

'Sorry,' I said. 'I'm about to be married. But I'll buy you another beer.'

I looked around at the dance floor and saw that other men were similarly engaged with various women, dancing close. A pattern developed: a couple would disappear for fifteen minutes and then return; the same woman might then leave with a different man. It was a conveyer belt.

Sydney saw me checking out the scene.

'Douglas,' he said, shaking his head. 'These women – they are not their wives.'

'No, I don't think they are,' I told him.

The gazelle was at my side again, and I bought her a third beer. The denim miniskirt was walking out with one of the gents, a drunk in a suit. Saddam and Beckham ignored it all and watched soundless images on TV. The president was at a political rally now, still making use of his fist.

'Sydney, who are those guys?' I said, nodding at the two.

'Settlers,' he said. 'New farmers from across the road. Maybe you can say they are squatters. They come here for TV, then they go back.'

I drank another Zambezi and smoked a last cigarette. Then I complimented Sydney on his music and said good night.

The gazelle followed me to the door.

'Fifty thousand?' she asked.

She was going down in price, much like the currency itself.

'I'm sorry, I can't.'

'Come back next week?'

'Maybe.'

Walking past a chalet on the way home, I heard the moaning of people humping. For some reason I thought of *Lonely Planet*. The Bible for international budget travellers had written glowingly of Drifters over the years and had helped make it the hot spot it became on the Cape to Cairo backpacker trail. I wondered what a new edition might make of the current scene: *Pizzas have given way to prostitutes at this rustic lodge in the beautiful Eastern Highlands. Comfortable chalets are ideal for coupling, even if the beds are a bit narrow, but the women in the bar are friendly and charge a bargain rate. Good music, too.*

My parents would be horrified.

At breakfast the following morning, sipping the rich, fresh-brewed coffee Mom always made, I gently broke the news to them about the night before. I told them what I had seen: the goings-on at the bar, the women. I didn't tell them about the two settlers. I knew they'd be appalled as it was. So much for the dignified and leisurely retirement they'd always dreamed of: a life of golf, bridge games, garden parties, holidays to visit their children abroad. Instead, their beloved backpacker business had become a brothel, an informal knock shop.

They listened, nodding, as I spoke.

Then they blurted out together: 'Yes, we know! It's bloody unreal. Been going on for months!'

My mouth fell open. 'What do you mean, for months?'

'Well, since we leased the place out,' said Mom.

'You leased out the lodge?'

'Yes, darling. It was no use to us. No tourists. We got this great guy in to take over.'

'Who leases it?'

'Black guy called Dawson Jombe. Lovely fellow. He was a manager on the De Klerk farm.'

'Why isn't he managing that farm?'

'Darling, you've got lots to catch up on. That farm was taken. Dawson lost his job there, so he approached us about renting out the restaurant-bar. We agreed.'

'So you get rent for the lodge and income from the chalets?'

'Well, we hardly charge him anything at all, but yes, we get money from the chalets.'

They looked at each other and giggled.

'Business is booming!' said Dad.

'So, the new fence, the computer, the TV? You paid for that with …'

Suddenly any initial embarrassment they felt gave way to gales of laughter.

'Yes,' said Mom in amazement. 'The place is bringing us in some money at last. It's been a bloody lean few years, I can tell you.'

I still couldn't believe what I was hearing.

Under my parents, Drifters had been mostly a white hangout. Under Dawson, it had become a black joint. He'd installed the new hi-fi system and the secondhand TV, and hired his cousin Sydney as bartender. Word got around town: a quiet place in the bush, just over the pass. At first, well-to-do black professionals

– businessmen, lawyers, accountants, civil servants – would just drive out for a few evening drinks. Soon they began bringing mistresses and hookers with them, able to spend time unseen by wives or prying neighbours. Then local prostitutes in Mutare caught on. When public buses were running, they would ride out to Drifters and stand at the bar waiting for trade.

That afternoon we walked down to the camp and I saw that it wasn't only evening trade. John Muranda was giving a chalet key to a man standing beside a Toyota Hilux, who then handed over a fat wad of dollar notes. An attractive young woman sitting silently in the passenger seat of the Toyota got out of the car and followed him into the chalet, closing the door behind her.

Muranda wandered over to us, his faded floppy hat low over his bloodshot eyes, awkwardly carrying a small red metal money box as if it was a school lunchbox. It was great to see the old man again. Just hearing that saxophone voice and seeing the lopsided smile made me laugh.

He greeted me effusively.

'Douglas! So, you are here. Very good. How is United States?'

'How's business, John?' Mom interrupted, getting down to business.

'It's okay,' John told her with a grin. 'Little busy.'

He handed her a wad of Zimbabwe dollar notes. He was an unlikely Heidi Fleiss, this wise old headman from the Honde Valley, hardly as glamorous as a Parisian brothel madam. But this was remote rural Zimbabwe. He fit the part. My mother took the money and counted it with excessive thoroughness.

The new direction Drifters had taken was a messy business.

Mom shook her head in disgust when she told me that the drains regularly got clogged with condoms, and the sheets had to be washed *twice* a day. For all the new financial benefits, she felt queasy just being down there, seeing what it had become. Dad pointed to the back of the Toyota Hilux. A bathing towel had been draped over the licence plate. Many of the men who drove out were government officials, civil servants, businessmen in town. They had jobs, wives, families, and could easily bump into someone they knew.

According to Muranda, one man arriving with a mistress encountered his own daughter exiting a chalet. So the men covered up car licence plates and even drove their vehicles into the thick bush behind the chalets, somehow squeezing them between rocks and trees.

In what was a vague attempt at morality, my parents had at least decided not to rent the chalets by the hour. Not that my father hadn't thought about it.

'You should see this hotel in town,' he told me. 'One of those big colonial houses at the top of Herbert Chitepo Road. A budget place like ours, but no more tourists, of course. The owner started doing rooms by the hour at lunchtime. Now all these buggers go there to screw around. The place is packed. Guy's making a killing!'

Only half jokingly, Dad had suggested to Muranda that they offer hourly rates, but John advised against it.

'You can try, sa, but in three months, I promise – *Manica Post* first page.'

The Mutare newspaper loved salacious stories, and the scandal of a white farmer running a brothel, however informal, would make for banner headlines.

A new world opened up when you read the pages of the Zimbabwe press. I'd seen some gems over the years. 'Prostitutes Demand Payment in Diesel' was one that wasn't made up. There were also 'Police Run Away from Goblins' and 'Marondera Man's Penis Erect for Five Days.'

'Unlikely,' was my father's response to this one. 'You can't get any Viagra out here.'

But I could hardly judge my parents for cashing in on the trade. Prostitution appeared to be the only growth industry in the country. For the first time in five years they were making money from their business. And it dawned on me now that they weren't facing up to their own mortality at all. They were adapting, surviving, hanging on.

Not all the new clientele at Drifters were punters or prostitutes.

John Muranda told me that the men who drove out with mistresses or hookers usually did so Mondays to Thursdays, because those were the days they could tell their wives that they were at work or away on business. And among these men were some who were simply having a quiet time alone with their second or third wives. Traditional Shona culture is still polygamous.

'They call it "small house,"' Muranda explained to me one afternoon as we sat at a picnic table beside the pool – a spot he liked to call his office. 'First wife is big house. Second wife is small house. Drifters, this place, is for small house.'

In such tough economic times it appeared that keeping a second or third wife in the comfort she might usually be accustomed to – her own home, for example – was no longer financially viable, and would also infuriate the first wife, who had a hold on the tightening purse strings. Many of the men who were coming to Drifters were just downgrading their second wives to a shared afternoon in a budget chalet in the bush – a small house.

Small-house culture is in fact a huge social problem in Zimbabwe. There's even a successful soap opera about it on ZTV, *Small House Saga*, about the secret lives married men are leading with other women, and the attendant health hazards.

Ironically, a health study in Zimbabwe had reported that as the economy got worse, the HIV infection rate dropped, since men had less money to spend on 'small houses'. Drifters could not have been helping lower the infection rate. It was cheap to get a room out here. No more than US$8.

Weekends, meanwhile, tended to be a far more wholesome scene. Families, couples and husbands and first wives would come out. Sometimes a school would rent Drifters for a dance, or the university near the Methodist mission would book it for a graduation party. There had even been a wedding with a live band on the lawn where the camp site used to be.

My parents had grown fond of Dawson Jombe, the man responsible for this new scene, and I discovered that he was not only leasing the lodge from them, but also living in one of the cottages on the property, their very first black resident. I met him one evening at the bar. He'd come to take stock before rejoining his wife, Patricia, a schoolteacher, in Cottage 1.

He took the opportunity to ask Sydney to keep the music down.

'Listen, Syd, less volume, hey, people are trying to sleep on this farm.'

Sydney, bashful, apologised profusely. That night he managed to play it even louder.

I liked Dawson instantly. He was the same age as me, mid-thirties, with a permanent toothy grin and a cackling laugh like a hyena's that could go off at any second.

If John Muranda was no Heidi Fleiss, Dawson was no brothel keeper. He wore a typical Zimbabwean farmer's uniform: khaki shorts, khaki shirt, rolled-down khaki socks and bush boots, out of which poked two skinny, hairy legs like matchsticks.

He came from the Honde Valley, the same area as Muranda, and had attended the College of Horticulture in Chipinge, south of Mutare, before becoming a senior technical manager on Kondozi, a highly successful horticulture farm owned by the De Klerk family in the west of the valley. That farm had been invaded, and he and six thousand others had lost their jobs.

Clearly he saw running the bar as a stopgap. He wanted to get back to agriculture.

'I am a farmer, Douglas. This game is temporary.'

I asked him what he thought of the goings-on down here, the prostitutes.

'When did you realise what was happening?'

'The first day. A man and woman came in. I thought: *Good, some business.*' He clicked his fingers and whistled. 'They took one beer, then went to bed.'

A male customer walked in just then, accompanied by a woman half his age.

'And how's business now?' I said softly.

'Put it this way,' Dawson cackled louder than ever, 'they don't stay for breakfast!'

He seemed as amazed by what was happening down there as my mother.

I was surprised to discover, however, that my parents had made black friends down at the camp now, people every bit as interesting to them as their formerly all-white clientele. Dad spoke in amazement of an electrician he had met named Brian Ndlovu, who stayed for a week while fixing the wiring in the lodge soon after Dawson took over.

'He seemed like an ordinary bloke,' Dad told me. 'Matabele guy from Bulawayo, in his forties. Anyway, I go down to check on things one afternoon and I find him giving a lecture to the staff and a dozen guests by the pool. They're all sitting on the grass, listening to him talk. I'm thinking, *What's this bloody bugger up to?* Turns out he's teaching them about HIV/AIDS – how it's killing so many people, how to prevent it, using protection, et cetera. I'm impressed. I thought he was just some cheapo electrician.

'When he's finished I say, "Brian, that was interesting, how do you know this stuff?" He tells me he's a member of Rotary!

He did a course. He volunteers all over the country.

'Anyway, I offer to buy him a drink. We walk into the bar. We sit at the stools by the dartboard. I get him a beer, and before you know it he pulls out this silver box from his jacket pocket. It's got three darts in it. He says, "Excuse me a moment."

'He goes to the dartboard and throws three triple twenties first go. Top score. I say, "Bloody hell, Brian, that's good." He says, "Ja, thanks. I play in the big leagues. We have a tournament coming up in South Africa in two weeks and I need to practise."

'I tell him that your mom and I are driving down to Joburg around that time, and maybe he wants a lift to the tournament. I mean, he can't have much money for transport. He says, "No, thanks, Mr Rogers. I was an electrician for Zimbabwe Railways before I went freelance and they always give me and my team a private first-class carriage to travel to South Africa. That way we can sleep in comfort and practice on the way."'

Dad beamed as he remembered the electrician. 'Brian Ndlovu – Renaissance man!'

But it was another group of black guests at the newfangled Drifters that had made the biggest impression on him. He told me that a few weeks into the New Year he received a phone call up at the house from a man wanting to book six chalets for a weekend.

'That's fine. What are your names?'

'We are priests,' the man said.

'Okay. But what are your names?'

'Just priests.'

Dad shrugged and made the reservation anyway.

Zimbabwe is a deeply Christian country. Missionaries were proselytising to the Shona and Matabele, Zimbabwe's second tribe, as early as the 1850s. There are Roman Catholic, Anglican and Methodist missions all over Zimbabwe today. Indeed, in 1979, the first black leader of the country, in the brief interim between white rule and Robert Mugabe, was a United Methodist bishop named Abel Muzorewa. Even President Mugabe, a graduate of a Jesuit school, claimed to be a devout Roman Catholic.

My mother, a decidedly lapsed Anglican, was horrified about the pending arrival of the priests. She was convinced they had heard about the 'den of iniquity' and were coming to cleanse it, to ask my parents to seek redemption. Instead, Dad walked into the restaurant on the Saturday afternoon and saw something remarkable.

'They were sitting at the far corner table in full robes and dog collars. But their Bibles were piled on a chair, and they weren't talking about God. They were holding a political meeting. They were MDC activists in disguise! They travel around with their notes and campaign documents hidden in hollowed-out Bibles or under their robes.'

Belonging to the opposition was as dangerous as ever. The government, to prevent the MDC from meeting or holding rallies, had invoked a law dating back to Rhodesian days banning gatherings of more than three people. The MDC got around it by holding 'prayer meetings'. But the state soon caught on. It would be at a prayer meeting that the young MDC activist Gift Tandare would be shot dead by police in March 2007, setting off a wave of state violence that included the beating of Morgan Tsvangirai with a metal pipe.

My father kept his political sympathies well hidden these days. The backlash from the last election had been brutal. But I could tell how proud he was of these brave men in liturgical vestments in his lodge, underground activists of the party he had joined, the party he hoped would one day come to power and get the country back to normal.

SIX
The Rogers Cartel

FUEL WAS HARD to come by, and if buses weren't running or petrol was too expensive, the men and the hookers didn't drive out over the pass. Often I would buy a case of beer from Sydney at the bar and take it over to the Murandas' small brick house by the swimming pool. There we would sit – John Agoneka, John and Naomi Muranda and me – around a wood fire, drinking, eating *sadza* and talking in stilted English about the doomed, depressed country.

The two Johns told me they supported the MDC, but they made sure to keep membership cards from the ruling party in their pockets in case they were confronted by soldiers or the feared youth militia. There was a militia training camp, Magamba, just up the road, and occasionally you could see these Green Bombers, squadrons of up to thirty uniformed youths in their teens and twenties, running in formation on the main road past the farm, chanting ZANU-PF slogans: *Pamberi nehondo, izvozui* – Forward with war, right now! *Pasi na Tsvangirai* – Down with Tsvangirai! Magamba once had been a farm school; now it was an indoctrination centre.

Dad had given the Johns a new radio in order to listen to secret nightly broadcasts of their favourite station, SW Radio Africa, run by Zimbabwean journalists and music DJs who had been expelled by the regime. I was proud to tell the two Johns that I'd recently written about the station for a British newspaper, the *Guardian*. It was the Johns, after all, who had first introduced me to it that night around the bar three years ago. I told them I had met the staff, including John Matinde, the legendary DJ who, in the 1970s, had secretly played the resistance music of the great Zimbabwe Chimurenga (revolutionary struggle) singer Thomas Mapfumo on Rhodesian airwaves before the Rhodesians found out and banned him. On 18 April 1980, Matinde had the honour of introducing Bob Marley to the crowd at Rufaro Stadium in Harare in front of the newly inaugurated Robert Mugabe at the delirious independence celebrations. Prince Charles was there, awkward and gawky in a safari suit among a band of Third World revolutionaries. It was Bob Marley's last-ever live performance.

I often wish I had been there that night, but I was eleven years old at the time, a white boy terrified of the future. Besides, I was unable to move. I had been in a serious car accident up in the Nyanga mountains on Easter Sunday, two weeks earlier, and spent all that month in Mutare General Hospital, in a bed next to my friend Brian Goble, whose father, Barry, had driven the car over a cliff and whose mother, Beryl, was killed in the crash. My parents, my sisters and Brian's brother, Mark, were in a car behind us. Mom and Dad dug us out of the wreck. 'It still makes me sick thinking about it,' my mother always says when I ask her about the crash. 'It's a miracle any of you survived.' All I remembered about Independence Day 1980 was being confused as to why all the beautiful black nurses who took such good care of Brian and me were so excited about it.

Now, those days seemed a lifetime away. John Matinde

and Thomas Mapfumo regularly denounced Mugabe from their respective exiles in Britain and America. Mapfumo now lived in Eugene, Oregon, and I'd interviewed him once, too, over the phone at 4:00 pm New York time while he sat in a bathtub and railed against the president who had betrayed a nation.

As for Matinde, John Agoneka beamed: 'What a DJ! He would play all the greats!'

The radio aerial was strung up in the twisted branch of a msasa tree above us, but the batteries were getting weak and the reception was hopeless. The government scrambled the signal, too – it was like trying to listen to a Second World War broadcast in a bunker during the Blitz.

One night, after we'd given up trying to get the signal to work, I was shocked when John Muranda pulled out a twist of newspaper filled with dried marijuana leaves and began to roll the fattest joint I've seen in my life. He used the pages of the *Herald* and the *Manica Post*, both government mouthpieces, as rolling paper. He had a whole pile of them next to him. So this was why John always had that slightly dazed look: he was stoned half the time.

I picked up one of the newspapers. It had an absurd piece of propaganda on the war in the valley and the great ongoing success of the 'agrarian revolution': *The area, which is known for its high agricultural productivity, has of late been turned into a political minefield, thanks to some gun-toting and bloodthirsty white commercial farmers. To most farmers, Odzi is like the biblical land of Canaan promised by God to the children of Israel. Some of the white farmers' being of Boer origin speaks volumes. These white farmers know there is no life after Odzi and they cannot just leave it without a fight.*

I passed the page to John to smoke next.

Mrs John sat on a reed mat laid out on the packed red dirt yard in front of the shack, her legs stretched out toward the fire, her head wrapped tightly in a bright red scarf. She looked like a shy, retiring grandmother. She turned out to be the biggest dopehead of us all. When handed the joint she would close her eyes, inhale for a minute until her face seemed about to explode, and then exhale in short bursts, like a puffing dragon, finally letting out a loud cackle with the last of the smoke, scattering the fruit bats from the trees. Her perfect white teeth flashed in the dark.

'I am old woman,' she coughed from behind billowing cumulus clouds in the gloom. '*Dagga* is good for my blood pressure.'

I couldn't help loving the woman.

John Agoneka didn't touch the weed, either, just as he didn't drink. I asked him how he'd come to speak such good English, and he told me he'd taught himself by reading a dictionary in a library in Bulawayo, Zimbabwe's second-largest city, and from speaking to his older brother, who was a successful soapstone sculptor in Cape Town.

As Mr and Mrs Muranda and I passed the joint between us, Agoneka told me how he used to take backpackers on daylong hikes up the Chikanga Mountains on the other side of the valley to see Bushman cave paintings and refuge ruins, stone sanctuaries where the Manyika used to hide from raiding Matabele war parties long before whites came to the valley. The hills also held the remains of ancient Shona gold-smelting works that dated back to their trade with Arabs and Portuguese on the East African coast as early as the seventeenth century.

The name Mutare comes from the Shona for 'place of metal', and it was not farmland but gold – dreams of El Dorado and the jewels of Ophir – that first attracted British pioneers to the valley in 1891. It was no coincidence that Cecil John Rhodes, the great British imperialist and mining tycoon, founder of the De Beers corporation, who would give his name to this country and his money to the scholarship that would later send the likes of Bill Clinton and Kris Kristofferson to Oxford, first set foot in

Rhodesia in this exact valley. Rhodes trekked in from Mozambique to oversee mineral contracts his emissaries had signed with the Manyika chief Mutasa, outmanoeuvering the Portuguese. It was 9 October 1891. There were already 160 gold reefs in the valley. Rhodes stayed only twenty-four hours, although he would later have a home in the Nyanga Mountains to the north that is still there today. He was thirty-eight years old, a self-made billionaire, prime minister of the Cape Colony, with an entire country soon to be named after him.

I took a drag of the joint. I was about to turn thirty-seven. What the hell. I could still make my mark.

The two Johns had an amazing grasp of much of this history, and I knew some of it myself, but mostly they spoke longingly of the recent past: the glory days at Drifters.

'Pizza night!' said Muranda. 'You should have seen it, Douglas. So many people. They would come from Mutare in their cars, a hundred, maybe two hundred people every Friday. Aish, it was too busy. Madam used to get very angry if we didn't make pizzas fast enough. Back then, we were thriving.'

They told me how they'd loved meeting foreign backpackers. Agoneka had met, and I suspect fallen in love with, a young New Zealand girl whom he had taken on one of his tours, and he had kept in touch with her for a while before stamps and envelopes got too expensive and he had to stop writing. He and Muranda said they missed the stories about England and America and Australia that the backpackers told them.

'In America I hear everyone has two televisions and a digital watch,' Muranda said.

'Not me,' I told him. 'You know how much rent I pay in New York?'

'How much?'

'Eighteen hundred dollars per month. One room with a garden. Smaller than yours.'

'Zim dollars?'

'No. *Usas*. American.' *Usas* was the local term for US dollars.

Aish! Eighteen hundred *usas*? For that sum of money we can buy this whole farm.'

'Easy, John,' I said.

I passed him more propaganda to roll another joint. This was a story about the De Klerk family, Dawson's former employers, farmers in the valley whom my parents knew. We had gone to the De Klerk farm for a lunch in 2002, just before the elections. It turned out to be more of a clandestine meeting than a lunch: the De Klerks funded the opposition party, and the meeting was to discuss transporting MDC agents to polling stations. The article quoted a government minister saying that the family were related to South Africa's former president FW de Klerk and that they wanted to bring apartheid back to Zimbabwe and 'enslave blacks'.

Muranda looked at the story before he rolled it.

'Mr de Klerk, Cottage Six,' he said.

'What's that, John?'

'Mr de Klerk live in Cottage Six. With wife.'

I knew the De Klerks had lost their farm. I didn't know the family patriarch was living on my parents' land. He must have been one of the new tenants Mom mentioned.

I looked up at the night sky, light-headed and dizzy.

Satellites and shooting stars pinballed the black velvet. Around me, the bush started to come alive. I wasn't hallucinating. First I heard voices approaching from the trees, floating clearly through the night air, and then, out of nowhere, a man would appear in front of us, stop and talk to the two Johns, and disappear back into the shadows. It was another world out here, away from the comfort of the big house.

Muranda said these were staff of the new residents in the cottages. I didn't realise the cottages had *this* many new tenants.

Two shadows emerged from where the game fence used to be by the road, and passed silently to our left, toward the bar: the kid with the Saddam Hussein T-shirt, and his pal with David Beckham on his chest.

'New farmers from Mr Frank,' said Muranda. 'They like to watching the television in the bar. Then they go back.'

'I know,' I told him.

It was incredible to think that some of the settlers who had raided my father's friend's home now spent the night at his bar watching TV. Perhaps they hated being stuck on that farm without TV. I wondered whether they wanted to move to town as desperately as I had when I was their age.

I asked Muranda where he'd scored the weed. It was strong stuff.

He took a long drag of the joint, closed his eyes, and said matter-of-factly, 'I get it from Youfada.'

'Youfada?'

'Yes, Youfada.'

'Where's Youfada, John?' I'd never heard of the place. I figured it must be somewhere in the Honde Valley, his tribal area.

'*Youfada!*' he said, exasperated with me. 'Mr Rogers! He grow!'

Mrs John cackled loudly again. Agoneka clapped his hands in glee. More bats flew off.

'What did you say, John? My father?'

'Yes. You fada! He grow it up at house. I teach him!'

'You what?'

'I teach him.'

I took an extra-long drag of the joint when it came round to me the next time. The things that happen when I'm not around.

It was apparent to me by now that John Muranda was far more than just an employee at Drifters. He had become my father's right-hand man, his ear to the ground, the reason my dad knew so much about the politics in the area and had, so far, been able to stay one step ahead of the game.

They had formed an unlikely partnership, the patrician white farmer and the Honde Valley kraal headman, but they were in many ways similar personalities.

When I'd first seen John twiddling the dials of my dad's old radio, determined to find the right station and furious when he couldn't, he reminded me exactly of my father. They were both headstrong, determined and intellectually cunning: they could play the game.

From his years as a lawyer, my father knew how to read and judge people: he knew when to charm and when to attack. John was similar, a chameleon, able to fit in anywhere in the valley. The young settlers across the road who sat at the bar and stared at the TV screen respected him as an elder, yet he could also drink beer with the authentic war veterans who occupied two of the larger estates in the valley, and he more than held his own with the more sophisticated urban clientele who checked into the chalets with their hookers and small houses.

They also both realised that John had just as much to lose if Drifters was taken as my parents did. Here, he and Naomi had a house, a job, a salary, regular food. Hell, they even had cheap beer and a marijuana supply. Who could beat that kind of deal? John must have known that if the war vets took over, all that would go. It was just as much in his interest for my dad to hold on to the farm, and he therefore kept my father abreast of the more important developments in the valley so he could plan ahead.

And yet in my wildest dreams, I never would have imagined John Muranda teaching my father how to grow marijuana. So the following morning, half jokingly, I said to my dad that I had heard a wild rumour down at the camp that he had become a *dagga* farmer.

'Oh,' he replied, looking up suddenly from his book.

He fidgeted in his chair. I could tell he was embarrassed. Which meant one thing: it was true.

'Muranda told you that, did he?'

'Actually, yes. He said he gets his *dagga* from you.'

There was an awkward silence. I suddenly felt sorry for my father. He was like a kid caught doing something naughty, worried about what to say next.

'Well,' he eventually replied, 'it's more *his* plantation than mine.'

'Come on, Dad. Are you growing it or not?'

'Don't worry,' he said guiltily. 'Your mom and I don't smoke the stuff.'

'I believe you, but where is it?'

I felt like I had become the parent, that some strange generational inversion had taken place in which my parents had become the irresponsible children I had to keep checking up on. Fooling around with weapons, running a brothel, experimenting with drugs. It suddenly occurred to me that my dream life in New York City was rather pedestrian in comparison.

'Okay, I'll show you,' he relented.

I followed him through the kitchen to the back of the house. I expected to find a few leaves on a potted plant. Instead, in my mother's herb and vegetable garden, cleverly hidden behind the laundry outbuilding, was a large bed of pungent green marijuana blooming wildly among her mint and basil and tomatoes.

'Behold!' Dad grinned. 'The Rogers cartel!'

It was an incredible sight. I had never seen so much marijuana in my life. When I was at Rhodes University I'd known students who would drive to the Transkei, fill up the boot of their car with sacks of Transkei Gold grown by rural farmers, and bring it back to sell on campus. In my squat in London I'd had a housemate who grew dope hydroponically in our laundry closet. But

he had just a single pathetic plant. This was on an entirely different scale.

Then, in the laundry building, Dad showed me dozens of
bunches of drying leaves hanging from the beams, like burley
in a tobacco barn. They'd been stashed there by John Muranda,
who, it turned out, once cultivated dagga in his village up in the
Honde Valley, where the weed was said to grow as strong and
wild as poppies in Afghanistan.

'How did you get into this?' I asked.

Dad explained to me that he'd come across the plant down
at the camp one afternoon. He'd seen some strange green weeds
growing in the flower bed below the restaurant-bar balcony.
He was about to pull them out when Muranda, in a mild panic,
rushed over from his 'office' – the picnic bench by the swimming
pool – and explained to him that this was a very valuable 'traditional vegetable' and it would be better not to uproot it.

'A valuable vegetable, John?'

I could imagine Dad's sarcastic voice.

'Yes, sa, this very valuable.'

'Rubbish. It's just a weed.'

'No, sa, it's very valuable.'

'It's *dagga*, isn't it?'

John thought for a while. 'Ah …'

'It's dagga, isn't it, John?'

'Ah … yes, sa! Yes. This *dagga*. But very valuable, sa! Very
valuable.'

He kept mentioning the value of it, which had the desired
effect. Muranda knew my father well. Dad could use a *valuable*
vegetable. He got John to dig it up and replant it up at the house.
Within a few months it had blossomed into a ripe plantation.

I thought back to the time Drifters had been such a hit on
the backpacker trail. Some Ivy League Peace Corps volunteer
or British gap-year students must have smoked a joint on the

balcony and dropped a few seeds in the flower bed below. Either that, or Muranda had actually brought some of his crop down from the Honde Valley and started cultivating it in my mother's flower bed. Who cared? My father now had a dope plantation.

'But what are you going to do with it, Dad?' I asked.

'I'm not sure,' he chuckled. 'There must be money in it *somewhere*. But of course your mother's getting all jittery. She keeps asking me to burn it.'

'Don't do that,' I said. 'Give it to Mrs John. She says it's good for her blood pressure.'

'I believe it does have certain medicinal qualities,' Dad said.

I had to confess, though, that I was with my mother in wanting him to get rid of it. Their security situation was tenuous enough, what with the squatters across the road spending nights in his bar and the camp becoming a brothel frequented by government officials. Growing marijuana might be going a little too far.

'What if the police find out?' I asked, sounding like the square I'd perhaps become.

'The police? The police are bloody useless. They're good at breaking the law, not much good at enforcing it. I'm more worried about the Americans.'

'What do you mean, the Americans?'

I followed him to his study. In two months' time he and Mom were due to come to New York for my wedding. It would be their first-ever visit to the United States, and they needed tourist visas. On his desk he showed me the visa forms they had to fill out. *Have you ever grown or sold illicit substances?* read one question. *Have you ever solicited women for the purposes of prostitution?* read another.

'Of course we'll say no in both cases,' Dad chuckled. 'But do you think they'll check up on us? The Americans have really sophisticated surveillance systems. They could see all our goings-on from a satellite.'

Mom walked past and heard us laughing.

'So he's telling you about our drugs and prostitution visa problem, is he?' she said with a grin.

'Yes, Ma,' I told her. 'And we've decided that when you come over to New York you're going to be the mule. You're going to stash all the marijuana in your suitcase. At JFK they'll never suspect you. The street value's going to be enormous – it'll pay for the rehearsal dinner.'

Mom ran off to the kitchen screaming, 'Not on your bloody life!'

We ate like kings. There was more than marijuana growing in those former flower beds. I discovered now why my parents looked so healthy.

There was a famine looming in Zimbabwe in early 2005, but if you could eat avocados you'd never go hungry in this neck of the woods. Every few days, scores of young black traders would make their way down from the orchards in the surrounding mountain valleys with huge hessian sacks filled with bananas, oranges, lemons, pawpaws, mangos and avocados. Mostly avocados: smooth green oval-shaped gems the size of cricket balls. The traders would wait at the bottom of Christmas Pass for transport to Harare, 290 kilometres to the west, where they hoped to sell the fruit at market, but there was no fuel, and the buses weren't running. Instead, they'd just sit for days, sleeping by the roadside, while their crop rotted away in the sun.

My father was outraged with this state of affairs. These were innovative, hardworking young entrepreneurs, trying to make a living. People were starving in Zimbabwe, yet here mountains of food rotted away. The state couldn't even get buses to work.

My parents had already begun growing most of their own vegetables, but now they started buying what they didn't grow from these informal traders, and it helped account for their excellent health. They ate fruit salads every morning, drank fresh-squeezed lemonade during the day instead of Coke or cordials, and cooked elaborate meals at night from recipes they got watching the Naked Chef, Nigella Lawson and Anthony Bourdain on their new satellite TV.

I told them I never ate half so well at home, and we decided one night they needed a Food Network show of their own, with a cookbook tie-in.

We came up with a title. It would be called *Recipes for Disaster: Adventures in the Kitchen of a Failed State*. In it they would be filmed buying produce from those informal traders on the road, asking them about their lives, how they got those heavy bags down the mountain. Did they own the orchards or steal the fruit?

My parents would also have to be filmed buying food from the new farmers in the valley who were trying to make a go of it.

'Oh, Christ,' said Mom. 'Will I have to jump up and down chanting ZANU-PF slogans in exchange for a maize cob?'

My father loved the idea.

'Yes, Rosalind, I can see you doing that. And just think of the appeal to a Western audience: ethnic dancing and an *organic* maize cob. These buggers have no fertiliser.'

Another episode, we decided, would be dedicated to the miracle of Zimbabwean cheese. My father had discovered that due to a shortage of one vital ingredient (or perhaps the loss of skilled staff), the usually tasteless Gouda that the state Dairy Marketing Board manufactured had now turned into a delectably rich and creamy Brie – as tasty as anything you might find in Provence. He bought several wheels of it at a time at the DMB warehouse in Mutare, worried that they might discover and correct their mistake and it would go back to tasting awful.

Finally, we decided that each episode would show them cooking up some masterpiece on that gas stove by candlelight on the kitchen floor during a power cut.

'We need more atmosphere,' I told them. 'A sense of *place*.'

'I know,' said my mother, warming to the theme. 'We could fire up the generator and eat each meal in front of the TV, watching a speech by Mugabe ranting about us "white imperialist running dogs of capitalism," or the "homosexual government of Tony Blair."'

We burst out laughing.

'You know what?' Dad guffawed. 'It could work. I reckon that Anthony Bourdain chap would come out here and present it. He goes to some really wacky places.'

My mother's eyes lit up at the thought of the dashing *Kitchen Confidential* star coming out to visit them.

SEVEN

The Refugees

THE WIDER SITUATION wasn't all fun and games. The country was still heading straight to ruin. My parents lived in constant fear that the car coming up their driveway would be the Top Man, a general or a ruling party chef arriving to inform them: 'This is my farm. You have 24 hours to leave.' The shotgun was always ready, just in case.

My parents rarely heard the howls of the poachers' dogs any more, but that was small consolation: their game fence had been dismantled, and they were resigned to the fact that all their animals had been slaughtered. Only a handful of settlers remained on Frank Bekker's land across the road, but judging by the look of Saddam and Becks, they were desperate. I still didn't have the heart to tell my parents about the two young settlers who spent their evenings in the lodge bar watching TV. They probably knew it anyway.

The lodge's becoming a knock shop had shocked me. Discovering my Dad was growing weed came as a surprise. But I was in no way prepared for what they would show me in the cottages on the back of the land during an afternoon walk a day later.

As a child I used to hate farm walks. They bored the hell out of me. I would rather be hitting cricket balls or sitting in the house watching videos. My parents always made us come along: Sunday afternoons, five o'clock, after coffee and pancakes with Golden Syrup on the veranda. Off we would troop – me, Stof, Zaan and Hel behind them, trudging through fields of stinking cowpats where the weed grass scratched our legs and ticks attached themselves to us like limpet mines. 'Isn't nature wonderful?' Helen would say sarcastically, but always under her breath so Dad wouldn't hear. 'Isn't nature wonderful?' became our catchphrase, code for everything we hated about being on the farm.

But recently I had begun to enjoy these ritual ramblings. Perhaps it was living for so long in cities – Johannesburg, London, New York – hemmed in by buildings, riding subways beneath the earth. I felt I could breathe out here. I loved the views of the valley from the top of the hill, and the smell of the earth after it rained, vapour rising up like the steam from a Manhattan manhole. It made me giddy, drunk.

The front of the property was now wildly overgrown and impossible to walk on, but the back of the land with the cottages in the hills was still immaculately maintained. Agoneka wasn't doing such a bad job in his new role as groundskeeper, really. We would take the dirt road past the cottages, all around us a wilderness of wind-bent trees, exotic plants and brightly plumed birds. Crimson wildflowers and flaming creepers splashed the hills with bursts of red. Paradise flycatchers, hoopoes and robins fluttered between the branches. All that was missing were the zebra and antelope.

Each of the sixteen cottages was numbered and named for a species of tree on the land – mahogany, cassia, knobthorn, acacia – the names painted by my mother on round steel plough discs that she hung on wooden poles outside the front gardens.

The houses were all built in the same simple way: two bedrooms, open-plan living room and dining area, a carport to the side, a tidy front porch leading out onto a garden. A year ago only four had had tenants, but now I saw something extraordinary.

Cars, battered trucks and even a tractor were parked outside the cottages or in those carports. Furniture was strewn on front lawns. I watched an elderly white man haul a rocking chair into number 9. Boxes of books and crates of clothing were piled high on porches or spread out in backyards like in a scene from *The Grapes of Wrath*. Old white people I had never seen before were watering plants or sipping tea on porches. They waved as we walked by. Mom and Dad waved back and said hello if they were within earshot. They asked them how they were doing, whether the water and lights were working.

'Jeez, who are all these people?' I asked my mother, a little spooked.

'They're white farmers. People who lost their land. We're the only place left in the area they could come to after they got booted off.'

'What, so it's like a refugee camp?'

She chuckled.

'I suppose you could say that. But don't worry, we charge them rent.'

Apparently, word in the valley was that if you lost your home and needed a roof over your head, Lyn and Ros Rogers at Drifters, the old pizza place, had cottages, good for short stays or long. They received regular phone calls about availability. One elderly widow turned up in the middle of the night at their front gate in tears with a harrowing story of a violent eviction, a mob running through her home. My parents took her in. They had become low-budget bushveld versions of Oskar and Emilie Schindler.

Eight farming families had found sanctuary at Drifters over

the past year, and more would do so in the years ahead. Most stayed just a few months, trying to sort out passports, visas and property shipments before leaving the country to start over again.

Others stayed longer, determined to fight to get their property or livestock back, or simply because this was home. They were Zimbabweans. There was nowhere else to go.

'You should interview them,' Mom suggested as we got down to the camp, where Agoneka was slashing the grass in a flower bed around Cottage 6, accidentally lopping the heads off some geraniums. 'You think we've gone a bit weird, but these people really are the last of a dying breed. The stories they could tell you …'

Right from the beginning my mother had encouraged me to write about their life and the farm. Originally, I suspected, it was the only way she knew to get me to come out and visit. But now, I realised, she was as amazed by what was happening around them as I was. She wanted a document of this time, a record, and who better to make it than her son, the writer, who was desperately looking for a story of his own?

And so now, just as I had started going down to the camp at night to hang out in the bar and to talk to the two Johns, in the afternoons I started visiting these old white farmers with a notebook and a tape recorder to hear about their lives.

They painted an extraordinary picture of a long-lost era in the valley that I knew nothing about, of a time dating back, in one widow's case, to the 1920s, and my maternal grandmother Evelyn Eggleston's era in Southern Rhodesia. They were bookends on a disappearing world, the last of a lost white tribe. Yet they seemed to recall the old days with extraordinary clarity and the current chaos with a remarkable stoicism and, believe it or not, humour.

The most recent arrival was an attractive, slightly built

Afrikaner, a widow named Unita Herrer. She was in her mid-to-late sixties, but spry as a teenage girl. She called herself 'one of the greatest cattle farmers in the valley'. I joined her on her porch one dusky evening in Cottage 2, Mahogany. She had dressed up specially for the occasion: bright red frock, silver slippers, a pastel blue scarf covering her head. A tiny pair of blue eyes darted from her pale, sallow face. She sat among a pile of wooden crates.

'My guns,' she sighed in a high-pitched, flat-vowel Afrikaans accent. 'I have to get rid of my guns. I have so many. An old Bruno. A twenty-two for hunting. My son Bredell's Beretta, a beautiful little pistol. I have to sell them to Africans. Whites don't buy anything any more.'

She sounded like an arms dealer, an Afrikaner Annie Oakley. Was Unita one of those 'bloodthirsty, gun-toting Boer farmers' the local paper wrote about? She seemed an unlikely candidate. As soon as she sold her guns, though, she was trekking back to South Africa, where she was born, outside Cape Town, in 1942.

She poured me a glass of vinegary white wine that tasted as if it had been bottled around that time, and she spoke in dramatic theatrical cadences – soft whispers followed by rising crescendos – like a 1930s screen star preparing for her close-up.

'I came to Rhodesia in 1962 to join my husband, Japie,' Unita said. 'I didn't really know him. He was the brother of a girl I worked with in Parow. He asked me to marry him after eight hours. Said he was going to get rich doing tobacco in Rhodesia. Tobacco was like gold then. I was engaged to a Hollander at the time. Not an Afrikaner, a man from Holland. My parents didn't like this Hollander. He wasn't a proper Dutchman. Back then us Afrikaners thought like that. We thought we were the really pure Dutch. Japie said he knew if he didn't get me to marry him I would go straight back to that Hollander.'

So Unita hitched her wagon to Japie and moved north.

But it turned out, as these things sometimes do, that her new husband knew little about farming and less about tobacco, which is a very difficult crop to grow.

She leaned in close to me, as if afraid her late husband would hear. 'All he wanted to do was play rugby. *I* was the farmer. But I had to be. My husband was a good man, but he wasn't a provider, or a worker, or a planner. I was a Maserati always pulling a Toyota.'

Suddenly something stirred under a blanket in a corner chair beside the crates. I leapt off the porch. The blanket fell to the floor, and I saw that an old man with glazed eyes and wispy shocks of white hair had been sitting there all along. He looked like a ghost. Drool was running down his shirt; there was a scrapbook open on his lap. I knew Unita's husband had passed away years ago in South Africa, and I was relieved to discover this wasn't his spectral presence but rather Frans, an old friend of Japie's, and Unita's farming partner for the past twenty years. Japie and Frans had bought the farm in the valley, the one she ended up doing all the work on, in 1963.

She looked at Frans and rolled her eyes.

'You know, all *they* wanted to do was play rugby. Rugby this, rugby that. People said to me, 'Unita, you are never going to make it with these guys. You will go bankrupt.' But I said, 'I am going to try.' So *I* went to get the loan from the Standard Bank. *I* decided we would do maize and cattle as well as tobacco. *I* pulled it up. And you know, in three years the whole farm was paid for. We did not owe anyone a cent! Let me tell you: I am a go-getter. A doer. I never give up. My husband was a good person, but he wasn't a — '

Frans stirred again. A bat flew onto the porch and back out. The scrapbook fell open. I saw it was filled with faded news clippings and photographs of old rugby matches. But I wondered what rugby had to do with this remote farming valley in eastern Zimbabwe, over six hundred kilometres from South Africa.

Frans raised his head. A smile crept across his face. Unita's eyes lit up.

'Don't you know why there are so many Afrikaners in this valley?' she asked. 'The first tobacco farmers here loved rugby.

Back in the 1950s they had so much money from tobacco they would travel all over South Africa to get the best rugby players to come up here and play for their clubs. The players would be given jobs as managers on farms, but they couldn't farm anything at first. *They were here to play rugby!*

Unita looked at Frans.

'These two' – she spoke of her husband as if he were still alive, sitting in the chair next to his old mucker – 'they couldn't farm at all. They were here for rugby!'

I was amazed to hear that from the 1950s through the 1970s several legendary Springbok and Rhodesian players lived in the valley. Two tiny farm districts, Inyazura and Odzi, were among the best rugby clubs in Africa. It was like a team of Yankee all-stars moving to grow beans and play baseball in a pueblo in Mexico. Unita reeled off famous names while Frans gleamed approval: 'Ryk van Schoor, Salty du Randt, Tienie Martin ... Piet de Klerk? Him in Cottage Six? Him, too. He was captain of Rhodesia! Go ask him.'

My parents had confirmed to me that old Piet de Klerk and his wife, Mienkie, were now living at Drifters. I knew that De Klerk was a famous rugby player who'd once scored a try against the All Blacks. I hadn't known he'd come to Rhodesia to play rugby. I was even more interested in speaking to him now, but he'd been hard to pin down.

Unita grinned and whispered again.

'You know, there were so many of us Boers here back then that when an English person came into a bar after a rugby game we would speak Afrikaans. And if they could speak Afrikaans we would speak Shona. *Us Afrikaners thought we were the real Africans!*'

I laughed.

Bad blood between the Afrikaners and the British lasted long after the Second Boer War. When my dad's mother, Gertruida Gauche, married his father, Kitchener Rogers, in 1923, her mother, Johanna, refused to speak to either of them for years: not only was her daughter marrying a hated *Engelse rooinek*, of the kind her own husband, Gerrit, had fought against as one of Smuts's commandos, but she was marrying one named Kitchener, after the notorious Field Marshal Horatio Herbert Kitchener, whose scorched-earth policy and chain of concentration camps across the veld (Johanna having been an inmate of one of them) had crushed and humiliated the Boer nation. My father – of half British descent, half Boer – straddled both sides of this divide.

In 1980, after independence, like so many white Rhodesians, Unita and her husband joined the stampede to South Africa, afraid of what would happen to them under a black government after the war. But Unita didn't feel at home in South Africa.

'I realised I wasn't a South African anymore. I was a Rhodesian. I decided I had to come back and become Zimbabwean. But Japie stayed down south. Soon we got divorced.'

Japie would pass away several years later.

Unita returned to the valley in 1986. Frans was still there but the farm was in disrepair. So she did it all over again.

'I pulled it up by myself. It was hard in the 1980s. This country was *communist* then. You couldn't get tractors or equipment. But I never give up. Frans was still on his part of the land. We did tobacco and cattle again. But you know, his cattle were always terrible. He wouldn't look after them. I told him: "If you are not in the field in the morning, your cattle will get pinched, they will get sick, and they will die." And of course they did. His cattle had ten horns and one eye! Man, they were *terrible!* But mine? I was one of the greatest...'

Frans stirred again. He wanted to speak but couldn't get the words out. Unita went into a misty-eyed reverie at the thought of her herd. She'd still been farming alongside Frans in 2000 when the land invasions began. What she had feared would happen in 1980 instead happened exactly twenty years later. And yet by 2004 she was still there, untouched. She reckoned it was because of her guns. Which was when, she said, she made her fatal mistake.

'You know what I did? I decided to *give* my farm to the government. I was so tired by then. I had been working hard all my life. At that time they were killing white farmers. My son Bredell told me: "Ma, don't keep the farm for me. Sell it, enjoy your later years." He was never a farmer. He's mechanical. He lives in Michigan, there in America, working with engines. These young people don't want to farm any more like the old days. And so I decided: before they kill me, let me offer it to them because I am old.'

She went to the Ministry of Lands in Harare and cut a deal. In exchange for her giving her farm to them they would allow her to harvest her final crop and pack her belongings unmolested. They agreed to protect her. She would leave by early in the new year.

Her voice grew softer, graver as she spoke now, her eyes watery blue pools.

'And of course they broke their word,' she whispered. 'They broke their word ...'

Unita was attacked in her home just before midnight a week before Christmas. A truckload of militia arrived, locked her and Frans in a bedroom and began to ransack the house. They were held captive for a day and a half. A black friend of Unita's came to plead with the gang leader, a ZANU-PF official from the local rural council. The leader gave Unita three more days to pack everything.

That Monday, 150 settlers arrived at her home and began offloading chickens and goats on her lawn, while she frantically tried to gather forty years of her life. When the sun fell and she was still not packed the leader came to her. 'He had a stick. He stood there like Hitler, tapping that stick on my floor: "Out! Out! Out! I want you out before dark!"

'I fell down at his feet. I said, "Please, I can't. I am tired. Please, just let me sleep, let me sleep on the carpet here tonight, I am so tired." And he said: "You are out. *Tonight!*"'

Tears were rolling down her face as she spoke. She was whispering again. 'And you know, at eleven o'clock that night we drove away, and the gates closed behind us.'

She spent that night at the home of a friend. Another friend called my parents. She arrived at Drifters in a convoy of battered trucks in a state of shock. 'Your parents were good to me, God bless them. They would take in all the destitutes.'

My father said later: 'I'll never forget what they did to that woman. I will never forget.'

Unita spoke with contempt of the councillor who'd kicked her off her farm, but she reserved particular vitriol for the official in the Ministry of Lands she had gone to see. When she spoke of him she clenched her teeth, and her tiny fingers rolled into fists.

'He was very nice to me that day. Oh, very nice. He smiled and he promised me in all fairness. But he broke his word. He broke his word.'

I had the distinct impression that if she ever ran into him again she would draw her guns: perhaps the Beretta in one hand, the Bruno in the other, both barrels blazing.

It was dark outside now. The humped hills behind us were

domed shadows. Frans was snoring. It was time to go. I thanked Unita for her time and hugged her on the porch.

She saw my tape recorder and said she had one more thing to tell me. She gazed up at the stars and whispered: 'I am returning to my place of birth, but my first love is Zimbabwe. This is where my heart is, this is where my blood is, this is where my roots are, this is where my children were born. My Zimbabwe. My Zimbabwe ...'

It was a beautiful theatrical flourish, and tears welled in my eyes.

Then she switched back to her normal voice.

'Did you get all that? Come on, give me another go – I can do it better.'

And she said it again. She had finished her final close-up.

Friends of Unita's, Mary Ann and Gerard 'Hammy' Hamilton, tobacco farmers in their late fifties, would find sanctuary in Cottage 8, on the lower slopes of the hill. Cottage 8 overlooked the reservoir that mysteriously had never filled with water again since the visit from the Top Man, and to me it was the prettiest house of all, shaded by a dense thicket of creepers and palms. It reminded me of a jungle guesthouse I'd once stayed at in Laos.

Mom arranged for me to meet the Hammies, and she was rather excited at the prospect.

'You're going to meet the red Indian,' she said.

'The red Indian?'

'Yes, Hammy's daughter, Angie, is married to a red Indian. From America.'

'Um ... Ma, I think you mean a Native American.'

'He looks like a red Indian to me,' she said, perfectly convinced.

I arrived in time for sundowners.

Hammy, Mary Ann, Angie and the 'red Indian' were tucking into beers and menthol cigarettes on a cluttered back porch, a mound of newspapers, documents and magazines – *Farmer's Weekly*, tobacco monthlies – piled high on a wrought-iron table in front of them. A fat black crossbred mastiff waddled around the yard with a bone in its mouth.

The 'red Indian' was Chris, a handsome forty-year-old pony-tailed part-Cherokee from the Midwest who had been a US Navy chef on ships sailing in the Persian Gulf. He'd been in Africa for three years and had no interest in returning to America.

'I'll never go back, man. Too many people, too developed. How can you live there?'

'I like all the people and the development,' I said.

Angie had studied hotel management, and she and Chris had worked together at luxury safari lodges and resorts all over southern Africa. Which helped explain why Chris liked it out here. They were currently on leave from an island resort they were managing in Pemba, northern Mozambique, the same area where Helen had her plot of land and where I'd tried to get Mom and Dad to move eighteen months earlier.

Hammy and Mary Ann were glad to have their daughter and Chris home, and it was touching to hear Chris, this all-American boy, call his Zimbabwean father-in-law 'Pa'.

Hammy and Mary Ann had lost their farm in the valley to a brigadier in the Zimbabwe National Army. It was what was called a 'slow bleed', a gradual takeover, and the stress of trying to hold on to it while their fields were trashed, their fences and machinery stolen, and their lives threatened had taken a heavy toll. Soon after they moved to Drifters, Hammy suffered a heart attack. They were planning a trip to South Africa so that he could get a bypass.

I asked him how his health was.

'I'm lucky,' he said. 'My wife's the best-qualified person in Zim to look after me.'

'How's that?'

Hammy took her hand. 'Should I tell him, doll?'

Mary Ann smiled and nodded.

'She's a nurse. And not just any nurse. Picture it: Groote Schuur Hospital, Cape Town, third of December, 1967. My wife was in the operating theatre with Christiaan Barnard during the world's first-ever heart transplant. My wife – can you believe it?'

'You worked on that operation?' I said, impressed.

Mary Ann smiled and nodded again.

'I tell you what,' I said. 'My dad's stressed, too. Can you help him if his ticker goes?'

'Of course,' she said, and we toasted the medical agreement over more cold beers.

For a man who had lost his home, his farm, and nearly his life, Hammy seemed surprisingly upbeat, and it wasn't just the early evening booze talking.

'I think I'm going to get my farm back,' he confidently told me.

Seeing my surprise, he explained, 'I know the vice president, Joice. Mrs Mujuru. I phoned her, told her what happened to me. She said I should come and see her. I have an appointment in Harare next week.'

Hammy did indeed know the vice president. He had been for many years a prominent member of the Commercial Farmers Union, the mainly white farmers' union that had held talks with the government since the 1980s on how to conduct proper land reform before it all blew up in their faces with the invasions in 2000. Joice Mujuru, a hero of the liberation war, was the wife of the former ZANLA guerrilla leader Solomon 'Rex Nhongo' Mujuru, and she had been part of those land reform talks over the years. Hammy said he got on well with her, and the fact that she had recently been named a vice president had given him a lifeline, access right to the top.

I wished him luck, but I wasn't sure it would work out. No white farmer had ever gotten his farm back. It simply didn't happen. Besides, my dad already had told me Hammy had been to see Mujuru before.

'Good luck to him, but I'll believe it when I see it,' he told me with a shrug.

Hammy and Mary Ann had other projects besides trying to get their farm back. As stalwarts of the CFU, they were determined to correct what they called 'the great lie' that had been propagated around the world about white Zimbabwean farmers like them.

'It's all bullshit, you know,' he told me.

'What is?'

'All this crap about us owning all the land. It's bullshit. You saw it all the time on the BBC and on CNN and in respectable foreign newspapers: "Whites owned seventy percent of the land in Zimbabwe." "White farmers had seventy percent of the fertile land in Zimbabwe." The media kept repeating it again and again until it became a fact, but it's a lie, total bullshit.'

'So how much land *did* whites own before the invasions?' I asked.

Hammy had the stats, Mary Ann had the documents. She passed him notes and pages from the files and magazines on the table, and he read extracts. They were a good team.

'Let me tell you,' he said. 'Commercial farming makes up only twenty-eight percent of this country's land. But there's a black farmers' union that represents six percent of that. The Development Trust, which is government, has three percent. There are black tenant farmers with four percent. And Forestry has one percent. That leaves whites with about fourteen percent of the country's land. Doesn't sound the same as seventy percent, does it? And that fourteen percent produced about sixty-five percent of all agricultural produce and fifty percent of foreign earnings, and employed or supported almost two million people. But all you ever heard about was us greedy white farmers.'

Everyone has their truth in Zimbabwe, but Hammy was correct. The Mugabe government's figures *were* routinely quoted by the world's media, and they gave the impression that in a country as fertile as Zimbabwe, a mere forty-five hundred white farmers controlled seventy percent of its land mass. Who wouldn't be outraged by that? But the seventy-percent statistic used by the state and repeated elsewhere ad nauseam applied in fact to only one region: the fertile Mashonaland tobacco farming belt around Harare.

The bitterest irony for Hammy, though, was that he'd bought his farm in 1985 after attending a meeting the president called to *ask* white farmers to stay in the country. Incredibly, it is estimated that by 2000, 76 per cent of white-owned farms had in fact been purchased *after* independence, and it became illegal after 1987 for anyone to sell a farm without first offering it to the government. My father made sure, before buying Drifters, that it had a Certificate of No Present Interest – confirmation that the government had been offered the land but didn't want it. No one in their right mind bought a farm in Zimbabwe after 1987 without such a certificate.

'You want to know the real reason for the invasions?' said Hammy, taking a deep drag on his cigarette. 'The government had run the economy so badly into the ground that they needed a distraction for all the people without jobs. And who took the hit? Us whites.'

Hammy had another theory that flew in the face of much that I had come to believe: that very few Zimbabweans – black or white – actually *wanted* to be farmers. 'You know how hard it is to farm? Let me tell you: bloody hard. And who wants to be on a farm when you have an education? This country was educated!

Mugabe did that. People want to wear suits and ties and sit at desks and work on computers in town. Now he's telling them to go back and sit on the land? It's mad, year-zero stuff.'

If I looked in the immediate vicinity I could see his point. I was a farmer's son; I had no interest in farming. Angie had managed her dad's farm, but she preferred hotel management. Unita's son was working in the United States. The only young person on this farm who actually wanted to farm was Dawson Jombe, and he had been thrown off a farm and was now running my parents' lodge – as a brothel.

Hammy was on a roll. He could have gone on longer, but we were suddenly interrupted by a loud blast of music emanating from the backpacker camp. It was 8:00 pm, Sydney had his sound track on, the brothel was open, and 50 Cent, New York's finest, was giving it his all, echoing up the hill: *You can find me in the club, bottle full of bub, look mami I got the X if you into takin' drugs...*

Chris and Angie rolled their eyes.

'It could be another long night, Pa,' Angie groaned.

They sounded like homesteaders in an old Western movie, except they were afraid not of a late-night attack by bandits but rather of a musical assault by a DJ in a backpacker camp.

'Ya, *again*,' said Hammy. 'We were kept awake by this rubbish the other night, too. Jeez, Drifters used to be so great. Pizzas. Braais. Tourists. Now? Now it's just like a brothel.'

I wanted to tell him it wasn't *like* a brothel. It was pretty much the real thing.

Another widow lived in Cottage 14, closer to the top of the hill, which appeared to suit her lofty social status. Her name was Charlotte Kok, but my parents called her Lady Charlotte. She was an Afrikaner blue blood, a true Boer Brahmin.

'Don't be late for Lady Charlotte,' said Mom. '*No one* is late for Lady Charlotte.'

Charlotte had invited me round for 'tea and biccies', and I made sure I wasn't late.

An elegant, slightly built woman, one year shy of her eightieth birthday, she stepped out to greet me in the garden, the breeze playing with her imperious bouffant and a rope of pearls around her neck. She spoke in a cut-glass accent more Victorian English than Afrikaans. Her daughter, Tess, an artist visiting from Harare, made us tea.

Charlotte had *pedigree*.

'Do you know that the city of Pretoria, the capital of South Africa, is named for my great-great-grandfather Andries Pretorius?'

'Major Andries Pretorius,' piped up Tess from the kitchen.

'No, Tess,' scolded her mother. 'He was a general. A Boer leader at Blood River.'

'Oh, sorry, Ma. Big stuff.'

It was the aftermath of the Second Boer War that brought Charlotte's family to Rhodesia.

'I was born in the Orange Free State in 1926, and my father moved us up here in 1929. In South Africa it was brother against brother back then – the Boer War had divided whole families – and my father wanted to get away from all the fighting.'

'Ironical, hey, considering …' began Tess.

'Okay, Tess, that's enough.'

Her father had bought land outside Rusape, a small settlement in the west of the valley.

'Land was cheap then. A pound an acre. This government says we stole it, but the country was empty back then. No one around. We had to recruit workers from Mozambique and Malawi. We cleared the bush and planted tobacco. We were the only family in the whole area to have a car, an old blue Essex, which you had to crank to start. It would take us two days to drive to Umtali [Mutare]. Strip roads. We would pack a picnic. Those were the days.'

Charlotte liked saying *Those were the days*. She got a dreamy look in her eyes.

'Staying at the Cecil Hotel in town. You know, we used to order all our clothes from a shop in England called Swan & Edgar in Piccadilly Circus. The catalogues used to come regularly and we would choose: linens, silks, cottons. And in no time at all they would have sent a parcel out to us in the bush in Africa. They were never pinched in the post like they are now. Of course, it would never even get to you now. Those were the days.'

By the 1950s she was married to a rugby-playing farmer named Basie Kok, and they'd established one of the country's richest tobacco estates in Inyazura.

It sounded as grand as a stately southern mansion: deep porch, sweeping lawns.

'You had some wild parties there, didn't you, Mom?' teased Tess.

'Oh, Tess, I don't want to speak about *that*,' said Lady Charlotte.

Tess had heard about them, though. Apparently her mother would host fancy soirées, and all the rough-hewn tobacco farmers would come from miles around. They would always scrape off the black muck she put on thin slices of bread – they didn't much care for caviar shipped via London.

Speaking to my parents and other farmers, I heard similar tales about life in the valley: the swinging fifties, a very happy valley, key parties – apparently it would take a while for a newcomer to work out who was whose husband. There was a horse-racing track on one farm, even a motor-racing circuit with vintage cars zooming through the red dust. Landed white gentry and remittance men and their mistresses got sozzled on gin and tonics served by black servants in white gloves and fezzes.

Then came the sixties. The good times rolled.

'Mom, you went to parties at La Rochelle, didn't you?' Tess said.

'Oh, Tess, I don't want to speak about that,' repeated Lady Charlotte, rolling her eyes.

But Tess knew all about La Rochelle, too. It was the estate of Sir Stephen and Lady Virginia Courtauld, wealthy English philanthropists who flew the length of Africa in their own plane in the 1950s and landed up in the eastern corner of the valley. The estate was in dense tropical forest, the top of which we used to be able to see from the lawn of my parents' chicken farm. Irises and tulips and acres of pruned white roses rolled for miles, and in the afternoons guests sipped tea and played croquet on the lawns under parasols as clouds of black butterflies flew overhead. Inside, the walls were hung with Turner paintings; the ballroom supposedly had the biggest Persian carpet in the world. The couple threw lavish parties, hosting visiting royalty, British stage actors who came to town and a few lucky locals. My parents never got the nod – "We were just bloody chicken farmers," Mom noted. The Courtaulds were famous liberals, too. It was said that La Rochelle was the only place where white Rhodesians rubbed shoulders socially with black political activists, who were frequent guests. The first ZANU constitution was signed at La Rochelle in the 1960s, and the house was never attacked by Mugabe's guerrillas during the war.

'Do you know,' said Tess, 'guests had to carve their names on the glass windows in the ballroom with a diamond-tipped stylus? It's still there – you should go and see it.'

But, in truth, Lady Charlotte wasn't much for talking about those days. Like Unita, she was getting ready to move to South Africa.

She didn't want to relive losing the family farm, either. Charlotte had moved to Drifters when her eldest son, Christo, lost that estate in Inyazura. This poky cottage must have been something of a comedown.

I asked her if she knew who took the farm.

'Oh, yes,' she said, 'the minister. Who else? He has *five* farms in the area.' *The minister ... the Top Man.*

'Hang around and you might get to see him take this place, too,' I told her.

'I couldn't bear it,' she said. 'Why do you think I'm leaving?'

Christo was now working in real estate in Cape Town, selling wine farms to wealthy Germans and Americans, and Charlotte would soon join him there. I could see Charlotte retiring to an estate in the Cape, that far southern tip of Africa, where her ancestors, like mine, had landed three hundred and fifty years ago before trekking into the interior of Africa. Charlotte was now trekking back. It would be a homecoming of sorts, a closing of the circle. Whites were gathering there in increasing numbers, their backs to the godforsaken continent, their feet on the edge of the ocean. It was, quite literally, the last stop. Still, I had the feeling Lady Charlotte would be okay. She had that air about her.

EIGHT

The Old Boer Wants His Cattle Back

THE MOST FAMOUS farmer on the property was harder to pin down.

Piet de Klerk – Oom Piet, as he was known for miles around – and his wife, Mienkie, occupied Cottage 6, Cassia, the one farthest from my parents' house, in the saddle of the hills, under the shadow of a tall blue-gum tree.

He was hard to pin down because every morning we would see his battered jalopy clatter down my parents' driveway, turn left on the main road, and disappear.

'There goes Piet,' Dad would say. 'Off to try to get his cattle back.'

He would be gone much of the day, and I didn't want to disturb them in the evenings. Piet was 76, Mienkie 74, and while they were in excellent health, they were very much the senior citizens of the property. I had heard about Oom Piet since I was a skinny kid kicking a rugby ball around the fields of Chancellor Junior School. His youngest sons were my seniors in high school and very good rugby players, but Piet was a legend: not only had he captained Rhodesia and come close to playing for the Springboks, he'd also once scored a try against the mighty All Blacks.

I finally got to meet him the week before I returned to New York, but only because his car had broken down. I ended up spending several evenings with him and Mienkie on their porch, gazing out at the giant blue gum casting a long shadow across the *vlei*.

Piet was a giant of a man. Over six foot five tall, with legs like baobab trunks and hands the size of baskets, he had to stoop just to get through the doorway to the veranda. Like Frans, he too had a scrapbook, but it wasn't filled with rugby clippings. It was a collection of articles from foreign and local newspapers that chronicled the destruction of his farm, Kondozi, a story that had taken on the dimensions of Shakespearean tragedy in the area. It was said that even senior members of ZANU-PF were ashamed of what they did to that farm.

It was a 3,500-hectare horticultural farm 24 kilometres south-west of Drifters that exported runner beans, baby corn, sugar snap peas, mangetout, red peppers and other vegetables to Sains-bury's and Tesco. The mangetout I bought at the Clapham Tes-co down the road from my London hovel in the late 1990s were grown on Kondozi.

It hadn't always been a horticulture project.

Piet, who'd come to Rhodesia from Cape Town in 1953, bought the farm in 1968 and originally grew tobacco and raised cattle. He stayed on the farm throughout the guerrilla war, mi-raculously escaping with his life after being blown up by a land mine while driving in an armoured truck on the edge of his land in 1976.

After independence he became the chief instigator in the construction of Osborne Dam, finally completed in 1990, which overnight brought irrigation to the driest parts of the valley. You never could have grown vegetables for export in the area before the dam.

By 2000 Piet and Mienkie had retired to a farmhouse on Kondozi – named for a river on the land – and three of their four sons, Piet junior, Thewie and Koos, ran the operation. Kondozi was unlike other large commercial farms in the area in that it operated on an outgrowers system. The De Klerk sons trained teams of black agronomists and technicians to travel the area on motorbikes teaching black peasant farmers to grow vegetables to the standards demanded by European supermarkets. Dawson Jombe was one of their first technical managers.

Kondozi provided small-scale black farmers with seeds, fertiliser and advice, and then bought the vegetables from them at harvest (minus the inputs they had given them), thereby guaranteeing a market. Six thousand people were directly employed on the farm – the biggest employer in the valley. But eighty small-scale black farmers in the area had become prosperous and successful through its outgrowers scheme, and the project supported some seven thousand black families in the region – probably as many as thirty-five thousand people.

'We had a beautiful thing going there,' purred Mienkie, a classy Afrikaner who spoke in fast, clipped sentences between elegant drags on her Kingsgate extra-longs. 'We had a bus that would drive out from Mutare every day with our accountants and technicians. We had a modern office complex filled with computers. A clinic with a doctor, four nurses and an ambulance. We had a very beautiful thing going there.'

Kondozi earned US$15 million a year in vital foreign currency for the country, and under the government's own land reform laws was classified as an export processing zone, which meant it was exempt from resettlement. In 2001, hundreds of settlers began staking out plots in fields that were supposed to grow prize vegetables. Instead of confronting them, the De Klerk sons started training them to grow vegetables. In two seasons, settlers with little farming experience were suddenly producing food fit for European markets.

But if Unita Herrer's mistake was to offer her land to the government, the De Klerks' mistake was much bigger. They were involved in politics. The sons secretly funded the opposition, and had hosted that clandestine meeting before the 2002 election for MDC volunteers. The government, it turned out, knew all along.

The sons were warned by the area's local MP, Chris Mushowe, to stop funding the MDC. The sons refused. The backlash was brutal – and personal. In the end it wasn't ordinary ruling party officials who claimed Kondozi farm: it was the country's Minister of Agriculture, Joseph Made, and Mushowe, who by then had been promoted to transport minister.

In 2003 Koos de Klerk and his young family were tied up in their home for two days, their young daughter threatened with rape. When they left the farm, Mushowe moved into their house. On Christmas Day 2003, Made arrived and declared that Kondozi was being taken over by the Agriculture and Rural Development Authority, which already owned a twenty-thousand-hectare ranch, Transsau, right next door, on which nothing grew. Made ordered Kondozi's workers to leave. They refused.

It was common by now – and astonishing, given the colonial history of Zimbabwe – for black farmworkers to side with white landowners. What was not so common was for farmworkers to attack and repel better-armed invaders. But it happened at Kondozi.

'It was amazing,' Piet recalled. 'Some of our female workers were picking green beans when they were approached by thirty war vets. The leader told the female supervisor to get off the land because they were taking it. She refused. He started beating her with a stick. She screamed for help on her mobile radio. The call was picked up by a team of fifteen young men erecting trellises for runner beans with fence posts. They each grabbed a post and ran to the rescue.'

Mienkie chuckled.

'Some of the men were the settlers who first occupied us in 2002. They were making a good living now. And they didn't take kindly to the war vets beating their women.'

A fight ensued in the middle of the bean field. The war vets were routed. Three were badly injured, others scattered, and one disappeared. The next day the police arrived searching for the missing man and accused Thewie de Klerk of abducting him. The man was finally reported spotted in a town thirty-two kilometres away.

'It seems that he didn't stop running,' said Mienkie.

But the fight back was only ever going to be brief. When the war veterans returned weeks later, they came with the force of an army. Water cannons were used to crush the last resistance. Within a month, one of the most productive and progressive farms in Africa collapsed.

Millions of dollars' worth of equipment, including forty-eight tractors, a dozen high-tech transport buses, twenty-six motorbikes and tons of fertiliser and chemicals, were looted. European supermarkets cancelled their contracts. The outgrowers scheme folded. Outraged at what had happened, a local chief named Marange, whose villagers worked and farmed for Kondozi, went to Harare to confront President Mugabe himself. He got an audience with Vice President Joseph Msika, who launched an investigation. It was said that even the Top Man was ashamed. The fallout from the collapse of Kondozi went right to the very top.

Incredibly, Piet and Mienkie remained on the farm after all their sons had been evicted.

'At one point I went to the Odzi police station,' Piet said. 'I told them: "Go tell Mr Mushowe that if he wants my farm, he must come and shoot me and bury me there."'

The message got through. When the police produced a map

of how Kondozi would be divided, a red circle had been drawn around Oom Piet's house and section. It was marked *Mr de Klerk's land*. He would be allowed to stay. But by then the old couple were isolated: their sons had all left, and the farm they had created out of raw bush thirty-six years earlier had been ransacked. They joined the convoy of refugees to Drifters.

I paged through the scrapbook as Piet and Mienkie spoke, and I came across the same article I had read – and then smoked – down at the camp with John Muranda a week earlier, the one that reported a government minister's telling villagers at political rallies that Piet de Klerk was related to FW de Klerk, the last white president of South Africa, and that he wanted to enslave blacks and bring apartheid to Zimbabwe.

'What did you think when you started hearing that?' I asked.

Piet smiled and shrugged. Then he said something that almost made me fall off my chair.

'But I am related to FW de Klerk. I come from the same Burgersdorp De Klerks. That was about the only thing the bloody minister got right about me.'

I was stunned, but now that I looked at him again, I could see the resemblance. They had the same bald, ostrich-egg head, the same receding crown of hair, even the same wire-rimmed glasses. Oom Piet was a decade older and about a foot taller, but they could almost be mistaken for brothers.

Mienkie said, 'They look the same, but of course my husband is much sexier.'

The De Klerks, I discovered, were more than just new residents on my parents' land. They had become close friends with my parents. Dad and Piet would watch rugby games together on TV and talk about what the best possible Springbok team was. Typically, Piet being Afrikaans and my father a half-English South African, they never came close to agreeing. When a dear friend of my mother's – the last of her bridge ladies – died of cancer, Mienkie walked up to the house with flowers and a fresh-baked *melktert*. 'Ros, I know you've lost someone very dear and I can never replace her,' she said, 'but I want you to know I am here for you always.'

Mienkie was a former teacher like my mother, but even better read, given to quoting Shakespeare and Proust one minute, dirty one-liners the next..

'Look at your husband, Minks,' Dad once teased her. 'Struggling all day to get his cows back. A good man is hard to find.'

'A *hard* man is good to find,' she said, deadpan, between drags on her cigarette.

It was wonderful for me to see that my parents had these new friends. They were helping one another, adapting, hanging in.

One of the reasons they got on so well was that they were in the same boat. Like my parents, the De Klerks had invested all their money in their farm; they hadn't filtered a fortune out of the country, as other white farmers – wisely, it could now be seen – had done. They were paying a price for investing in their own country. Their children were scattered, too, but not to foreign cities. Thewie was farming in Mozambique, Piet junior and Koos in Zambia – countries whose black governments welcomed skilled white farmers.

News of the tragedy at Kondozi had reached as far as Zambia. Mienkie told me that she and Piet had recently been to visit their sons there. 'We were driving through immigration on the Zambia side and this uniformed black customs lady ran after our car. I got such a fright. She came and tapped on my window. "Are you Mrs de Klerk? The farming De Klerk?" I was horrified. I thought, *Oh, God, what have I done now?* I rolled down the window, and she said: "I am sorry about what happened to your family in Zimbabwe. It is an honour to have your sons in our country." I mean, what could I say? I had tears in my eyes. What a beautiful thing to say.'

I loved the evenings I spent with Piet and Mienkie, and I especially enjoyed Piet's old rugby stories. He told me about the try he'd scored for Rhodesia against the All Blacks. In that 1960 game he locked against Colin Meads, one of the greatest rugby players of all time. Piet chuckled as he recalled the story.

'At one point I was on the ground and Meads was standing right on top of me in his big boots. I thought, *Meads, you bastard!* Our captain caught the ball at the next lineout. He kicked it ahead. I went charging full speed after it. I was pretty fast at that time. I used to train by running through my tobacco fields at night with a flashlight. I collected the ball on the twenty-five-metre line. Meads was chasing me. He caught me about three metres out, but I carried him on my back over the try line. I had scored! Hell, ja, I enjoyed that. It was a good try. Of course, Meads stepped all over me after that. Like he was crushing grapes.'

Piet was still in touch with all his rugby friends in South Africa, many of them famous Springboks, and he said they all thought he and Mienkie were mad to still be living here. One had even offered to build a house for them on his farm if they just would leave.

'That was nice of him, ja, but ag no, we can't go live down south.'

I thought I knew why. The deaths of fourteen white farmers in Zimbabwe had made front-page international news these past five years, but it was a little-reported fact that far more white farmers – some said as many as a thousand – had been murdered on their land in South Africa since 1994. But that wasn't the reason Piet and Mienkie wouldn't go live there.

He looked out at the pretty garden in front of him, the grassy vlei, and the smoky pink sunset turning to black behind the blue-gum tree.

'Ag no, man. Mienks and I, we're Zimbabweans. We love it here. I mean, look at this place. It's beautiful. A cottage, a garden, our friends around us. What more could we want?'

But there was one thing I knew Oom Piet did want, and very

badly. It was what made him get up at dawn every morning, clatter down my parents' driveway in his battered white Mazda, turn left on the main road and drive out toward that farm he had started out of virgin bush nearly forty years ago. He wanted his cattle back. When he and Mienkie left Kondozi, they had left behind 300 Simmental cattle, 170 head of sheep, some goats and a pet zebra named Stripey that thought it was a horse. For Piet, the loss of his livestock was never part of any land reform programme, and he was now fighting with the new occupants of the farm and meeting with local chiefs and ruling party officials to try to get them back.

'All I want is my cattle,' he told me one evening. 'All I want is my cattle …'

My heart sank when I heard those words. I thought of Hammy believing he would get his farm back. It would never happen. They were gone forever.

And yet it wasn't only an eccentric band of refugee white farmers who now occupied the cottages at the back of my parents' land. I was surprised to discover that my parents had several black tenants besides Dawson, and as the likes of Unita and Lady Charlotte moved on, more black families moved in.

It wasn't as if my parents had turned down black tenants before. The cottages had all been purchased by whites back in the 1990s when they were first built, and when those owners left the country they either sold or leased their homes to friends or relatives. As the white population dwindled, however, those absentee owners knew no one left to rent to, and the houses stood empty. Empty cottages were routinely burgled by bandits, putting everyone's safety at risk, so my father took it upon himself to find tenants. Cottages he didn't fill with white farmers he leased to black families from Mutare or the valley.

Growing the bush on the front of the land was a physical barrier, a camouflage; having the cottages occupied made sense politically. 'Anyone coming to take this place will have to do more than just evict us,' Dad reckoned. 'They'll have to evict a whole lot of black people, too. It might make even them question the morality of their behaviour.'

My father was starting to play a cunning political game.

I had already got to know Dawson on those evenings down at the bar. He had been referred to my parents by Piet and Mienkie de Klerk, who viewed him as the best technical manager they'd ever had at Kondozi.

The next black tenant, however, was chosen out of pure self-interest.

One of the original cottage occupants, a stalwart of the community named Dave Burnett, mentioned to my father that a black businessman he knew from Mutare, a dapper, middle-aged gentleman named Charles Mhlanga, was interested in leasing number 11.

'What does he do?' Dad asked.

'He's a senior financial manager at ZESA in town,' said Dave.

Dad's eyes lit up as if charged by a kilowatt of power from the national grid. ZESA was the Zimbabwe Electricity Supply Authority. The power on the farm was starting to fail regularly. The lights were frequently out. Bandits stole power cables and valuable copper wire to smelt down and export to China. It was hard to get ZESA technicians to tend to all the faults. But with a senior ZESA official living on the land? That would be different.

My father practically pushed Charles Mhlanga into number 11.

'ZESA Man,' Mom and Dad nicknamed him – a superhero with a magical ability to create light – and for a while Drifters had one of the most regular power supplies in the valley. Within minutes of a blackout Dad would phone ZESA Man or simply drive around to his cottage. 'Sorry, Charles, lights are out. Can you call your men?'

Even Charles couldn't perform miracles, though. Within a year the entire country was, quite literally, beginning to go dark. The power turbines at Hwange, near Victoria Falls, were collapsing because of mismanagement and the loss of skilled staff, and the government, unable to pay the bills for the power it now had to import from Zambia, Congo and South Africa, started introducing rolling blackouts known as load-shedding.

'What did we do before candles?' went the local joke. 'Electricity.' The joke became dated fast, because soon shops ran out of candles.

My parents eventually bought a generator, but as the load-shedding got worse, Charles, with typical Zimbabwean ingenuity, 'made a plan'. He persuaded my father to lease some of the other empty cottages on the property to ZESA colleagues of his who needed homes, and soon four more black tenants – all ZESA technicians and engineers – moved onto the land. Drifters once again had a reasonable electricity supply.

It was the discovery of the relative of another black tenant in the cottages, however, that most amazed me. On my very last evening before returning to New York I was walking back from Piet and Mienkie's, and passing number 4, Acacia, I saw a small, elderly, well-dressed man with tortoiseshell glasses sitting on the front veranda writing in a notebook by candlelight. The old man nodded as I walked past.

'Evening, sir,' I said.

He looked familiar. Where was he from? How did I know him? I carried on up to the house, racking my brain. Then it came to me, clear as a lightning bolt, all the way back from the grape farm in 1979.

In that year Rhodesia was briefly known as Zimbabwe-Rhodesia, and the first black leader of our country, for all of seven months before President Mugabe won power in the 1980 election, was the Methodist bishop Abel Muzorewa. Muzorewa's United African National Congress (UANC) had clinched a democratic election in April 1979 and agreed to share power with whites. The two guerrilla movements – Mugabe's Shona-dominated ZANLA and Joshua Nkomo's Zimbabwe People's Revolutionary Army (ZIPRA) – considered Muzorewa a puppet and refused to participate in the election. No Western leaders recognised Muzorewa, either, and the war and the sanctions continued until new elections in February 1980.

Muzorewa was still the choice of most whites for that election, and we all thought he would win easily. He was a moderate and an anti-Communist; Mugabe was a Marxist. Stephanie, Helen and I informally campaigned for Muzorewa. Driving to school in the morning from the grape farm, we threw UANC fliers out at pedestrians. We waved our hands out the windows, shouting '*Pamberi ne UANC!*' (Forward UANC) and 'Vote the Bishop!' We were young kids caught in the first thrilling flush of a democratic awakening. Sandra just sat in the back of the car polishing her nails. She wouldn't get involved, so we accused her of supporting ZANU. It's why we started calling her Zaan, a name we still use for her today. As for the bemused black people we implored to vote UANC, they waved happily back at us. Of course, few of them ended up voting for the bishop at all: Robert Mugabe won in a landslide. We all felt like fools after that. Except my mother, that is. She kept her counsel in the lead-up to that election, too. She had a sense, even then, that nothing was as it seemed out here.

The man on the veranda looked *exactly* like Abel Muzorewa. I knew it couldn't possibly be him. That had been twenty-five years ago, and I presumed he was long dead.

I got back to the house and found Mom cooking my farewell dinner on a gas stove on the kitchen floor. The power had gone out again, and Dad had gone to call ZESA Man. I mentioned that someone who looked just like Abel Muzorewa was staying in number 4.

She looked up at me, barely impressed, concerned more with her chicken casserole. 'Oh, it is him. He comes and visits his brother Ernest, who's living here at the moment.'

I wasn't sure I had heard correctly.

'What? Bishop Muzorewa, the former prime minister, lives in number 4?'

'No, darling, his *brother* lives there. Ernest and his wife, Florence, farm down the road. Their house burned down on their daughter's wedding day a while back, so they've moved into one of the cottages while they rebuild. The bishop comes and visits from Harare. Piet and Mienkie have got to know him. They say he's a nice man. Do me a favour, pass the salt.'

I reached for the salt. The albino frog blinked at me from the copper coffeepot. The lights came back on. ZESA Man had done the trick. A light came on in my head, too.

My parents had a relative of South African president FW de Klerk in one cottage and a former political activist and African prime minister in another? I couldn't believe what she was saying. And it suddenly dawned on me that their farm was more than just a piece of land. It had become a stage set, a metaphor for the state of the nation. You could literally see the fortunes of the country unfolding in microcosm from their front lawn: the struggling squatters tearing up the land across the road; the desperate prostitutes and the men with SUVs who paid for them down at the camp; the eccentric white farmers and their new black neighbours out back; and my parents and a staff of three in the middle of it all, conducting operations, manipulating, planning, scheming, trying to stay alive.

I was now filled with admiration for my parents. What they had built here out of virgin bush fifteen years ago had become central to the events of the country. Things could rise or fall depending on what happened right here.

Of course, what I didn't know then – what none of us knew then – was that the danger was about to get closer. Much closer. It was about to move in right across the road.

NINE
Friends and Neighbours

MY MOTHER DIDN'T smuggle marijuana to New York when she and my father came for my wedding in the last week of April 2005, much to my relief. Customs officers at Newark airport didn't bother to search her suitcase, but if they had, they would have found two cartons of Kingsgate cigarettes, a bottle of Bols brandy and the rolled-up canvas of an oil painting.

The cigarettes and the booze were for her. She always travelled with them now to save money. The painting was our wedding gift.

It was a shimmering landscape of Osborne Dam by Itai Nyagu, a young black artist my mother, a painter herself and an avid collector, had come across in the valley, and whose work she exhibited and sold in the gallery on the ground floor of Drifters during the tourist years. The gallery no longer functioned, but my mother loved Itai's work and had bought the painting five years ago. In it, two fisherwomen in blue headdresses cast nets into the shallows, and cotton clouds reflect in the water around them. An old bicycle leans against a msasa tree on the banks. It's a beautiful, bucolic scene. My parents wanted me to hang it in our bedroom – 'to remind you where you come from'.

It was accompanied by a near-indecipherable note written by Dawson Jombe and signed by the two Johns and Naomi down at the camp. It took me a while to work out what it said.

Douglas, they had written, *we are happy you are to married. Please to be faithful. Don't forget us in Zimbabwe.*

My parents took to New York City the way country people the world over take to big cities: with wide-eyed wonder and confusion bordering on panic.

Within an hour of his arrival my father contrived to lose the South African credit card he had acquired specially for the trip. On that first evening in the city my three sisters, who had flown in on the same day, took them to see stand-up comedy in the East Village. Urban rookies, Mom and Dad insisted on sitting at a mysteriously empty table closest to the stage.

'This, I discovered, is a big no-no,' Dad told me the next morning, tucking into the steak I had left over from my bachelor party at Peter Luger steakhouse the night before, 'since the comics picked on your mom and me and seemed to find it rather amusing that we'd come all the way from Africa. I'm not sure why. It's not like we're from somewhere weird, like Texas. Or Florida.'

At the rehearsal dinner in a Mexican restaurant in Manhattan, Dad made a speech of surprising tact, telling Grace's family, 'You're welcome to visit us in Zimbabwe,' before adding, 'if our house hasn't burned down yet.'

Grace's dad, Ed, boomed with laughter.

'No, thanks. I think we'll stick around here!'

We were married at two o'clock on 30 April in the Church of the Guardian Angel, at Tenth Avenue and Twenty-first Street. Helen told me she saw Dad wipe away a tear during our vows. Grace and I had joined an exclusive club: only my father's deceased uncle and dead dog had ever made him cry.

Two Gypsy musicians – violinist and accordion player – whom Grace had met busking at the Broadway-Lafayette subway stop a week earlier marched us all up Tenth Avenue to the Chelsea loft we had hired on Twenty-eighth Street. There my parents proceeded to drink most of our supposedly hard-partying friends under the table.

One London friend, Anna, passed out before the dinner after three mojitos. My mother, well into her fourth, watched her go down.

'Can't handle her drink too well, can she?' she said, and ordered another.

At dinner they sat next to a dear friend of mine, Jim Zug, who had stayed at Drifters once in 1994, while en route to Mozambique. They hadn't seen him since then.

'Jim, how was Mozambique?' Dad boomed.

'I contracted cerebral malaria and almost died.'

'Yes, that can happen,' said Dad. 'Bloody good game fishing, though.'

I had told several of my mates – and certainly not Grace's parents – about the brothel and marijuana plantation back home, and my father took to his assigned role as sixty-eight-year-old pimp and dope farmer with some pride. *'Meneer Rogers, luister, hoeveel ruk 'n zol en 'n cherry 'n ou deesdae in Zim met die inflasie en als?'* [How much would a joint and a lady put you back in Zim these days with inflation and all?] our Afrikaans buddy Deon asked him straight up.

'Vergeet dit Boet, jy kan dit nie bekostig nie.' [Forget it, young man, you can't afford the ladies we have.] Dad chuckled.

Mom handed out her Kingsgates on the rooftop, and I enjoyed a cigar up there with my brother-in-law Rob as a mist came in over the Hudson.

'Do you ever think it was all a big mistake?' Rob asked me as he gazed down on the city.

'Jeez, Robbie, give me time. I've only been married three hours.'

'No, not that,' he said. 'You know. Us. Africa.'

Rob owned a software company in Harare and was a brilliant businessman. He had somehow kept his company afloat all these years while watching the staff he trained emigrate, the economy plummet and the government threaten to raid his business and take it away, just as it had done with white farms. Like all Zimbabwe business owners not in bed with the regime, he faced ruinous fines or even prison if he failed to pay every punitive new tax the state passed without warning.

Now he pointed in wonder to the city around us: the Empire State Building shrouded in mist, the canyon streets below humming effortlessly with the thousand cars of a New York night, a cruise ship easing down the Hudson.

'Do you ever think our ancestors got on the wrong boat?' he said.

I thought about Rob's words a couple of days later when Grace's mother, Barbara, took my mother to see *La Damnation de Faust* at Lincoln Centre.

I'd long been of the belief that my parents and Grace's parents were so far removed from one another's experiences that they would have little in common. Barbara, half Irish, half English, and Ed, an Armenian, lived in safe, upscale American suburbia; my parents lived on a besieged farm in a chaotic, lawless country. And yet, when Grace and I watched our mothers walk out together from the opera that night, arm in arm, chatting excitedly about the performance they'd just seen, they looked as if they had been friends forever. They were the same kind of people, with the same values and love of family, art, culture and a game of bridge. But a simple quirk of geography meant they lived wildly different lives: *their* ancestors had taken different boats.

I dropped Mom and Dad off at the airport bus to Newark in lower Manhattan days later. It had been a whirlwind week, but I hadn't seen them this happy since that millennium family reunion five years earlier, and I imagined they would be devastated to be leaving, to be going back *there*. But it turned out they were quite excited and rather relieved.

'It's lovely here, darling,' Mom sighed as she hugged me goodbye, 'but really, it does make your head spin. The noise. The traffic. So many people. Phew! I don't know how you do it. We're looking forward to some peace and quiet.'

'Peace and quiet?' I spluttered.

'Well, of course, we have a few problems of our own.'

I waved goodbye. As the bus pulled away, the gaping hole in the ground where the World Trade Center towers had once stood came into view. My parents were going back to their own ground zero.

Grace spent the first five weeks of our married life in Iraq, working on a documentary about the upcoming trial of Saddam Hussein. Some honeymoon.

'You think your country has problems?' she said on one satellite phone call she made from a mass-grave site in Halabja, Kurdistan.

We took a late honeymoon in Argentina and Brazil, and I wrote pieces about it for various publications. I was now writing for glossy American travel magazines, which paid better than UK ones, including expenses. I was starting to feel like a proper writer. *Travel & Leisure* flew me to Mozambique to do a story on Pemba, where my sister's plot stands on a beautiful bay – the plot I'd wanted my parents to move to. I did a story during the same trip for London's *Saturday Telegraph* magazine on a remarkable white Zimbabwean farmer named Jake Jackson who, unable to farm in Zimbabwe, had transformed a desperately poor, war-torn part of northern Mozambique into rich farmland by training more than forty thousand black Mozambicans to grow tobacco and other crops for export. Peasants who had recently lived in mud huts, dependent on food handouts from the West, were now building houses, driving four-by-fours and sending their children to school. Men like Jake Jackson are lost to Zimbabwe. They now live as expatriates in many remote rural parts of Africa, where their skills are used to help feed and develop those countries, as they once did in Zimbabwe. Few of them will ever return.

I confess I paid little attention to my parents at this time. For two months in late 2005 I didn't communicate with them at all: their phone lines were down, which meant the Internet, too, and besides, I was busy making a life with Grace and loving New York and our perfect Brooklyn neighbourhood.

Then, early one Saturday morning in late January 2006, Grace shook me awake.

'Bubba, your mom's on the phone.'

'What?'

'Your mother's on the phone.'

It was still dark outside; I was hung-over.

'My *mother*? Surely not.'

My parents never called me. They couldn't afford to, for a start. I was amazed my mother had even worked out the dialling codes. There were a lot of numbers to get in the right order, zeroes to drop, ones to add; she couldn't even work a VCR. She had the time zones all wrong, of course: it was midday in Africa, but there was a blizzard outside our window, and it was only two hours since I had staggered home from the Brooklyn Social, my favourite haunt on Smith Street.

Then it hit me. She hadn't gotten the times wrong at all. This was the call. The call I had been dreading all these years, the call everyone who has elderly parents dreads. We all know it will come. We just never know when.

My mouth was rough as sandpaper, but I was suddenly wide awake, and I ran to the phone, heart racing, blood beating back the headache.

'Hi. Mom. What is it? What's happened?'

'Hello, my darling,' she said.

Her voice was soft, gentle, a mellifluous purr through the static. *So this is how I hear about the death of my father? A phone call on a cold and dark Saturday morning from a voice that sounds like birdsong?*

'Oh, everything's fine,' she said sweetly. 'I just want to wish you a happy New Year.'

God. Is that it? My heart slowed to a panic.

'Jeez, Mom, thanks, but it's the middle of January.'

'I know, my darling, but we haven't heard from you in ages, and the lines have been down for so long. They say it's "maintenance", but we all know the Chinese have been brought in to install monitoring devices. They're probably listening to us now. Anyway, your dad's gone to Mozambique today to get supplies. I'm home alone and the bloody power's gone off. Again! I can't even watch the cricket. So I thought I'd give you a call.'

I was relieved, but suddenly filled with an aching sadness at the thought of my mother all alone out there, in those faraway hills, in a dark house.

I Skyped her back, and we spoke for an hour on a signal so clear that she sounded like she was in Manhattan. It always amazed me how my computer could connect so easily to them on the farm, where the fried telephone cables were severed to make animal traps, the telegraph poles chopped down for firewood.

She seemed so calm, and she managed to convince me, as she always did in that unfussy way of hers, that everything was perfectly fine with them.

But in fact things were not fine with them at all. They had been robbed on New Year's Day. They had a dangerous new neighbour: a man with intentions on their home. And my father was spending his nights sitting under the giant fig tree with a loaded shotgun on his lap.

Things were not fine at all.

No one knew exactly when the Political Commissar moved into Frank's house across the road, but my parents found out one lunchtime in December 2005. They were sitting on the veranda working on the *Recipes for Disaster* cookbook idea. Mom had more than a dozen recipes by now, and they were coming up with new ones all the time. One chapter would be about bread. There were bread shortages across the country – since the state set the price of bread at such a low rate, bakeries could not afford to make it. They made croissants instead; it was easier to find croissants than loaves in Zimbabwe. My parents had now bought a bread machine, and the loaves they made were as rich and chewy as the baguettes I'd taken them to taste in the old Italian bakeries on Court Street in Brooklyn.

Another section was dedicated to procuring meat. Zimbabwe's currency was devaluing so fast now that instead of getting rent for Drifters in cash, Mom occasionally charged Dawson Jombe in chickens. He and his wife, Patricia, had a chicken coop in their garden at Cottage 1, and it was worth far more to her to be paid with a hen or a rooster, which they could roast, than with a brick of Zim notes that would be worthless in a few days. She was calling that chapter 'Jombe's *Jongwes*' – *jongwe* being the Shona word for 'rooster'.

They were interrupted from the creative flow by John Muranda, who suddenly appeared on the front lawn, having run up from the camp.

It was a warm, dreamy day, one of those lazy days when all they could hear were the calls of the cuckoos in the sycamore trees and the gentle ripple of the wind through the blonde grass.

Everything seemed right in the world.

John punctured the mood.

'Sa! Sa!' he said to my father, out of breath and a little bit too excited for Dad's liking.

'Yes, John, what is it?'

'Sa! A very important man has moved into Mr Frank's house. A very important man!'

Dad shifted in his chair and looked down at John on the lawn.

'What do you mean, John? Who is this important man?'

'A very important man, sa!' said John. 'He is organising the new farmers. He has made himself headman for the valley. He is replacing Chief Mutasa. He is the Political Commissar.'

My father looked over at my mother and rolled his eyes.

'Shit,' he said. 'This is all we fucking need.'

My mother's heart sank. She turned to him and said with a weary, seen-it-all-before smile: 'Now this is what I call a recipe for disaster.'

There were lots of ways to lose your farm. In the beginning it was mostly violent. Now, though, the process had become highly formal, and in many ways more chilling. Ordinary citizens who supported the ruling party and claimed they wanted to farm simply applied to the Registrar of Deeds for a farm and, if approved, got what was called an offer letter. This applicant, known as an A2 farmer, simply drove onto the farm he had been allocated, handed his letter to the farmer if he was still on the land, and told him he was the new owner. 'It's like winning the lottery, except you don't even have to buy a ticket,' Dad told me. 'You pay nothing at all.' Incredibly, a white farmer could be prosecuted for squatting on his own farm if he didn't vacate.

As far as my father knew – and he would have known, for Muranda would have told him – Frank's land had neither a chef nor an A2 applicant on it. Perhaps it was because the farmhouse looked so run-down and the land clumpy and overgrown with bush. Muranda reckoned there were only ten settlers left on the property. Across the country similar scenes played out: most of the early land invaders had given up and returned to towns or rural districts or fled the country altogether, along with three million other Zimbabweans.

My parents had reached an uneasy standoff with the remaining settlers. True, they had ripped down my parents' game fence, poached their animals, and stolen furniture and TV sets from the cottages. Two of them watched TV in their lodge bar at night. But generally they had been true to the words they had written in that note back in 2002: *Open your gates, we come in peace.*

The arrival of a Political Commissar – a title given to high-ranking guerrilla war veterans and senior military enforcers – threatened to destroy this delicate balance. The last thing my parents needed across the road was an organiser, a militant, an ideologue, someone who might get the settlers riled up about more land and eyeing my parents' own home.

They hadn't had much time to think about the Commissar before they were robbed. It was a hammer blow: on New Year's Eve, the one night of the year they were likely to be out. What a start to the new year! They had spent the night with their close friends Joe and Claire up at their lakeside cottage in the Nyanga, the range of purple-crested mountains you could see from the front lawn of the house, and had driven back on the afternoon of 1 January 2006.

Dad knew something was wrong as soon as he got to the front gate. The door to his workshop was flung wide open. He always locked it, especially when they went away. He ran to it, and his heart sank: the padlock was shattered, and his fuel was gone. He had kept two 38-litre drums of unleaded petrol in there – a rarity these days – and it had cost him a fortune. Now it was gone. But his tools were gone, too, and that enraged him more: an electric drill, some wrenches he had bought in Pietersburg, even a shitty old pair of pliers.

From the safety of the kitchen, my mother watched him erupt. He started by kicking the garage door and screaming: 'Who takes a man's tools, for fuck's sake? Who takes a man's tools?' Then he bellowed for the two Johns and charged off down to the camp. He accused them first, shouting that they were the only ones who had keys to the main gate. He knew they hadn't taken the tools, but he felt an atavistic need to assert himself, to get back some boundaries, to let them know who was boss. Several days later he was still in a rage. He was lost without his tools, unable to fix the pump for the borehole, the grill on the coffee roaster, the leak in the geyser on the roof.

For a while he suspected John Muranda's teenage son, who had come to stay for Christmas. He'd seen him down at the camp one evening on their walk. He was unemployed, like every other youth in the country, and where had he got that fancy new pair of running shoes?

But the more he thought about it, the more he suspected the Political Commissar. It seemed too much of a coincidence to be robbed for the very first time so soon after he had arrived in the neighbourhood.

One weekend in the middle of January 2006, the weekend my mother called me out of the blue, Dad drove to Mozambique and spent a fortune he didn't have buying two new barrels of un-leaded fuel. When he got home he made a good show of letting the workers on the farm know he had a new supply. He had John Agoneka and John Muranda offload it, and watched Sydney the barman notice it as he walked past the gate down to the camp. Word would get around, he reckoned. It always did. This was Africa, and you couldn't stop talk. He figured whoever stole it would hear that he had a new supply and would return. And this time he would be waiting.

That night he did something he had never done before. At ten o'clock, when Mom took a book to bed, instead of leaning the shotgun behind the curtain and joining her as he usually did, he opened the gun cabinet, shoved a handful of cartridges into his pockets, and walked silently out into the dark night, the gun over his shoulder.

Mom sat up in bed, open-mouthed, as she watched him go. With the picture in her mind of an old man lying in a garden, a newspaper wrapped around his head, she leapt out of bed, threw on her dressing gown and slippers, and ran outside.

She found my father sitting in a garden chair under the giant fig tree facing the front gate. The shotgun was on his lap. The moonlight pressed through the leaves of the tree and shimmered on the barrel of the gun. He sat perfectly still.

'Lyn, darling, what are you doing?' she asked.

'I'm keeping guard,' he said.

'Come on, darling. Come to bed.'

'They stole it before, they'll try again.'

'And what are you going to do when they come?'

'Shoot them,' he replied, exasperated. 'What do you think the gun is for?'

He sat outside keeping guard every night for the next two months.

He got used to being out there, to the soft sigh of the night, the whisper of the grass, the sweet scent of the fig leaves. Some nights he heard Sydney's music, other nights familiar voices from the camp – Muranda's baritone, Naomi's cackling laugh. He wondered why it was that African voices seemed to carry so easily in the darkness. Did it have something to do with the oral tradition? He thought about that tradition. *What a clever thing. So open to interpretation. When your history isn't written down, who knows how it changes in the telling? How it's modified, improved* upon, exaggerated over generations? It just becomes storytelling after a while. And everyone had some bullshit story about how they really owned the land and how they were here first. It did nothing to quell his rage.

Then one night he fell fast asleep in the chair. His arms had grown heavy and the leaves and branches of the fig tree seemed to sink warmly around him, enveloping him like a blanket. His grip had loosened on the gun. It was then that the noise came from the bushes beside the front gate. He woke up with a start. *Christ. What time is it? How long have I been asleep? Someone is out there!* He gripped the gun and leaned forward, trying to keep silent while adjusting his position. It came again: a light rattle of the chain-link fence. Someone was out there! His heart pounded, the sudden exhilaration making him dizzy. He saw two red eyes in the darkness, staring straight at him. He stared straight back, trying to focus, easing the gun up to his shoulder now. It was happening – they had come back. At last, it was payback time!

And then he saw it as clearly as if it were day: a giant full-grown antelope, a magnificent bull eland, with tall twisted horns like acacia branches, grazing in the long grass beside the fence. His heart was pounding. *Jesus. An eland!*

He had presumed the settlers – the Commissar's men – had killed every last one of them, but now one had showed itself. It stared at him with those magnificent sad eyes and he stared straight back. He had never felt so much pity for a mere animal before, and yet so much love for one, so much elation that something out there – something *else* out there – was surviving.

The animal bent its neck, chewed more grass, then looked up at him again. It seemed to be nodding at him. He wanted to nod back, but he didn't want to scare it. Then the creature wheeled away and loped off into the long grass past the avocado trees, toward the camp. My father watched it go. And for the first time in two months, the rage inside him disappeared. He felt light-headed, faint. He walked back to the house. He set the gun by the dresser and rolled into bed next to my mother. He thought: *Maybe now I can get some sleep.*

The Commissar didn't take long to announce his presence. Mom was in the kitchen in early February, adding some flour to the bread machine, when two young black men appeared silently and suddenly on the back patio.

She got a fright at first, but they seemed more frightened of her. They stood there edgy, nervous, rubbing their hands, not armed or threatening.

'They could hardly speak English,' she recalled, 'but they had a letter.'

It was a note from the Political Commissar introducing himself by proxy as their new neighbour and the new headman in the valley, and requesting that they give his men a donation for the president's birthday celebration.

Mom read the note, then looked at his two men. They were listless, infected with fatalism. They were no more than twenty years old. If she had spent time down at the camp at night she would have recognised them: one wore a Saddam Hussein T-shirt, the other the face of David Beckham.

She considered the president. And then she considered the thought of giving money to celebrate his birthday. And then she exploded.

'I beg your pardon? I beg your pardon? Money for the president's birthday? No! No! I am not giving you any bloody money for the president's birthday party. Why don't you go and ask the president for money for his own fucking birthday party? After all, he has all the money in the country. No. Go away!'

The young men stared at her, blank-faced, open-mouthed.

And then they trudged disconsolately away.

Two days later the Commissar himself turned up. Dad was in his workshop near the front gate, siphoning some fuel out of one of the new drums of petrol he'd just bought. He saw a large man lumbering up to the back of the house, mumbled to himself, 'Who the fuck is this, now?' and then called out: 'Hello, can I help you?'

The man turned slowly and ambled toward him. He was heavy and thickset, with a round, puffy face and dull blank eyes. He wore a tatty khaki farmer's shirt and trousers but had on a stylish, long grey Columbo-style raincoat, even though it was a hot day. His shoes were scuffed and covered in dirt, but he carried a brand-new businessman's leather briefcase.

'Yes, can I help you?' my father said again.

It always made him nervous when a car drove up to the house, as that was how the chefs and A2 farmers arrived to claim a farm. But this man was on foot. Dad presumed his car had broken down on the road and he needed some help.

'I am your new neighbour,' the man announced in a slow, deep voice. 'I am here for a donation for the president's birthday party. I sent my men up here two days ago and for some reason you turned them away.'

Dad stared at him. At last, this was the famous Political Commissar! He had wondered how they would finally meet. He had wondered how he would react to the man who was now living in his friend Frank's farmhouse, a man he suspected had sent his men to steal his fuel and his tools, a man whose settlers had already stolen his fencing wire and poached all his wildlife and were now giving him sleepless nights.

He considered the attire: expensive briefcase, scuffed shoes; stylish raincoat, frayed shirt. It all made perfect sense. Here was the embodiment of a ZANU-PF man: part urban, part rural, caught between the trappings of the modern world and the traditions of the tribal. My father was convinced that this was the root of all the country's problems: that its leaders existed in a cultural netherland, a schizophrenic state between two worlds. They spoke of tribal customs and traditions, then bought Armani suits and BMWs. They railed constantly against the West, then complained when the West stopped investing in them. My father could go on and on about the contradictions, but he knew right away he hated the Commissar with the passion of a thousand burning suns.

He also knew he had to play a clever game. He couldn't get angry and insult him, as my mother had done with his settlers. This man had power and could make things very difficult for them.

So he surprised even himself when he shook the Commissar's hand and said politely, 'A misunderstanding, I am sure. My wife, she gets very stressed – the economic situation. You want a donation? How about some beer?'

In the outbuilding where the marijuana was drying were several cases of three-year-old Castle lager that my parents had kept back from the Drifters bar for a party one year. Three-year-old lager – my dad was happy to give him that.

The Commissar shrugged.

'Thank you, that will be fine. I will get my men to come and take it away.'

Saddam and Becks came to collect it that afternoon.

My parents heard the party from the front lawn a few nights later, the drumbeats coming up the hill.

'Who knows,' chuckled Dad. 'If the beer has gone off, they might all get terribly ill and we'll never hear from them again.'

They met the Commissar together a few weeks later.

Dad and Mom were on their way to town in Dad's twin-cab bakkie when, turning onto the main road and passing the entrance to Frank's place, they spotted a thickset man in a long grey coat with a leather briefcase, hitchhiking from a bus stop.

'My God,' said Dad, 'it's him!'

'Who?'

'The Political Commissar.'

He slowed to pull over.

'Why are you slowing down?' asked Mom, incredulous.

'I'm going to give him a lift.'

'No, you are not! I don't want that man in this car.'

'Rosalind, relax. It would actually be good to meet him.'

'I don't want to meet him!'

'Rosalind, it's better to get to know him and try to find out what he's after than to ignore him and get a big shock later down the line.'

My father had been modifying his approach to those in authority in recent weeks. In a departure from his previous habit of silently seething – the method he had used with the CIO officer at the roadblock – he now often tried to charm and probe, but also, for his own sense of dignity, to mock with irony and sarcasm, a technique that had served him well as a lawyer when dealing with corrupt magistrates or lying clients. He was convinced they wouldn't get the sarcasm. These small triumphs kept him sane. 'Besides,' he once told me, 'your mother's angry enough to play bad cop for both of us.'

'I already know what he's like,' she seethed. 'I don't need to *meet* him.'

But Dad pulled over anyway.

The Commissar clambered into the back and very politely said, 'Morning, Mr Rogers. Morning, Mrs Rogers. Thank you for this ride.'

'Morning, Commissar,' said Dad cheerily. 'Where's your car?'

'I don't have a car, Mr Rogers. I travel by bus.'

He didn't have a car? Dad didn't like the sound of that. The man was high enough on the party ladder to get a farm, but not high enough to get a car? Dad suspected that meant he was high-ly ambitious, and like ambitious middling-to-average people ev-erywhere, all the more dangerous.

'Where are you going this day?'

'I am going to my town house,' said the Commissar calmly.

Which was when my father almost crashed the car.

'Your town house?' he spluttered.

'Yes, my house in town.'

Dad's face went red. The Commissar had two houses! Frank's farm was his country estate, his dacha. *Christ! What was it with these people?* Dad was about to ask him how he could own two homes but no car when he heard Mom chuckling to herself in the passenger seat.

'I told you I knew what he was like,' she muttered under her breath.

Now he was fuming at her, too.

The relationship with the Commissar soured badly soon af-ter that. One afternoon in May, Dad heard dogs barking near the main road at the bottom of the farm. He had long ago stopped bothering to get out his gun when he heard the dogs now, since he presumed all his animals had long since been slaughtered.

Just then Agoneka ran up to the house in a blur of orange.

'Sa! Some poachers have caught a buck! They are chasing it to Mr Frank!'

Dad was stunned: there was an animal alive on his land? And suddenly he remembered: the eland.

There was no time to get his gun. He and John jumped into his bakkie and raced down the drive, hurtled across the main road and barrelled onto Frank's place.

The poachers, six young settlers with sticks and metal pangas, had chased the animal into the barbed-wire fence around Frank's house. The dogs were snarling at it. Trapped against the fence, its corkscrew horns caught in the wire, it reared to try to defend itself. The poachers attacked it from behind with pangas, severing its hamstrings, until it fell to the ground. Blood was seeping from one flank. Its head twisted sideways, contorted in the trap of the fence. It had broken its neck.

'What the fuck are you doing?' Dad screamed, leaping out of the car and running over. 'That is my animal!'

The settlers skulked off, their blades dripping blood, their dogs cowering. He wished now he had brought his gun. He would have shot these people. But it was too late. The animal was dead.

He looked at it lying there, mutilated. It had round, glassy eyes that stared mournfully up at him as he hovered over it. It was a magnificent bull eland.

He wondered whether it was the offspring of one of the does that he and Mom had christened after my three sisters, back in 1991. He felt sick looking at it. But there was no way he was going to let the Commissar and his settlers – his poachers – eat the creature.

'Okay, John, you and Muranda, you want this meat, you take it,' he said, and he and Agoneka hauled the heavy, still-warm beast onto the back of his bakkie.

That night the two Johns made a blazing fire and roasted the eland, sharing the meat with the staff of the cottage owners at the back. They had not eaten so well in a year. The animal was devoured in two nights. A few days later, however, Muranda arrived up at the house to speak to my father. He was agitated and angry. The Commissar had apparently turned up at the camp in a rage the night before, demanding the return of 'his' beast. 'I am the headman for the valley,' he had shouted at John. 'I am entitled to the best meat from this animal.'

But the staff had eaten it. All that remained were the hind legs. The Commissar was outraged. He physically threatened

John and demanded his due: the best meat. Eventually he settled for what was left of it.

Muranda's initial enthusiasm toward the Commissar had already cooled before this point. When the Commissar first arrived in the area, John had been excited that he was going to get the settlers producing food again – food that he and Naomi could buy. That hadn't happened. He had also since found out that he wasn't a war veteran at all. He had been a collaborator, but he hadn't fought in the war. He was connected, though. He was a committed member of the ruling party. He had seats on the boards of various government utilities, and a string of failed businesses behind him. It was his political connections that had gotten him here. His connections made him headman of the valley.

My father knew of only one way to get back at the Commissar for the eland. All wildlife in Zimbabwe is owned by the state. It is illegal to hunt without a licence. The National Parks and Wildlife Department was one of the few organs of government that still functioned reasonably effectively. So he phoned the department, and an official drove out with three National Parks scouts armed with FN rifles. The official fined the Commissar for being found with 'bush meat'. My father made sure they fined the two Johns, too; he later reimbursed them, but he didn't want the Commissar to believe that he had been singled out.

Which was, of course, when the Commissar paid him another visit. He confronted my father on the back patio one morning and spoke slowly, sombrely, in a low, menacing tone.

'I expected you to be a good neighbour,' he said. 'But now you have reported me for this beast. In my culture the best meat is due to the chief. I do not expect to be fined for it. The meat of that beast was due to me.' He kept going on about the best meat, how it was supposed to be his.

Which was when my father's effort at charm gave way to red mist.

He thought of the eland bull twisted in the fence, those dead glassy eyes staring up at him. And he recalled how the animal's eyes had looked at him that one night as it grazed. If only he had known, he would have shot the animal right then. One clean shot. An assisted suicide. Instead it had been hunted down by mongrel dogs and hacked to death with pangas.

He started shaking. His face went purple and his fist slammed the refrigerator.

'You expected me to be a good neighbour? I *am* a good neighbour! I give you donations for your party when you want them. I give you lifts into town, in my car, to your town house. Your people cut down my fence for traps and hunt my animals. You expect to get the meat from this buck they poached and what do I get in return? Their footprints lead straight to your door! And now you come tell *me* to be a good neighbour? It's your turn to be a good neighbour!'

He wanted to say more. He wanted to say: *That is not even your house. You stole that house. You did not build it. My friend built that house; now you live in it.* But my mother had heard him from the living room and came rushing out. She grabbed his arm and ushered him into the house. She remembers all too clearly the face of the Commissar as she led Dad away.

'He just stood there. Inscrutable, staring, not blinking. He looked neither angry nor shocked. He just had a dull, blank look. You couldn't tell what he was thinking.'

There was a theory among some farmers that it was best to be confrontational with the regime, that they would leave you alone if you stood up to them. Unita Herrer was convinced she had been violently kicked off her farm only because she'd made concessions to the ruling party in her area, offered to give up her land, and they saw this as weakness: even the weakness of a sixty-four-year-old woman would be exploited. Oom Piet reckoned he had been allowed to keep his home and land because he had sent a message to the minister: 'If you want my place, you must come and shoot me and bury me there.'

My father had been in the habit these past few years of asking the few white farmers he knew who were still on their land how they did it.

'What's your method?' he would say.

I was with him one morning in Mutare when we bumped into Chris de Lange, a reedy maize farmer from the far western part of the valley. With his veld hat, khaki shorts, bush shoes and squeaky, high-pitched voice, Chris was straight out of a Herman Charles Bosman story.

'So, Chris,' said Dad, 'you're still on your place. What's your method?'

'My method?' he shrieked. 'Ag, man, they've come for my place a few times. When I see them come up my drive I just stand at my front gate and I start screaming. I jump up and down, wave my hands in the air like crazy, and just keep shouting at the top of my lungs: 'Fok off! Fok off! Fok off!' Eventually they think I'm mad and drive away.'

Chris indeed sounded mad to me. I couldn't see my father using this method.

Of course, resistance hadn't worked for many others. My father now worried what effect his outburst would have on his future.

TEN

The Political Commissar

I think I should go and speak to him,' I told my parents.

'You what?'

'I think I should go speak to the Commissar.'

My mother was incredulous. 'Why would you want to speak to that crook?'

'Well, you said there are lots of stories out here. He's bound to have one, too.'

'Yes,' she said, 'but he's a bloody crook!'

'You don't know that.'

Dad remained silent in his leather recliner.

It was late one night in June 2006, and I had just flown in, the beginning of a month-long visit. This trip would be different: Grace was coming out in ten days' time, her first visit to Zimbabwe. We would spend four days with Piet and Mienkie de Klerk on their houseboat on Kariba, the giant man-made lake in the Zambezi Valley in the west of the country, then come back out here for two weeks. I was excited for Grace to see my parents' strange world and where I grew up.

But it was a different trip for another reason: I knew now that

I wanted to write a book about the farm. On my past visits I'd always been thinking in terms of writing articles, but now I felt more comfortable out here, at home, and I wanted to write about the farm as a metaphor for the condition of the country. To do so I needed to speak to the other side: to the Commissar. I even thought I could help my parents by doing so.

What had I ever contributed to their struggle? I always just flew in, took notes, then flew back home to regale Grace and my friends with stories of my crazy parents over bottles of wine in Bar Tabac and Raoul's. Now, though, it occurred to me that if I got to know the Commissar, I might be able to persuade him to leave my parents alone.

Dad broke his silence.

'Your mother's right. The man is a charlatan. I used to come across people like him all the time in court. I defended some of them. He's come out here with his spiritual mumbo jumbo to con these rural people, to build a power base for himself. He says he's going to help them, but I guarantee you he won't. Still, that's no reason *not* to talk to him. Tell you what – when we drive in tomorrow, I'll introduce you.'

'How will you manage that?' I said.

Mom shrieked from her chair, 'Because after all that's happened your bloody father still insists on giving him lifts to town! I mean, it's outrageous!'

They had very different views on tactics.

'Look who,' said Dad.

The Commissar was standing at the bottom of the road, as my father had said he would be.

He was exactly as he had been described: heavy, thickset, slow-moving, with that dull, blank, expressionless face. It was a face of either authority or incompetence.

The car gently rocked as he clambered into the back seat.

'So, Commissar, how are your new farmers?' Dad asked.

My father was using his sarcasm plan again, probing, teasing, his rage at the Commissar since the confrontation on the back patio a month ago shelved for the moment.

I expected the Commissar to tell him how well things were going, as the government still claimed the land reform programme was a great success.

'*These people,*' he said instead, waving his hand in the air, talking about his settlers. 'They think they can get a piece of ground for nothing and it will just grow food. They don't realise farming takes hard work.'

Dad gulped in surprise. It wasn't the answer he was expecting.

We were soon driving past Margaret Matongo's place.

There were three productive farms left in the immediate area, and they were all owned by black farmers. The Muzorewas, who had now left Cottage 4, were to the west of Drifters; Dr John Pfumojena, a physician who'd once treated my father for malaria, was next to them; and their neighbour to the east, Margaret, was the dynamic wife of a bus company tycoon named Didymus Matongo. The Matongos were erstwhile ZANU-PF stalwarts, but my father had always liked them and really admired Margaret. If Unita Herrer used to be the greatest woman farmer in the valley, Margaret now held the title, and her immaculate fields of winter wheat stretched a kilometre and a half to the river bank to our left, in stark contrast to the dishevelled ground under the Commissar's control next to it. My father told me once he could only laugh when, in 2003, after it was clear that the government had utterly destroyed agriculture in the country, reporters from the state-run ZTV came to film Margaret Matongo in her fields as a shining example of the great success of the land reform programme. They didn't tell viewers that the Matongos had bought their farm in the 1980s and that Margaret, like any other farmer, had become successful only after years of trial, error and hard work. Dr Pfumojena and the Muzorewas had bought their farms, too.

Dad tried a new angle with the Commissar.

'You know why this is a good farm?' he said, ready to give him a subtle lesson on the basic laws of commerce, drive and hard work.

'Yes, I know,' the Commissar replied with a tired sigh. 'Matongo bought this land. She learned to farm it herself. You can't get something for nothing in this world.'

Dad gulped again.

'You can't get something for nothing,' the Commissar kept muttering.

It occurred to me that either he was playing his own games with my dad or he actually genuinely agreed with him. Either way, he was no fool.

Dad finally introduced me.

'So this is my son. He is a writer. He wants to find out about the history of this area and the story of your people.'

I felt a flush of annoyance. I didn't want my father to introduce me as a writer, certainly not to a ruling party official. But my father had judged the Commissar well.

His face lit up.

'A writer? This is good! I know all this history. I can tell him many stories.'

The Commissar did know a lot of history. He told it as we drove.

'My great-great-grandfather was a famous chief in this area,' he began. 'He was the spiritual adviser to Chief Mutasa when Rhodes first came to this valley in 1891.'

I had no idea the Commissar had royal lineage. Coupled with his political connections, it helped account for his power base here.

'Your great-great-grandfather met with Rhodes?' I asked.

'When the whites came, they asked Chief Mutasa for land to do mining. Mutasa sent one of his men to my ancestor for spiritual advice. My ancestor was informed by his spirit medium, 'People will come without knees. Do not fight them now, you will not win. They are too well equipped.' So in this way my ancestor advised Mutasa to agree to Rhodes's request, and Rhodes was allowed to settle in the valley and start mining here.'

I didn't know what he was talking about.

'What do you mean, "people without knees"?'

'People without knees were the whites,' said the Commissar.

'Why?'

'Because they wore shorts. Their trousers had no knees. This is what was interpreted by my ancestor.'

'What about "well equipped"?' asked Dad.

'The whites had guns, of course. They were *equipped*. It would have been a mistake to fight. We would fight them later when we were more prepared.' Then he added wryly: 'Which we did. As you have seen.'

The Commissar had a sense of understatement.

We were nearing the top of Christmas Pass now. A familiar domed granite hill appeared to our right, beyond the edge of the road. The Commissar pointed at it. 'You see that mountain? That is my ancestral burial ground. A sacred place. That is where my ancestor lived, in the caves on top of the hill. Before the whites came, the Matabele were coming. They used to raid us and take our belongings, including our beautiful wives and daughters. My ancestor lived in a cave up the hill for security from war. Our people lived in the Mutare Valley we now see below.'

The town had come into view.

'My clan had all the land from the border of Mozambique to Dangamvura to the Mutare River. It was all ours. But then in 1897, as you know, after the railway line was built by the whites between Mutare and Beira, the site of Mutare was moved to here and my forefathers had to leave. That was how some of them came to settle in the valley we are now in by the river.'

The Commissar had a deadpan, baritone delivery that matched his blank, expressionless face, but he knew his history. Even my father couldn't argue with what he was saying.

'All was smooth here until the Second World War. After that war, those British who fought in Europe were allocated land here for commercial farming as a reward for their success in that battle. Many of them settled in the valley my forefathers had been moved to. But our people were now educated. We were educated by British missionaries. We did not want to work on white farms, so the native commissioner, Cripps, moved us again, this time to Zimunya.'

Zimunya is on the other side of Mutare. There were many forced removals of blacks in Rhodesia, moved to what are now known as communal lands but then as tribal trust lands.

My father listened intently. He had a few quibbles, but not many. The Commissar was certainly right about the Second World War. I recalled the story John Muranda had told me down at the camp about how his father was repaid with a medal after the war, while white veterans were allocated land. I had always been under the impression that it was the original white settlement in the 1890s that caused the rupture over land in our area. But, according to the Commissar, the real problem had come much later, after the Second World War.

But then, just as I was beginning to think my father had completely misread the Commissar, the man drifted off into the old tribal world, a realm of visions, dreams and spirits. It was as if he couldn't resist it.

'But let me put it clear,' he suddenly boomed. 'When I was two years old in Zimunya and just beginning to talk, I told my father my name: "The Big One. Mukuru." He was shocked. That was the name of *his* father. So he knew then that I was a leader. When I grew up I said to my father, "I belong to where *your* forefathers lived." It took me a long time, but only now, after this land reform, did I finally get it. My wife received a call from the district administrator's office in 2004 that I had been allocated land, and that was when I moved to where I am now.'

My father couldn't help laughing. 'Two years old? The Big One? What?'

'Yes, Mukuru, the Big One,' he said seriously.

But he wasn't finished.

'But also I had a *conviction* that we came from that place. In 1980 I had a dream. I was driving through that area and I saw a beautiful house just by these hills and a white man handing me over the keys and saying, "This is the house that we are giving you." There was a beautiful lawn around it.'

He was flitting between his two worlds: the ancient and the modern.

'Interesting,' said my father. 'A dream, hey?'

I suddenly worried that the Commissar really *did* have designs on my parents' home. Frank's place didn't have a lawn, but theirs did. A beautiful one. I decided to change the subject.

We were cruising down the pass now, the green ribbon of Mutare revealed in its dappled valley. The Commissar's ancestral hill towered above us. I knew the hill well. As a boy I used to climb it with a friend, David, whose father managed the Wise Owl Motel just below. It gave me the creeps. Once David and I thought we would camp on it for a night, but when dusk came, the air suddenly turned cold, the monkeys started screeching and we thought we heard a leopard growl. We scampered home, terrified. Later, in my early teens, my dad, to get me fit for cross-country running season, would make me run up the old pioneer road that wound around its foothills. The hill still gave me the creeps, but I knew that a good way to get to know the

Commissar's intentions would be to ask to see his burial ground with him.

'Can you take me up there?' I said as we descended into Mutare.

The hill was framed through the back window of the bakkie. The Commissar considered my request as we pulled up outside ZANU-PF headquarters.

'Yes,' he finally said, 'but first we need to ask permission from the spirits. Come and see me at my house at two o'clock on Sunday.'

'Which house would that be?' Dad said, 'your town house or your farmhouse?'

My father had got in a late dig, but even so, their duel was a draw.

And so it was that the following Sunday, half an hour into the 2006 Federer-versus-Nadal French Open tennis final, I drove across the road to attend a spiritual ceremony. Up on the hill my parents would be watching the world's greatest tennis players on satellite TV; down in the valley I would be throwing bones.

'Have fun,' said Mom. 'Tell him we say hello.'

'Yes, good luck,' Dad grinned. 'Wish we could go with you.'

I took a tape recorder and notebook. I was suddenly nervous. The Commissar had seemed amiable enough in the car, but he was a powerful ZANU-PF official. I was entering his realm. Some of his settlers could have been the invaders who assaulted Frank in 2001; they were certain to be the poachers who'd cut down my father's game fence and killed his zebra and antelope. How would they react to me, the son of the white farmer across the road who shot at their dogs and had chased them from the eland? I hoped Saddam and Becks would be there. I was at least on nodding terms with them.

I had never seen Frank's farmhouse when he lived in it, so I could make no comparison, but it was a hovel now. The windows were broken. Chickens were shitting in a doorway. A snotty-nosed baby cried in the backyard. A mongrel tied to a fence post howled and then yawned. I wondered if it was one of the dogs the settlers used to hunt.

I found the Commissar addressing nine settlers seated in a circle on the ground in front of a mud hut erected in Frank's garden. He was instructing them to go to the other occupied farms in the valley to get the settlers to choose headmen who would now report to him, their new leader. I hadn't expected agricultural college, but this was a Soviet-style lecture, all about war, peasant struggle and the Commissar's power.

'Only those who are committed should be chosen,' he was saying. 'Bring names of people who are troublesome to me. Then I will know if they came here for land reform or not. If they did not, I will deal with them. If they are not members of the party, then I will know. I will deal with them.'

As for the settlers, they were a sad, listless, defeated bunch, hardly the fearsome war veterans I had half expected. Five were youths in their early twenties, as bored as the yawning dog. Saddam was there, eyes down, fiddling with a stick. There was no sign of Beckham. Perhaps he'd found his way to a TV and was watching the French Open. I caught myself wondering what the score was.

An old man in a tweed cap and tweed jacket next to the Commissar was the spryest of the lot. He smiled at me. He cut a dapper top half, huntsman to hounds, but his bottom half let him down: ripped trousers and muddy, laceless brown shoes. Three old women, skirts emblazoned with the president's face, sat off to the side on reed mats. One of them was fast asleep.

The Commissar nodded at me and carried on talking.

After half an hour the meeting broke up and the younger settlers ambled off drowsily to their scrubby plots marked out by stick fences at various points on the land. Tweed Jacket and the three old women stayed behind.

The Commissar said: 'Some formalities. Before we ask permission from the spirits to go up the mountain, we need to approach the elder. We will go see him and then we will return for the ceremony.'

'The elder?'

'The elder is the most senior man in the valley.'

'How far away?'

'It is short. Eight kilometres. We can drive.'

He instructed Tweed Jacket and the women to wait, and we jumped in Dad's bakkie.

We drove sixteen kilometres west and turned left onto a rough dirt road. The bakkie lurched over rocks and anthills; there was barely space for an ox-cart. We came to a clearing outside a brick shack and a circle of huts where an old man sat alone under the shade of a giant knobthorn tree. He wore tortoiseshell glasses, the bridge held together with a Band-Aid. One of the lenses was shattered. He was blind in one eye. His bad eye had the good lens. He looked up as we approached, and nodded. I didn't know how he could possibly see us. He was thin as a rail, over six foot five inches tall if he stood, and as ancient as the branches of the tree above him.

The Commissar knelt in front of him and clapped three times.

'I am with the son of our neighbour, Mr Rogers, and we want to visit the burial ground of the ancestors,' the Commissar said.

The old man smiled. He had a mouth like a rusty can, with six jagged teeth. They spoke in Shona for a while. I could make out the name Rogers several times.

'What did he say?' I asked when I heard it the fifth time.

The Commissar looked at me quizzically.

'He asked if your father is Mr Rogers the lawyer.'

My heart jumped. What did this guy know about my father?

'Yes, he is. What did he say about him?'

He spoke to the man in Shona again. The quizzical look returned to the Commissar's face. He seemed surprised at what the old man was telling him.

'He says your father represented him once. In court. A legal issue.'

I couldn't believe what I was hearing. This old black man had been a client of my father's?

It must have been for a liquor licence. My father began specialising in liquor licensing in the 1970s. Back then, few white lawyers represented black clients, but my dad did, and he soon built up a base: licences had to be renewed every year. By 1990 he was processing so many that he couldn't walk down the main street in Mutare without some black tavern owner or buxom she-been queen coming up to shake his hand, ask him how he was. The very first manager at Drifters had been a former client: a formidable Shona woman named Maude Magondweni who was built like a late-period Aretha Franklin. When her husband divorced her and stole her bottle store, Dad offered her the job at Drifters, a task she performed with fierce distinction, terrifying most of the black male workers. In 1998 Maude left to care for her daughter, who had AIDS. She died soon thereafter of a heart attack.

'Was it about a liquor licence?' I said. 'Did this old man own a beer hall?'

The Commissar shrugged.

'No. He said your father represented him during the war.'

'Over what?'

'Some court issue with the *gandangas*.'

My heart pumped faster.

Gandanga is Shona for 'guerrilla' – a ZANLA soldier.

'What about the *gandangas*?'

The Commissar smiled at me for the first time. He seemed suddenly impressed.

'It appears this old man was accused of supporting the guerrillas during the war. He said your father defended him. He said you have permission to go up the mountain.'

I recalled the words of my mother: *They have long memories. They know who did what in the war, and they know who is doing what now*, and a thought occurred to me. If this elder, whom even the Commissar had to respect, remembered that my father had defended him many years ago during the war, then perhaps he had some say in whether the land invaders would take Drifters. Was he protecting my father? I walked over to the old man and shook his hand. He smiled that tin-can grin and looked away, cackling loudly. Then the Commissar and I drove back to Frank's place to get in touch with the ancestral spirits.

The ceremony was held in the hut in the yard. It was cool and dark inside, with a smooth mud floor and a clay ledge around its walls. I sat on the ledge next to the Commissar. The three women sat on reed mats in the gloom opposite. I was introduced to Tweed Jacket, who sat cross-legged in the middle of the floor.

'This is my nephew,' said the Commissar. 'I summoned him from Mozambique when I became headman. He is older than me, but in our culture he is still my junior.'

The nephew was tasked with summoning the spirits. He pulled a leopard skin over the shoulders of his tweed jacket. On the floor behind him, leaning against the wall, was a pangolin skin. In front of him was a small pile of pebbles, bones and bits of dried maize. He closed his eyes, threw the bones and pebbles on the floor, as if rolling dice, and started chanting in Shona in a slow, sonorous voice as the three old women began to clap their hands, slowly, in time.

The hut suddenly seemed to get cold. In the darkness, one

of the old women began to burp loudly over the chanting. The spirit was appearing through her.

The Commissar said: 'The spirits require a token to proceed.'

'Do they accept US dollars?' I asked.

'Yes, that'll be fine.'

'I thought it might,' I said.

I handed him a five-dollar note and he passed it on to the nephew. The nephew put it in a chipped enamel bowl next to him and resumed his chanting. The three women clapped in unison, and the burping lady burped ever louder.

The Commissar spoke again.

'Our forefathers, we have a visitor, Mr Rogers, the son of our neighbour Rogers, who wants to know about our history. We are asking permission to see the burial ground.'

In the darkness of the hut, the burping woman suddenly ceased burping.

'Mr Rogers?' she said, her voice high-pitched, incredulous.

'Er, yes,' I replied, trying to make out her face in the gloom.

'Douglas?'

I almost fell off the ledge. Tweed Jacket opened one eye, then the other. The dull, blank face of the Commissar slowly turned to stare at me, then at the old woman.

'Do you remember me?' she squeaked, her teeth gleaming in the dark.

'No,' I said. 'I can hardly even see you.'

'I am Gracie Basket,' she said. 'I was looking after you when you were seven years old.'

'What?'

'I was looking after you when you were seven years old,' she repeated. 'Don't you remember?'

'No, Gracie, I don't.'

'I was taking you from your home Friday to Mrs Russell's

house, and on Monday we make breakfast for you and Michael and then take you down to the road and Mrs Rogers collect you to take you to school.'

I realised that I *did* remember some of that. The Russells had been our neighbours down the hill from the chicken farm. Michael, their son, was my best friend. They had a television. I used to love staying weekends at the Russells' house. I could watch TV: *Lassie, Batman, Hawaii Five-O...*

'How is Helen?' she asked.

Christ, she knew my sister, too!

'She's fine, Gracie. She lives in London. My wife is called Grace.'

'You were seven years old, I was fourteen,' she said mournfully.

She was only seven years older than me. She looked ancient.

'So what are you doing here, Gracie?'

'I am a settler,' she said. 'A new farmer. Now that I have land, I don't have to work for white people anymore.'

I gulped.

The Commissar turned to me and smiled.

Douglas,' he said, 'this is good. You two have a history together.'

He had called me by my given name for the first time.

'This woman,' he said, 'I had to fight tooth and neck to make sure she was allocated a piece of land here. Lo and behold, she is my best farmer. She is better than all the others. You should see her field. She has good maize. But these others ...'

He waved his hand dismissively, as he had in the car with Dad when complaining about his settlers. Tweed Jacket gazed sheepishly at the floor. Perhaps he wasn't producing the goods. The ceremony had lost its impetus. Everything appeared to be fine with the spirits. We made a date to go up the mountain in a week's time. Gracie and Tweed Jacket would come with us.

The Commissar walked me back to the car. I was still in a

state of shock. He seemed pleased at how things had turned out, and smiled again.

'So tell me, do you have farming activities in America like we have here?' he asked.

I stifled a snigger. 'Um, I wouldn't say it works *exactly* like it does here.'

He shrugged. 'I agree. There have been mistakes. Believe you me, there are advantages and disadvantages. But please understand. Us Zimbabweans are a good people. A kind people. Only when pushed ...'

He paused, then redirected his thought. 'So tell me,' he said, 'what did you think of the ceremony?'

We had reached the car. I still had no idea what to make of the Commissar. He was clearly a bright man, but he was also a manipulator, if not an out-and-out con artist. I thought of his diatribe at the settlers: *If they are not members of the party, I will deal with them.* I thought of the dismissive manner in which he spoke of his nephew: *He's older than me, but he is still my junior.* But most of all I thought of my five bucks in the enamel bowl. I knew *he* would be getting it.

Then it hit me – what I had to do.

'The ceremony was great,' I told him, 'really great. I tell you what – if you did it for tourists, you could make a lot of money. A lot of money. Do you know that my parents' place is a tourist business? There are none now, but if things get better here the tourists will one day return and then you can charge them a lot of money for a ceremony like that. Usas. American dollars.'

A tiny ember burned in the back of the Commissar's brain.

'Say hello to your parents, Dougie,' he said after a while, but his mind had wandered off to a bright and prosperous future.

ELEVEN
Miss Moneypenny

THE ANCESTRAL SPIRITS had taken the last of my money, and I needed more. A few days after the ceremony my father took me to meet his money dealer in town.

The condition of Mutare shocked me now, its decay a pitiful reflection of the country as a whole. The main street, Herbert Chitepo Road, ran tired and ragged through the centre of town, its asphalt potholed and yawning, the untamed roots of blazing flamboyant trees and pastel-flowering jacarandas buckling its pavement. The tops of the parking meters had all been beheaded, stolen long ago not for the worthless coins inside them but to smelt down the metal and sell to traders in Mozambique and on to China. Metals were a prized commodity: the aluminium street signs had all been ripped away, too. They made for good coffin handles. The city was eating itself. Once-elegant shop fronts looked on in vacant resignation, their shelves mostly empty, the display windows deserted.

Commercial activity had moved from the shops into the streets and parking lots, where young men, crafty urban hustlers, whispered like drug dealers as you walked by: 'Bread', 'Oil', 'Sugar', 'Soap'. They had to keep their eyes peeled for the police, who regularly beat and arrested them, but then the police and the ruling party ran much of this illicit trade anyway, and took bribes from those they didn't control. An entirely informal economy had sprung up; the black market ran the show.

'But where do people get any money to buy these goods?' I asked Dad. We were driving through the Indian quarter now, toward the industrial estates on the southern outskirts. 'Eighty percent of the country is unemployed. Aren't they all broke?'

'Remittances,' said Dad. 'There are now three million Zimbabweans living outside the country. Everyone needs a relative outside sending back foreign currency. That's how they survive. They can transfer it through the banks, in which case the government takes a big cut, or they can exchange it on the black market and get a much better rate.'

The world would soon come to know all about Zimbabwe's hyper-inflation. The figures were flabbergasting. Companies had to use smaller fonts to fit budget calculations onto a balance sheet; people walked around with bulging rucksacks and suitcases full of cash – Zimbabwean wallets. Shop clerks wandered the aisles of their stores changing the prices of goods twice a day, while customers, carrying pocket calculators to add up their costs, tried to stay one step ahead of them.

Inflation had spun out of control as a direct result of the land invasions. In breaking its own laws and dispossessing its own citizens, the state not only destroyed the sector of the economy that provided fifty percent of its foreign revenue, but it also frightened away foreign investors. Without foreign currency to pay its bills, the government simply started printing money. Then more money. And still more. Once they started, they couldn't stop; it became an addiction.

In turn, the currency black market had boomed because the Reserve Bank set the local currency at a fixed rate against the US dollar. It was currently Z$101 000 to US$1 – ridiculously low. Only the chefs, the fat cats – ministers, bankers, senior ruling party officials – could buy US dollars at this rate. The black-market rate was a more realistic gauge of the strength of local currency: Z$300 000 to US$1, three times the official rate. In two years it would rise to two thousand times the official rate – which, incredibly, was how the government wanted it. Conventional wisdom said that inflation and the collapse of the Zimbabwe dollar would finally bring down the government and cripple the leaders. The opposite was true: the worse it got, the better it became for the chefs.

Dad explained why.

'The chefs buy US dollars at the cheap official rate. They take that money and exchange it at the black-market rate. Then they take that money back to the bank and buy US dollars at the cheap rate again. And so on. Within a few dozen transactions they can become millionaires – in US dollars. And they don't have to do any work!'

By 2008 ministers were literally buying brand-new Mercedes-Benzes for US$50.

The great discrepancy between the two rates kept the chefs in Armani suits, flat-screen TVs, mansions, cocaine, Johnnie Walker Blue and Hummer limousines. Remittances exchanged on the black market kept millions of ordinary people alive – and my parents survived in a similar way.

My sisters and I didn't send them money – they were too proud for that – but the few thousand rands my father had left in South Africa from the sale of the Knysna home were now worth far more to him on the black market in Zimbabwe than they ever would be if my parents actually had to try to live on it in South Africa.

It was the ultimate irony my friends in New York could never get their heads around.

'Why don't they just leave?' they would ask me.

'Because they're *better off* where they are!' I would say.

They were stuck: Estragon and Vladimir, waiting for God knew what.

The secret, of course, was finding a reliable money dealer. Foreign currency was a drug for the chefs, who needed it like locusts needed leaves, and they did anything to get their hands on it, especially raiding and arresting money dealers.

My parents had a dealer, and they spoke of her in the reverential tones we might reserve for a movie star or a great musician. They rarely called her by her real name, but instead used code names. In addition to Miss Moneypenny, they called her Moneybags, Madame Bureau de Change or my favourite, the National Treasure.

'She *is* a national treasure,' Dad would say in wonder. 'If anyone deserves to be buried at Heroes Acre when their time comes, it's her.' Heroes Acre was where they buried guerrilla veterans of the liberation war.

I wanted to change US$200 into Zim dollars. I didn't *have* US$200 on me, but that didn't matter. Moneypenny had accounts in London and South Africa. All I would have to do was transfer the US$200 when I got back to New York. It was as simple as going to an ATM.

Dad had his own business to discuss with Moneypenny.

'She got in big trouble with the Reserve Bank,' he told me.

'What happened?'

We were driving past Blue Star Motors now, a fuel station where a four-day queue of battered cars and rusty trucks stretched for several kilometres along a pavement and up a grassy shoulder. Street kids hired by the motorists to look after their vehicles dozed on bonnets and back seats. Eventually word would came through that a fuel shipment had arrived and the motorists would find their way back to their vehicles. It was better to have a donkey cart, and I saw that they were making a comeback: we stopped for one at a broken traffic light.

'The government is so short of foreign currency that they run ads in the *Herald* encouraging people to inform on anyone who they believe is dealing in foreign currency. They offer a ten per cent reward on any money recovered. Although it's illegal to own foreign currency, they pay this reward *in* foreign currency.'

'The government advertises for spies?'

'Yes. They encourage people to inform on their neighbours, friends, family – all in the cause of "national unity", of course. Anyway, Moneypenny has a brother who emigrated to South Africa a while ago, and she managed to sell his house to a black Zimbabwean girl who lives in New York. This girl wanted it for her parents, who still live here. She paid US$110 000 for it into Moneypenny's overseas account. But the girl's brother lives here, too. He found out about the deal and informed the Reserve Bank. So the bank made Moneypenny return the US$110 000 and paid her out in Zim at the official Z$101 000 rate. It was either that or jail.'

'Jesus. And what about the brother?'

'Get this: he got his ten percent cut – US$11 000 – and now lives in the house!'

'Christ, Moneypenny must be furious.'

'You have absolutely no idea.'

'So you're going to give her some legal advice?'

He thought about that for a moment.

'Well, of a sort,' he said.

I was pleased my father was getting back into the law. I knew that with his experience he could help people.

We came to a sprawling warehouse complex and a row of low-slung brick buildings in the industrial estates on the edge of town. The complex was surrounded by a high wire fence. A sign on the open gate read *Latex: Balloons. Gloves.*

A tan sedan was parked on the grass outside. Two black men

sat in it, one sleeping, the other smoking a cigarette. We drove in.

'So this is it,' said Dad. 'Moneypenny's lair.'

'She makes balloons?'

'Used to,' said Dad. 'Now she's pretty much just a bank.'

I half expected a glamorous businesswoman in a Donatella Versace power suit barking orders into banks of cellphones and checking currency markets on a flat-screen TV hidden behind the walnut panelling of a plush, air-conditioned office. But Moneypenny sat on a wooden chair behind a chipped Formica desk littered with paperwork and dirty teacups. An old desktop computer that sounded like it was powered by steam whirred away on it. An electric fan scattered her papers. A set of ladies' golf clubs leaned in one corner; a large, black metal trunk of the kind I used in boarding school was on the floor beside the desk.

She was a plump, beaming, middle-aged redhead with a laugh as loud and ready as a foghorn, dazzling green eyes and a jumble of crooked white teeth. She wore a frumpy fifties-style floral dress. She reminded me of my old primary-school teacher.

Dad greeted Moneypenny in the manner he greeted all his friends, male or female: boisterous pat on the back, jokey jab to the ribs and a loud ironic tone.

'Miss Moneybags! I've missed you! How is the *bureau de change*?'

'Morning, Lyn,' she said, swinging her feet up on the desk. She looked at me and shook her head. 'Your dad's so full of shit.'

Dad pulled out a three-iron from her golf bag and started practising his swing.

'So, Lyn, did you see my friends at the gate?' she asked.

His follow-through made a dent in a pine wardrobe against the wall.

'Oops, sorry about that... Ja, I saw two buggers sitting out there.'

'My Charlie Tens. Just checking who comes and goes.'

Charlie Tens? That was slang for the CIO – the secret police. I was horrified. And yet she sounded so cavalier about it. Dad didn't seem too bothered about them, either. He put the three-iron back, pulled out a putter and introduced me.

'So, Madame Bureau de Change, this is my son. He wants to bake two hundred gringos in a backie pie.'

'Two hundred? Excellent. I think I can do that.'

'And I'll bake a thousand japies.'

'Hmmm ...' She glanced at the metal trunk. 'Not sure I have enough. I might have to send you to the vault in town. I'll call Enoch.'

They were speaking in code, but it wasn't too hard to work out.

Gringos were US dollars. Japies were South African rands – after a common Afrikaans Christian name. Backie was an abbreviation of her actual surname. A backie pie was the name they gave to a transaction. It was unlikely the office was bugged, but they had gotten into the habit of e-mailing and speaking to each other on the telephone in this way, and so they stayed in character. You could tell they quite liked the intrigue of it all, too.

Moneypenny's secretary, Faith, a beautiful twenty-something black girl in high heels and a miniskirt – she was the glamorous woman I had expected Moneypenny to be – brought us cups of strong Tanganda tea.

'He also wants to ask you about the *bureau de change* business,' Dad continued. 'He's writing a book about all us weirdos. Rosalind and I told him you're our national treasure and that he should dedicate it to you.'

I suddenly felt embarrassed. I didn't want to compromise her safety.

'Only if you're not worried,' I interrupted. 'I won't use your name.'

She cackled loudly and slapped her thigh. 'A little nervous, your boy, hey, Lyn?' She turned to me. 'Listen, darling. I've got spies sitting outside my front gate. The Reserve Bank wants to send me to jail. Some son of a bitch has stolen US$11 000 from me and is living in my brother's house. My name in your book is the least of my worries. Ask me what you want as long as you make me famous.'

Dad stepped out to make a phone call. Moneypenny got up and kicked open the metal trunk. I saw it was filled with neat pink bricks of Z$20 000 notes, a million's worth tied together at a time with rubber bands. She gathered a pile in her arms and I fired questions at her while she counted out US$200 worth at Z$300 000 to US$1, forming a cash mountain on her desk.

Where to begin? How do you ask a sweet middle-aged lady to tell you how she became a money launderer? I felt as if I was asking my old primary-school teacher how she'd come to moonlight as a hooker. It didn't seem right.

'Um, so how much do you deal in a day?' I asked.

'Well, this is Mutare, darling, we're pretty low-key here. Harare, that's where the big bucks are. I guess I change about US $4000 on average. The problem is getting enough Zim cash. The government has to print so much of it now since it's basically worth toilet paper. But luckily I have a guy who drives to collect trunks of it for me near Harare. Someone from Harare meets him halfway at this lovely old tea shop on the Harare road. The Charlie Tens sitting outside my gate should go to that tea shop. That's where the *really* big deals go down.'

I knew the tea shop well. I would never look at it again in the same way.

I wanted to know how the black-market rate worked – how it was decided what the local currency was to the US dollar. It seemed to fluctuate wildly from town to town and from day to day – Z$450 000 to US$1 in Harare, Z$300 000 here.

'There's a lot of us in the game,' she explained. 'We get a newsletter by e-mail from a guy in Harare who helps set it. Something to do with Old Mutual. They take a variant of Old Mutual shares in London and what the same share price is in Harare, and by dividing one by the other get the rate. Very complicated. There is a way to work out what the value to the dollar *should* be.'

'What's that?'

'The egg rate.'

'The egg rate? What, like a local equivalent of the Dow or the FTSE?'

She cackled loudly. 'No, darling. Go to a street dealer and ask him for seven boiled eggs. The price he charges is the rate of the Zim dollar to the US dollar on that day. It's highly scientific.'

I burst out laughing. 'Come on, that's bullshit.'

But it was, in fact, entirely true. A financial journalist in Harare named Jonathan Waters, a graduate of Prince Edward School and Rhodes University, had established a highly respected economics subscription service called Zfn. He e-mailed a daily guide to the markets and currency rates that included the Hard Boiled Egg Index, the HBEI. Everyone in business in Zimbabwe subscribed to his service, including Reserve Bank and Finance Ministry officials. It was easy to believe they learned more about the economy from Zfn than they did from actually running the economy.

Moneypenny continued counting the cash on the desk, skimming through each brick with her fingers like a Vegas croupier counting a deck of cards.

'Z$29million … Z$30 million … halfway there.'

'So how on earth did you get into doing this?' I asked.

She laughed again.

'Well, I didn't set out to be a criminal, my dear. I studied accountancy at university. My parents had the rubber business here in town making balloons and gloves, and I came to work for them. That was in the 1980s. The business was pretty successful, and my brother and I eventually took it over. But then, by the late nineties, the government started controlling the US dollar rate and printing local currency like mad. The economy began to slide. The rubber business was kaput, and we had to adapt. I had all these clients with cash out of the country who needed cash here, and they didn't want to put it through local banks, where they control what you take out. So I got into *bureau de change*. I take a small cut and I manage to get money out of the country. I learned the ropes pretty fast.'

She gazed out the window at her now idle balloon factory. A pyramid of oil drums was piled high on top of a rusty old truck that had four flat tyres. A plume of smoke drifted over from a neighbouring factory. Somewhere out there, a wheel of industry turned.

'Condoms,' she muttered.

'Condoms?'

'Condoms. I told my brother once, if only we'd made condoms instead of gloves and balloons, I wouldn't be doing all this Chinese accountancy bullshit today. There's still a huge market in Africa for condoms. But balloons? Not so much. Z$39 million … Z$40 million …'

'Aren't you worried about being caught, though? I know about the Reserve Bank business and the problem with the guy who took your house.'

I got a big smile. I could tell she liked speaking about her job.

'Well, in the beginning, yes. I got raided a couple of years ago. Totally unexpected. Someone informed on me. These two guys from the Criminal Investigation Department [CID] came in. I had the trunk of Zim money, but they're not really bothered about that, and all my US is in offshore accounts, so they wouldn't find any actual cash. But I did have a shopping bag under my desk with paper printouts of transfers into my UK account by some Catholic priests in town I play banker for.'

'The printouts had all your foreign account details?'

'Ja – and theirs.'

'Shit, did they find it?'

'They were looking in the wardrobe, going through everything very slowly, moving on to the desk. I told them I had to make a call and I buzzed Faith and said, 'You know the thingamajig for Father O'Reilly? Can you come in and get it?' She knew what I was talking about. She came in and I gently kicked the bag under the table with my foot. She bent down, picked it up, and walked out, cool as a cucumber. Ja, that was a bit scary.'

It must have been terrifying, but she giggled now at the thought of it. I knew it was small victories like that that kept many people sane.

'Okay, but what about now? You have those guys waiting by the gate. Isn't the government more desperate? Isn't it worse?'

Her green eyes sparkled.

'Yes, but now, darling, I have my *own* informers. Ha-ha! You must understand, everyone is a criminal in this country. You have to be. These days I deal cash for guys in the police and the CID. Just the other day this CID chappie whose friend is one of my clients phoned him to tell me he was typing a warrant to search my house and office and that he should make sure I cleared things away fast before his crew arrived. So they warn me, which is nice. The first raid was the big one – like a rite of passage. You have to stay calm and polite. After it happened I got so many calls from other dealers saying, "Now there, that wasn't so bad. We're all thinking of you. You've had your baptism."'

She made it sound like they were a needlework group or a netball team, all in it together, part of a club. It was heartening.

'Also, this place might look shabby, but I keep it this way on purpose. You don't want to look flush. I'm pretty careful, too. When I make calls to my overseas bank, for example, I drive up to the Vumba. There's a turn on the road in the cliffs up there where your cellphone switches to a Mozambique signal. They can't listen in on that. So I do a lot of my work in the mornings up the mountain. It's a nice view, but shit, it's bloody cold in winter.'

I was still amazed she was so calm about everything. Then I remembered something Dad had told me in the car: *Look at her fingernails*. I looked as she counted the cash and I saw they were chewed to the quick, the cuticles blood-red half-moons. She was highly stressed, but her personality – all dynamism and gusto – hid it so well. Being able to laugh at the absurdity of their situation was a trait all Zimbabweans picked up; if they didn't, they all would have had heart attacks.

So I asked her why she didn't just leave. Unlike my parents, she had a decent amount of money out of the country and a brother with a business in South Africa. She could live well there. For the first time she seemed vulnerable, unsure of herself.

'But what about my golf?' she said.

Dad had told me she was a passionate golfer. She wasn't a brilliant player, but she loved the game, and Dad said it helped her relax. Her house overlooked the twelfth hole at Hillside, and she played all the time. She also got to meet new clients at the club. Her black book was full of golfers.

'But you can play golf in South Africa, too,' I pointed out.

She shook her head. She wasn't having any of it.

'I don't think so, darling. They have so many good players down there. I would just feel too intimidated on their courses.'

So Moneypenny hung around partly for the sake of her golf game.

My sixty million was a high mound on the table, a beautiful

pink volcano. Dad came back in, twirling the putter. Moneypenny made a quick phone call.

'Enoch? Hi, listen, Mr Rogers is coming round. Can you give him sixty litres? Any colour … Thanks. And let me know when the trunks arrive.'

She turned to him.

'Okay, Lyn, your bucks are at the vault. Now let's talk revenge.'

She beamed, leaned back, and took a sip of tea from a chipped mug.

'Revenge?' I asked.

'What's the latest with this witch doctor business?' she said to Dad.

Seeing my puzzled look, she laughed. 'You haven't told him? Oh, my, you have to hear this. It's brilliant. We're putting a spell on the chappie who took my house!'

I stared at my father. He looked at me and shrugged.

'I didn't say I was offering her *conventional* legal advice.'

'You hired a witch doctor? From where?'

'Muranda found him,' said Dad. 'Some old bugger in the valley.'

I wondered whether it was the old man Dad had called in all those years ago when they first opened. Before she accepted the job as manager at Drifters, Maude Magondweni had insisted Dad first bring in a *n'anga* to bless the property. She wouldn't take the job without it. Then again, maybe it was the Political Commissar's nephew doing a bit of freelancing. Everyone seemed to be into sorcery these days. You either were a traditional healer or you needed one.

'So what did he recommend?' I asked.

'Well, Moneypenny came out to the camp a while ago with a suitcase full of cash to meet him. We sat in one of the chalets. He wore a suit, spoke well, nothing exotic. It was a bit like going to a regular doctor. You tell him your problem and he suggests a remedy. Except he gives you several choices and tells you that the more you pay him, the better the results.'

I still couldn't believe they were going down this path, but I was quietly thrilled by it. It reminded me of my father's growing the bush at the front of his land to hide the house; it was the same principle. You had to go back to Africa, back to the old ways, to survive. There was a mad genius to it.

'So what were the options?'

Moneypenny took up their tale.

'Well, he asked me if I wanted my money returned in US or Zim dollars. I said gringos, of course. He told me what it would cost and said to pay him ten percent up front, the rest when I got my bucks back. He seemed pretty confident it would work. Then he asked what I wanted done to the guy, what kind of revenge. Did I want to scare him, make him sick or kill him? He had a menu.'

'Christ, killing him was an option?'

'Ja! Of course I don't want to kill the bastard, but you know, I wouldn't mind scaring the shit out of him a bit.'

'So how would he do that?'

'Well, there were two ways. First of all he said I could get a mirror and write the man's name on the glass in tomato sauce or red lipstick. Then I should hammer a nail into the middle of the mirror and pour pig's blood over it, put the mirror in a box, and post it to him. The idea is that he opens it and sees his face with a nail through his head and his name on it.'

'That would scare the crap out of me.'

Moneypenny nodded.

'Ja. In fact, I was worried that that option might actually kill him.'

'So what was the other suggestion?'

'Well, that's the one I went with. He just said that he needed to see the house. So I drove him past it one evening and he got a feel for it. Then he said he would go to the Save River, where the spirits live in the water, and they would speak to him and sort it all out. Anyway, he phoned me and said I would have my house and my money back on the twenty-fourth. That was a month ago.'

'So it hasn't worked?'

'No,' said Dad. 'I went to Muranda and told him, 'John, no more of these namby-pamby herbalists. Get me someone powerful. Someone who can do a proper job here.' Anyway, I was speaking to someone down at the camp the other day, some guy I did some legal work for years ago, and he told me about another *n'anga*. Said he's the most powerful witch doctor in the country. All the ministers go to him. He apparently helped win the liberation war.'

'Jeez, who is he?' I asked.

'Well, he lives up in the mountains near Chipinge and his name is – get this – the Destroyer!'

I burst out laughing.

Moneypenny chuckled and slapped her knee. 'He sounds like just the man!'

'The problem is, he's hard to get hold of, and the guy who told me about him doesn't have any access. But I'm working on it.'

'Okay Lyn, I love it. Let's find the Destroyer. And maybe in the meantime this other chappie's little spell will work its magic. I live in hope.'

The session of legal advice over, it was time to pack up my cash. I handed Moneypenny a paper bag I had brought from the car. She laughed at it. It wouldn't be big enough.

'No, my dear. You have a lot to learn.'

She opened her wardrobe and pulled out a large blue nylon rucksack.

'I'll loan you a Zimbabwean wallet. Return it when you can.'

She piled my fortune into it. Dad put back her putter and we said goodbye. The Charlie Tens were no longer waiting outside when we left. I wondered whether they had our licence plate number and were following us. I kept looking in the rear-view mirror and down side streets as we drove back to town. I found that I was chewing my nails.

The vault was in a paint shop that Moneypenny owned in the centre of town. Enoch, the black floor manager, greeted us and led us to a shelf of paint tins lined against a wall. He drew a lever and the shelf pulled out to reveal an enormous steel security vault. He twirled the wheel on it, the vault opened, and we walked down into a well-lit cellar stacked with boxes of paintbrushes and tins of enamel paint. The shelves were lined with neat bricks of Zimbabwe notes in orderly piles of separate denominations. It looked like the vault of a bank.

Dad's 'sixty litres' – Z\$60 million – was already counted out on a table.

'Thanks, Enoch,' he said as he shovelled the money into his own rucksack.

Flush with cash – 'We're multimillionaires! We could buy this place and install a jukebox,' I cheered – we walked out onto the street and went off to spend the stuff.

I needed to purchase food and booze for our boat trip. Grace was arriving in ten days' time. We would meet her in Harare and drive on to Lake Kariba, where we'd join Piet and Mienkie on their houseboat. Kariba was my favourite place in Zimbabwe, and I was sure that being on the water, seeing the sunsets and listening to the cries of the fish eagles would ease Grace into the country, the calm before the storm of my parents' world. It would be good to see Piet and Mienkie again, too. Dad said Piet still had not got his cattle back, but he had told him that he had met up with a soldier in the Zimbabwe National Army, a staff sergeant, who claimed he could help. 'I'll believe that when I see it,' Dad muttered.

We returned to the Indian section to stock up on meat and seafood at Salim's, a butchery owned by a former classmate of mine whose family were local tycoons. Like all the Indian traders in town, they seemed to stay in business no matter the circumstances. Salim smuggled fresh prawns in from Mozambique and sold six-inch kings for less than US$20 a box. For my parents, finding such fine seafood in this flailing landlocked town was a gift, a minor miracle – and another chapter for Mom's *Recipes for Disaster* cookbook.

We stocked up on biltong, too It was virtually impossible to get hold of biltong now since the country's beef herds had all been slaughtered and butcheries were going out of business because of the power failures. But somehow Salim's freezers worked and he had rows of the tasty strips hanging from steel ceiling hooks behind the counter. Dad reckoned he knew how he got it.

'You still poaching, Sal?'

I squirmed when he said it.

Salim was standing behind the counter. I remembered him from primary school as a shy, skinny academic. Now he was plump, prosperous and totally bald. He was still shy, though, or maybe he was just like that in front of my dad.

'I am not a poacher, Mr Rogers,' he said guiltily, eyes down.

'But weren't you caught on Droppie's farm with a spotlight and a twenty-two?' Droppie was a white farmer in the west of the valley, still on his land.

I jabbed my father in the ribs. 'Leave him alone, man.'

'That wasn't me, Mr Rogers,' said Salim, looking away.

Sal had lost all the hair on his head, but he had grown a long, thick beard, black and shiny as shoe polish, and Dad gave him a hard time about that, too.

You joined the Taliban now, Sal?' he said.

It was getting embarrassing. My dad had no filter.

'Not the Taliban, Mr Rogers. Just a good Muslim.'

'Okay,' said Dad, 'well, how about a discount on these samosas, then? I promise I won't tell Droppie you've been shooting his animals again and I won't tell the Americans you're with the Taliban.'

Dad's approach seemed to work. The samosas were warming in a glass box behind the counter, and Salim piled a dozen of them into a bag and said they were on the house. We were devouring them before we left the shop.

The supermarkets weren't completely empty. Mom had given me a shopping list, and I bought a bottle of brandy and a cucumber at Spar. Cucumbers were one of the few vegetables my parents didn't grow or buy from the roadside traders. It was the last one left. I paid half a million for it and walked onto the street in triumph, holding it aloft like a bat, as if I'd just scored a century at Lord's. Sadly, Dad wasn't watching. He was distracted in the parking lot, haggling with a street vendor over the price of a bag of sugar and some rice. They came to a compromise and Dad handed the kid a brick of cash. Then the kid ran off down an alley without handing over the goods.

'Jeez, what now?' I blurted out. 'He's taken your bloody money!'

'Watch this,' Dad said calmly, and we drove slowly away. Suddenly the boy appeared, jogging by the side of the car in the face of oncoming traffic, innocently tossing bags of sugar and rice through the open window onto the back seat. Once the goods were safely in the back, Dad hooted and sped off, and the kid, acknowledging the hoot with a quick thumbs-up, wheeled away. This was a well-practised method of not getting caught dealing. 'Really,' said Dad, 'you'd think I was buying crack.'

Outlaw characters rolled forth like a scene from a mad Western. Mutare once had been a town for newlyweds and nearly deads; now only the nearly deads remained. Most of my school friends had long gone, but their parents were still here. It was astonishing to see how many friends Mom and Dad still had left. Spending most of my time on the farm, I was under the impression that they and their few refugee tenants were the last, the diehards. But now I found others popping up all over town, the last of the *bittereinders*, forgotten by history.

Outside Frank Meglic's plumbing shop Dad hooted at a demure white lady crossing the street, an old friend who was also in the backpacker business.

She grinned. 'How are your prossies, Lyn?'

Everyone seemed to know about Drifters and its prostitutes. Dad quite liked the notoriety it gave him.

'Ah, Anne, why don't you join the game? It's the way forward!'

'I'm leaving that to you, Lyn. It's my own house we're talking about.'

They gossiped for a while about the backpacker lodge at the top of the main street that was now a full-time brothel, doing a booming lunchtime trade.

'Wall-to-wall prossies,' said Anne. 'He's raking it in.'

'I told you, my dear. Join us! Give it a go!'

My parents really admired Anne Bruce. They told me she helped bereaved people arrange cremations for the newly dead nearly deads. Zimbabwe's crematoriums no longer functioned because there was no gas to fire the furnaces, and the cemeteries in Mutare were too full because so many people had died of AIDS. But Anne had made friends among the Hindu community in the Indian quarter, and she had learned how to use their traditional wood pyre. Mutare's deceased white Christians were going out as Hindus.

A black man in a suit waved the car down. Dad stopped, wound down the window. It was Collius Chitakatira, a school-teacher and a sometime golf partner of his.

'Lyn, I haven't seen you for a while. Did my superior game scare you away?'

'What crap, Collius. I'm giving my game a rest, let you brush up on your technique.'

My father hadn't played golf in years now. Couldn't afford fuel for the trip to town, the green fees, the caddy, or the cost of a round of drinks after. But he wasn't going to let Collius know that.

'Just call me when you've learned to hit the fairway, Collius.'

He waved at a white couple exiting the Meikles department store. The woman was a slender, attractive brunette, the man a tall, broad-shouldered farmer type with a handsome mop of thick salt-and-pepper hair. Dad pulled over.

'Wendy, Speros, how are the jailbirds?'

I had heard about Wendy and Speros Landos. They'd once had a farm next to the De Klerks. It was invaded, and Speros was attacked by a gang of war veterans one evening during a dispute between the veterans and his workers. He was knocked to the ground outside his gates and set upon with rocks, clubs and daggers. He had a licenced pistol under his shirt, and he fired a round off, killing one of the attackers instantly. Witnesses said the war vets got the pistol and tried to shoot him, but the weapon jammed. Speros was beaten unconscious and left for dead. He woke up in a hospital bed with two broken arms, shattered wrists, a pierced kidney, a broken nose, cracked teeth and bruises and lacerations all over his body. Although he couldn't move, he was shackled to the bed and had a 24-hour armed guard. After five weeks in hospital, he spent four months in Mutare's Remand Prison, awaiting trial for murder, a white man in a dangerous-prisoners' cell with fourteen black men. I'd expected him to describe the time with anger and depression. Instead, he spoke as if he had been on a spiritual journey.

'It was a very humanising experience,' he told me one evening up at the house. 'There were about fifteen of us in a five-by-four-metre cell. A lot of them were in for minor stuff. They just can't afford bail. I got my lawyer to bail some of them out. It freed up a bit of space.

'The first thing the hard-core criminals did was to tell the others to leave me alone. I speak Shona, so that helped. My arms were in plaster and I couldn't walk. The other prisoners took turns nursing me. They would wash me at shower time, undress me in the late afternoon when the dangerous criminals had to strip for inspection. It was very humbling.

'The toilet was in a corner of the room. They would carry me to it when I needed to go. Mutare had a problem with its water supply so the toilet didn't flush. But I worked out a system. Water would flow through our cell from the women's cells showers behind us, so I dammed it up and we used that to flush.

'I had to find ways to pass time. There was nothing to read. People used to be educated in prisons. Mugabe was jailed by the Rhodesians for eleven years. He passed three university degrees inside. Now you could never do that. Publications have to be vetted for incriminating material, and they don't get through. But Wendy started bringing so many boxes of reading material that they couldn't cope with vetting them all. *Reader's Digest*. Car magazines. Bibles.

'I handed them out. I read to pass time. The black guys read to learn. They would have discussions for hours about the cars they read about in the magazines; the benefit of one vehicle over the other. One guy said he had stolen a Toyota twin-cab five years ago and it was rubbish. Debates would go on for hours. Then it would go quiet. We had passed time.

'I read the Bible. I lent it out. I asked one of the hardened criminals to be in charge. He was very efficient. He would say, "I need it back at such and such a time," and it would be returned. The best debates were about the Bible. They would debate the meaning of the stories, the characters. They argued about Samson. The book of Job. The relevance of these stories to our lives. You realise people's humanity.'

Incredibly, many of the prisoners Speros was in jail with were farm invaders: war vets, youth militia, exactly the kind of men he had lost his farm to – and killed. Yet he didn't blame them, and they didn't blame him.

'These guys were told to do these things by politicians, police, soldiers. They did them for money or for food. The real criminals are the ones who told them to do this.'

If Speros's prison story was remarkable, his legal journey was just as astonishing. After four months in D Block he was granted bail, and he spent the next twelve months awaiting a trial date, reporting three times a week to the police station. But if the country's economy was in a shambles, by 2005 the judicial system appeared to be heading the same way. By the end of 2005 still no date had been set. It was then that my father casually suggested a wild gambit to Speros.

'This has been going on long enough. When you next see the magistrate, tell him they must either set a date or drop all charges.' Speros did so, and incredibly the magistrate agreed. A month later, all charges were dropped. By 2006 he was a free man.

Now, he says, when he walks down the street in Mutare, complete strangers come up to him to say hello. He doesn't recognise them. They say: 'We were on the inside together. You brought us books.'

TWELVE
The Rally

THE FOLLOWING MORNING Dad woke me with a cup of coffee. 'Brian James just called. He wants to know if you want to go to a rally.'

'A rally? Jeez. Okay, when?'

I was groggy, clearing away the rust of a cheap hangover. I'd spent a late night down at the camp catching up with the two Johns and Naomi, drinking beer and smoking some of their marijuana supply. Dad had dug up his *dagga* crop at Mom's insistence months before, and the Murandas had the remains stored above the rafters of their house. They were going through it fast, Naomi medicating her 'blood pressure' with liberal doses. It was great to see the three of them again. I gave them a wind-up radio I had brought from New York that didn't need batteries, and we tuned in to SW Radio Africa and Studio 7, a Voice of America station broadcasting from Botswana. We listened as a full moon, round and veined as a peeled grape, floated across the black sky.

The three were holding up well; Drifters, not as well. Dawson Jombe was struggling, unable to afford stock for the bar, so the shelves and fridges were empty. Often he didn't open the place at all. Sydney, his barman, had left and taken his music with him. Although there was eighty per cent unemployment in Zimbabwe now, it was strangely hard to hire anyone to work. The security guard had disappeared, too – no one knew where to. Dawson was applying for work with some Western NGOs who were trying to set up rural farming schemes in the area, but he and Patricia were increasingly reliant on her diminishing teacher's salary.

Yet the brothel thrived. More men in ever-sleeker motorcars drove out with their prostitutes, mistresses, small houses. They brought their own drinks with them now and would park their BMWs and twin-cabs in front of a chalet, turn the car stereos to a low hum, and drink in the dim glow of the passenger-seat lights as if at a drive-in theatre before staggering into a chalet for a quick session on the mattress. I watched these shadowy assignations from the warmth of the wood fire, and it made me depressed. The camp had become an open-air brothel, the scent of cheap perfume mingling with the tang of marijuana and wood smoke.

I sipped the strong Vumba mountain coffee Dad had brought me.

'It's on Saturday. Give Brian a call. He says Tsvangirai's going to be there.'

'Really? Wow. Ja, I'll definitely go.'

I had the chance to meet Morgan Tsvangirai, the leader of the opposition.

Brian James was a white friend of my parents' who'd become a prominent MDC member in town. He and his wife, Sheelagh, a slender brunette whose aristocratic demeanour belied a wicked sense of humor, had lost their chicken farm in the early days of the land invasions. Brian had never considered himself remotely political – 'I just wanted to farm and play cricket on weekends.' But he joined the MDC, and by 2006 he had became treasurer for the Manicaland province, replacing Roy Bennett, the famous Shona-speaking farmer from Chimanimani, known to his legion of rural black supporters as Pachedu, meaning 'one of us'. Bennett was perhaps the most popular member of the MDC after Morgan Tsvangirai and Tendai Biti, and he had won a seat in Parliament in 2000 in a landslide, thrashing the ZANU-PF candidate. In 2004, however, he was sentenced to a year in a maximum-security prison in Harare after he 'pushed' the justice minister, Patrick Chinamasa, during a confrontation in Parliament. After his release, fearing assassination, Bennett moved to South Africa, where he became the party's treasurer in exile and a prominent spokesman. Brian had big shoes to fill.

I knew him from my cricket-playing days as a good medium-pace bowler. An intense, soft-spoken man with wire-rimmed glasses and sandy hair, he'd always struck me as more academic than agricultural. My father said he was fearless, though – which helped explain his rise in the MDC. Sheelagh, whose brother Terry Coughlan was my former provincial cricket captain, strongly supported his new high-risk political career while at the same time managing to affect an air of amused detachment, as if it didn't worry her. Brian had spent four days in jail on trumped-up treason charges (several of my parents' friends had now been in prison). When Mom phoned Sheelagh to ask her how he was doing, she said, 'No idea, Ros. I don't *do* jail.'

I was excited about attending an MDC rally and seeing Tsvangirai speak, but I was nervous, too. I had no media accreditation, and I knew I would stand out in a crowd, the only white person apart from Brian, who was already well known in the area. MDC rallies were filled with informers, CIO spies. I phoned Brian.

'I definitely want to go, as long as no one finds out I'm a reporter.'

'Don't worry about that,' he said. 'Just bring a packed lunch.'

'Where's the rally?'

'Buhera.'

My heart sank. Buhera was a remote, arid rural area two hours' drive southwest of Mutare, far from any town. It was Morgan Tsvangirai's home district and it was there, one night in 2000, that two of his organisers, including his driver, Tichaona Chiminya, were burned to death in a firebomb attack on their vehicle by ZANU-PF hit men. I had also heard rumours that it was the home district of Joseph Chinotimba, a ruthless thug who, although he had never fought in the liberation war, had branded himself a war-veteran leader and become a feared government enforcer, leading many farm invasions and attacks on opposition activists.

There would be no hiding place in Buhera.

'Okay, just as long as I am not identified as a journalist,' I reminded Brian.

'So you are the journalist! Welcome. Welcome!'

It was 6:00 am. I was standing outside an MDC safe house in a suburb of Mutare, surrounded by a dozen young black activists in T-shirts emblazoned with the open-hand symbol of the party, all waiting for a lift to the rally.

They were thanking me for joining them, excited that a foreign-based reporter would be coming along for the ride. So much for being incognito.

'Guys, guys,' I hushed them, 'don't tell anyone I'm a reporter. Keep it quiet.'

They laughed and slapped hands with one another.

'Don't be afraid. You are safe with us!'

I was struck by the lack of fear. Rather, there was a sense of excitement, as if we were going to a soccer match. Which, in a sense, we were. Soccer was the country's national sport, and the MDC's symbols mimicked those of a soccer referee: the open hand was the signal a referee made when sending a player off. MDC members also brandished red cards and blew whistles, exhorting Zimbabweans to 'send Mugabe off'.

To the side of the group I noticed a handsome dreadlocked guy, similar in age to me, a notebook in his hand, calmly smoking Madisons. I introduced myself.

He said his name was Sydney Saize. He was a local journalist who filed radio reports for Studio 7, the Voice of America station that I had listened to down at the camp the night before. Sydney also wrote for local newspapers, but he mostly survived on assignments for VOA because they paid him in US dollars.

'Is it safe for me out there without accreditation?' I asked him.

'It should be,' he said. 'The police hassle the leaders and the supporters more, try to stop the rallies. Hide your notebook. You should be fine.'

'Have you ever been arrested?' I asked him.

'Yes, in January. I have to go to court for breaking the Access to Information Act – 'peddling falsehoods'. A story I did on some teachers who were beaten up by ZANU-PF youths in Marange. I filed my report by cellphone from the school, and a war veteran overheard and made a citizen's arrest.'

'What could happen to you?'

He shrugged.

'Twenty years in jail.'

Then he smiled and offered me a cigarette.

It was humbling to meet people like Sydney. Hundreds of local journalists worked in Zimbabwe for little money or recognition, and at great risk to their personal safety. Few of them could afford cars, offices or computers; they would hitch lifts and catch buses to interviews and political rallies. The stories I did for British and American newspapers were relatively well paid, and I risked little reporting them compared to these guys. They were on the front lines: followed, threatened, their offices bugged, their newspapers banned, even bombed, their friends bribed to become informers. But still they did it; it was their life. Just how brave they were would become horrifically apparent in March 2007 when Morgan Tsvangirai, the man we were about to see, would be brutally assaulted at the prayer meeting in Harare where the MDC activist Gift Tandare was shot dead. Tsvangirai's skull was cracked by police truncheons; he blacked out several times during a later assault in prison. The world never would have seen images of his bruised and battered face if Edward Chikomba, a freelance cameraman, had not smuggled out of the country footage he'd shot of Tsvangirai in the hospital. That one act might have helped change Zimbabwe's history: the MDC's struggle suddenly became a major news story. Tsvangirai was a symbol of resistance to brutality. Two weeks later Edward Chikomba was abducted from his home; his mutilated body was found dumped in the bush, on a farm south of Harare.

We drove off, Brian behind the wheel. I sat with an organiser from Buhera named T Chimonya in the front seat; the others piled in the back of Brian's truck, happily waving the open-hand salute at passing pedestrians as we left town.

Half an hour later we turned onto a rutted dirt road, and suddenly, as if we'd crossed a border, the cool green of Mutare's mountains and valleys gave way to the hot, dry breath of the communal lands. The earth – parched, cracked, the colour of bright copper – was semi-desert here; only baobabs, scrub and thorn survived the ruthless onslaught of the sun.

We passed no other cars and few people except, occasionally, at dusty settlements of mud-and-thatch huts set in the shade of rocky outcrops. And as we drove past these huts, a strange thing would happen. On hearing our vehicle, scores of villagers, most of them beaming middle-aged women in bright white skirts and neat red headdresses – the MDC colours – would run out at us, waving both hands high in the air in the open-hand salute, imploring Brian to stop and give them a lift to the rally. We piled so many of these women into the back of the truck that soon the chassis scraped over the bumps in the road, and we slowed to the pace of an ox-cart. They began singing in Shona as we drove. We must have sounded like a travelling gospel choir.

I noticed there were few young people in the villages we passed. Most had moved to the cities or out of the country to send back those remittances. But at one stop a group of snotty-nosed kids, barefoot children wheeling the rims of bicycle tyres through thick sand, ran up to my window to ask me for food, money – '*Mari, sa, mari, sa!*' – and writing implements. 'Please, mister, give me pen! Give me pencil! I need pencil. Books. Books.'

I had hidden my notebook under the car seat in case of a police roadblock, but I pulled it out now, gave a spare pen to one of the kids, and tore out several pages. I found myself thinking of John Agoneka during the war; how he'd hidden in terror as Rhodesian helicopters strafed his village, how guerrillas had forced him to carry weapons on his back when all he wanted to do was go to school, to study, to learn, to read. The urge to read is not uniquely Zimbabwean, but under Robert Mugabe in the 1980s and 1990s, Zimbabweans did learn. The country became one of the most literate in Africa. Now it was regressing. Schools were closing, textbooks were too expensive and pens and pencils were in short supply.

After two hours we came to a series of low, windowless cement buildings fronted by the parched grass of a soccer field. It was the Buhera high school, and the rally, I learned, would be held on the field. A white tent covering a row of dirty plastic chairs had been erected beside one goalpost. We were in the middle of nowhere; scrubby bush and sand stretched to the horizon.

I had always been under the impression that the MDC was an urban party, strong in the cities and among the young and the educated, but with little support in rural areas, where an older population with deep memories of the horror of the liberation war supported ZANU-PF, the party that had won freedom from white rule. And yet by midday five thousand people had gathered on that field in the blinding sun, many of them old men and women, wizened as prophets. They arrived like pilgrims – on foot, in creaking donkey carts, emerging from the thorny bush around us, dusty and bedraggled, yet triumphant. One old man smiled as he told me he had walked throughout the night, more than thirty kilometres, to hear Tsvangirai. He called him 'my president'.

I left my notebook and tape recorder in the truck, bummed more cigarettes from Sydney, and sat, a little self-conscious, on the grass to the side of the field, the only white person in the world, it seemed, apart from Brian.

Tsvangirai arrived suddenly and without fanfare in a bullet-proof red Isuzu twin-cab. He stepped out looking busy and purposeful in a floral dress shirt and a black leather cowboy hat. A frisson of excitement rippled through the crowd, a murmur that rose to a crescendo of whistles and open-hand salutes. He waved as he walked with his wife, Susan, two bodyguards, and Brian and T, and took his seat under the tent. Sydney sat at the back of the tent, the only official reporter present.

The rally turned out to be more a traditional Shona celebration than dull political stump speech. The crowd and the activists ran the show. Slogans were chanted in Shona by an activist near the stage, and the crowd responded, knowing every word. Since the MDC's formation in 1999 its manifesto, as its name suggested, had been democratic change, and the most common slogan at a rally, done in call-and-response style between an activist and a crowd, was '*Chinja maitiro! Maitiro ako ayo chinja, hezvoko bwaa!*' Change your deeds, bad ones, your deeds should change.

I knew this slogan fairly well by now, but soon the entire crowd had broken into song, a beautiful, mournful Shona ballad that I saw brought tears to the eyes of those singing it around me.

I asked the man next to me what it was about.

He whispered in broken English. 'A man and a woman were burned here some years ago. It is to them.'

Tichaona Chiminya and Talent Mabhika had been attacked at dusk, not far from this field, as the sun set. They had been trailed from a local bar by CIO agents and war veterans. Stones were thrown at their vehicle, then petrol bombs. Engulfed in flames, they stumbled screaming from the vehicle and rolled in the sand on the road trying to put out the blaze. They burned to death.

It was the same weekend that the farmer David Stevens was murdered. A message had been sent; Zimbabwe would never be the same again.

Another song was about Operation Murambatsvina – Operation Drive Out the Trash. Starting in April 2005 and continuing into the frosty mists of that year's freezing June and July, more than two million Zimbabweans living in slums and shantytowns on the edge of the country's cities were violently driven out by police and soldiers who arrived in bulldozers and tractors to demolish their shacks and homes. Many of the slum dwellers were former farmworkers already displaced in the land invasions, and after their shacks were destroyed they wandered the country, homeless, haunted, ghostly nomads. Some would have been in this crowd. It was said that the Ethiopian dictator Mengistu Haile Mariam, who lived in asylum in a posh Harare suburb, advised President Mugabe on the removals, since he knew the destitute slum population was a strong MDC base. However, the man who was really in charge of the removals was much closer to home: the Top Man.

The song described the Operation Murambatsvina clearances in nearby Mutare: 'Mutare residents were living peacefully until ZANU-PF came and destroyed their homes in cyclone tsunami style.'

I was so taken by the spectacle, the effortless repartee between crowd and stage, that I failed to notice someone standing over me, blocking out the sun.

'What media organisation are you with?' a voice commanded.

I looked up. A man, about fifty, in a filthy, torn white T-shirt, hovered over me. His face was hidden by the glare of the sun behind him.

'I'm not with any media organisation,' I said, shielding my eyes.

He cursed.

'You are! What media organisation are you with?'

I stood up now. He had a stringy beard, bloodshot eyes and alcohol on his breath. I was conscious of the people around me whispering and murmuring. For a moment I thought this might be Chinotimba himself.

'I'm not with any media organisation,' I said, more annoyed than afraid.

He moved his face close to mine.

'You are! You are a journalist!' I felt flecks of spit.

He grabbed my forearm and squeezed it, trying to pull me away.

Some of the people around me stood up, talking excitedly now, but the rally continued; our mini-commotion was too far from the stage to be noticed.

I am not a brave person. I try to avoid conflict, to run from confrontation. But, perhaps inspired by the people around me and the stories told in the songs and chants, or perhaps simply because the man was not in uniform, didn't have a weapon and was drunk, I pushed his hand off and shoved my face at his.

'Fuck off,' I said. 'I am a farmer. A farmer from Mutare. Fuck off.'

And then, out of the crush of bodies now standing around me, another hand appeared, grabbed mine, and pulled me away.

It was T, one of the organising officials we had come with.

'Come,' he said. 'That man is CIO. You are safer sitting in the tent.'

I was dizzy, pumped with adrenaline, and more paranoid than ever. I sat next to Sydney and told him what had happened. My hands were shaking.

'Spies,' he whispered. 'Everywhere there are spies.'

By the time Tsvangirai rose to speak, a dozen uniformed policemen had gathered on the goal line some way off. They were talking to two men in white shirts. I was worried it was about me. Was one of the white shirts the man who had confronted me? He pointed to the stage. This was it. I wanted to run.

Sydney shrugged again.

'Relax, Douglas. This always happens. The MDC have to get permission to hold a rally. They get it, then the police arrive and say, 'It was not for this time,' or 'It is too late,' or 'You have five minutes left.' They are always harassing. They want to stop Tsvangirai from addressing the crowd.'

The white shirts were MDC organisers trying to persuade the police to allow the rally to continue. I saw T among them. He had his work cut out for him.

Despite my paranoia and the constant threat of menace, it was inspiring being at the rally, watching the crowd. The open hand is a joyous sign – the very opposite of the violent clenched-fist symbol of the ruling party – and while the songs about struggle and resistance were emotionally wrenching, there was also great humour displayed at the proceedings, a remarkable ability to laugh at one's enemies. Sydney explained another song to me: *Tambirai Morgan pamusika weMbare, Bob NdiWhindi, pamusika weMbare.* 'It references Tsvangirai as a dignitary while Mugabe – Bob – is a tout at a bus terminus who should carry Tsvangirai's luggage.'

What struck me most powerfully, though, was that the supporters, the activists and Tsvangirai himself were not victims. There was none of the belligerent self-pity everyone now associated with the tirades of the ruling party, a party that constantly blamed the West, Britain, America, Blair, Bush, Tsvangirai, sanctions, sellouts, puppets, stooges, whites, the weather or the drought for the chaos in the country. They had held power for more than twenty-six years, they controlled every aspect of the state to the extent that you couldn't openly say what you thought, and yet someone else was always to blame. Aggressive victimhood is a mark of tyranny, an ugly and dangerous thing to behold.

The rally finally ended with a comic one-act play so shocking in its audacity – given the police presence – that I found myself too nervous to laugh. The crowd had no such fears. A skinny old man in a worn-out suit stood up unsteadily in front of the crowd. He held a walking stick in a bony hand and wobbled on it while reaching into his pocket with his other hand for a pair of sunglasses. The crowd whispered excitedly as they watched. The old man put on the glasses and staggered about, groping, falling, pretending to be blind. The crowd was laughing now, hooting their approval, and I suddenly heard what they were saying: 'Mugabe … Mugabe …' The man was playing President Mugabe as a lost, blind, out-of-touch old man. The policemen looked on sullenly from the side. I wouldn't have wanted to have been that old man afterward.

I made my way back to Brian's truck with Sydney. I wanted to speak to Tsvangirai, but his bodyguards hurried him back to his car, and the crush of people made it hard to get close to him. His vehicle sped off down the road in a cloud of red dust.

So much for meeting the leader of the opposition. At the same time I was relieved. I wanted to get out of there, get home. Who knew what dangers lurked as afternoon gave way to dusk? Then Brian came up to me.

'He's waiting for us at Birchenough Bridge.'

'Who?'

'Morgan. You can speak to him there.'

'You arranged that?'

'It's safer. Let's go before it gets dark.'

It appeared I had a meeting with the man who would be president.

We drove due south on a busier dirt road, which might have been a good thing, but it made me nervous again. A popular method of political assassination in Zimbabwe is to ram a military vehicle into a targeted car. Here I was in a carload of opposition party activists driving in the late afternoon on a remote rural road. We were obvious targets. But we passed no military vehicles, no police roadblocks. It was eerily quiet. Even that struck me as suspicious.

By four o'clock we had arrived at a run-down hotel on the banks of the Save River in the shadow of the Birchenough Bridge. The bridge is a gleaming single-arched steel structure, 329 metres in length, that rises out of the arid veld like the silver fin of a giant sailfish. A stunning, futuristic masterpiece built in 1935 by Ralph Freeman, designer of the Sydney Harbour Bridge, it seems utterly out of place, almost a mirage, in this dusty, primeval landscape.

The hotel was better suited to the surroundings: a sleepy, run-down property of airless, peeling chalets and bougainvillea-splashed bungalows, the only shade provided by the veranda of a bar and a baobab tree on a lawn. I remembered this bridge and this hotel from another time, and my mind drifted back to it. It was 1977, and we were waiting in our Chevrolet in a queue of cars in an armed convoy to drive to the border for our Christmas holiday in South Africa. The area was a hotbed of action, and the hotel was pockmarked with bullet holes and boarded up. My sisters and I sat and smiled at the Rhodesian troopies with their machine guns guarding the bridge, and counted the crocodiles basking on the banks of the Save River below.

I snapped out of the reverie as we pulled up.

Tsvangirai and his wife were sitting on garden chairs under the tree, outside the bar, relaxed as honeymooners at a desert resort. His cowboy hat was on the table. For a second I imagined we were in west Texas. His bodyguards drove off to find food in a nearby village, and I joined the Tsvangirais at the wrought-iron table. We spoke as the late-afternoon sun glinted off the steel arch of the bridge, and two vultures circled in the sky.

Say what you like about Morgan Tsvangirai – the ruling party branded him a puppet, a stooge of whites and the West; the MDC Senate faction that had split from his party a year earlier denounced him as an autocrat; intellectuals and many liberals in South Africa called him uneducated and inarticulate – but there can be few braver people in the world.

He was born in the southeastern province of Masvingo, not far from where we now sat, in 1952. The eldest of nine children of a poor bricklayer, he dropped out of high school to support the family, working for a while in the textile industry in Mutare, and then in the mines. He didn't fight in the liberation war but joined ZANU-PF after independence, rising rapidly up the ranks of the mineworkers' union. In 1989 he became secretary-general of the Zimbabwe Congress of Trade Unions. By 1997, however, he'd split with the party over its misrule and corruption, and he became an outspoken critic of Mugabe's dictatorship. He was promptly hung out of his tenth-floor office window by state security agents. They would have killed him, but his receptionist walked in. He founded the Movement for Democratic Change in 1999 and had been looking over his shoulder ever since, surviving two more assassination attempts, several assaults and arrests and a highly public treason trial. When I spoke to him, his worst beating was yet to come – that 2007 prayer meeting assault.

I asked him if he felt safe, and I glanced over my own shoulder as I did so. A white Mazda sedan pulled up, and three men in jeans and T-shirts stepped out. Tsvangirai had the round, compressed face of a chipmunk and talked in a deep, raspy voice that came out in a machine-gun staccato.

'I do not travel anywhere in the country where I feel in danger from the people,' he said. 'I feel insecure by the state machinery. But they would not dare do anything to me. It is too risky. My security comes from the people.'

The three men walked into the bar.

What did he make of South African president Thabo Mbeki's approach to Mugabe? Mbeki was the world's designated point man on Zimbabwe and for six years had advocated a policy of 'quiet diplomacy' to resolve the crisis. Tsvangirai rolled his eyes. I chuckled. My father always did the same whenever anyone mentioned Thabo Mbeki.

'Mbeki's quiet diplomacy will never work. It is quiet approval. The biggest mistake on his part is to endorse all the flawed elections. The human cost of that is enormous. He gives Mugabe the opportunity to defy everyone.'

I sipped a Coke as the sun dipped lower. The three men stood at the bar drinking beers. One turned his head to look our way, then turned back. Brian lounged by the truck, staring at his watch.

It was often remarked that Zimbabweans were a docile people, that they lacked the courage to stand up to Mugabe, to force him from power. From the safety of my perch in New York, I often expressed this view myself. Knowing it to be true of me, I asked Tsvangirai whether he thought it true of the majority of Zimbabweans. He shook his head forcefully.

'They are not docile. The people know the experience of the violence from the liberation war. It was not an easy experience, and they know this time it is not like we are liberating ourselves from a white oppressor. We are now fighting brother to brother, and the ruthlessness may even be much worse.'

'Worse?'

'Worse. I mean, look at the whole of Africa. We don't want that. We can't fight another independence war. We fought for that and won it. We are now fighting for democratic change so we can express ourselves freely again. But let me tell you – don't underestimate these people. They are not docile. Not at all.'

The three men moved outside now. They sat at a table across the lawn.

I asked Tsvangirai about white farmers. I wondered where people like my parents, Brian James and other whites would fit in if he came to power. His reply would have pleased my dad.

'White farmers are Zimbabweans. Some are third, fourth generation in this country. They know the climate, the soil, the agriculture. It's not like you can come here and just start ploughing. It needs a culture, long-term understanding of the culture. White Zimbabweans had this.'

He rolled his eyes again. 'Now Mugabe has a policy to "look east". To look to the Chinese to invest in us. What is a Chinese going to understand about Africa? It will take another hundred years! Mugabe's policies are denial. The base of the Zimbabwean economy is Western investment for over one hundred years since colonialism. The fabric of this economy is investment.'

The sun was setting, and it was beginning to get dark. I had one more question, and it was about what had struck me so much about the people at the rally. The support for the MDC has long been in the cities, among the urban working class. Rural Zimbabweans, especially the elderly, had always been Mugabe's constituency. Yet there were so many old supporters at that day's rally. Was this happening elsewhere? Was Tsvangirai starting to get rural support outside his Buhera constituency?

He nodded confidently.

'Let me tell you: Mugabe can never win an election in this country. Eighty percent of the people below the age of forty support us, and that is most of the population. But now what you are seeing is that the older people are overcoming their fear, too, influenced by their children in the cities. You can see that at our rallies – the drumming, the singing, the choirs. ZANU-PF has lost that spirit. People are coerced to their rallies. Forced. Our rallies are alive. Everyone volunteers; no one is forced to come. Between the leadership and the people there is a symbiosis.'

The sun had now set, and it was time to go. I stood up and shook Tsvangirai's hand and thanked his wife for their time. The three men sipped their beers. They were facing our way. Tsvangirai paid them no mind. I told him I was going to Kariba in a few days' time with my American wife.

He smiled. 'Watch out for elephants.'

I glanced at the three men.

'Watch out for yourself,' I said.

The heat of the day had rapidly given way to the cool of a winter evening. It was another starlit night. We piled into Brian's truck again and drove north. Brian hit the accelerator. I looked in the rear-view mirror for the headlights of a Mazda sedan to appear. Brian drove faster still.

'Are you worried they're following us?' I said.

'Nah. I have to get home soon. Sheelagh hates it when I'm late.'

In the back of the truck the activists sang Shona hymns. We sped on through the night.

THIRTEEN
The Helicopters

THE TRIP UP the Commissar's ancestral mountain was a disaster from start to finish, although not without its moments of dire comedy. I picked up the Commissar, Gracie Basket and Tweed Jacket at the bottom of the road in Dad's bakkie.

It was a blinding hot Thursday morning, not the best weather to hike up a hill, and the Commissar had on his long trench coat, his briefcase in his hand. He was dressed for a middle-management conference in midwinter Chicago.

We exchanged pleasantries – 'Morning, Dougie,' he said – but he soon started on a political rant. We passed the fuel station at the foot of the pass where a scrawled sign read, *No Petrol. No Diesel*, as it had for about four years.

'The British have diverted oil ships from Beira coming to Zimbabwe,' he said. 'They just hate the leadership of Zimbabwe. Britain wants to use its power to show the president and Zimbabweans that they cannot succeed without them. So they enforce sanctions on us.'

I glazed over. There were no sanctions on Zimbabwe. There were travel bans on leaders of the regime. Companies that disinvested from Zimbabwe did so because it was unstable; the government had broken its own laws and dispossessed its own citizens. Who would invest in a place like that?

But then the Commissar mentioned the United States, and I woke up.

'You know, I like America. It is known for advocating democracy. This teaching is good. Democracy would want to see everyone on equal footing.'

'In a way,' I said.

I reached for the tape recorder in my bag, keeping my eyes on the road.

'But we have a problem with our opposition,' he continued. 'The kind of opposition leader we have, Tsvangirai, was once a trade unionist, but in a sweet change he supported the employers. If you were represented by such a person, he is a sellout. Our opposition leader is a stooge, a puppet, being used for his personal gain by the British. Not for the benefit of the people.'

Gracie cackled in the back seat. She clearly agreed. I pressed what I thought was the Record button on the cassette player. By accident I must have pressed Play.

A deep voice came on, an extra passenger in the car.

Mbeki's quiet diplomacy will never work. It is quiet approval. The biggest mistake on his part is to endorse all the flawed elections. The human cost of that is –

It was Morgan Tsvangirai – the tape from the interview at the Birchenough Bridge hotel! The opposition leader was in the car! I panicked, tried to switch it off, dropped it at my feet, swerved in front of a bus and then swerved back again. Eventually I found the Stop button. The Commissar turned to give me a look. Then he faced the front again. He didn't speak for quite a while.

We motored down the other side of the pass, past the ancestral hill we were supposed to climb. It still gave me the creeps, that mountain, but I was excited to see the burial ground of his ancestors. I didn't think much of the Commissar's political views, but he had told a gripping story about the past. However, he needed to go to a pharmacy in town to buy some headache tablets before we resumed our journey.

I parked outside a pharmacy on the main street while Gracie harrumphed in the back. It was all taking too long. 'I have meetings,' she squeaked. 'Crops to harvest. I need to tend my fields. Farming takes time.'

Tweed Jacket smiled happily next to her. He had nowhere else to go. As we waited, a young black man standing at the entrance of a shoe shop across the road saw me and waved. Then he bounded over to my side of the car.

'Douglas,' he said quietly, almost in a whisper. 'The Red. How are you?'

I had no idea who he was.

'The Red?'

'The Red. Thanks for coming to the rally. Did you enjoy?'

Finally I placed him. He was one of the activists we had driven out to Buhera with. MDC supporters often said 'the Red' when it wasn't safe to wave the open hand. I hadn't recognised him without his white T-shirt. He wore the uniform of the shoe shop.

I grinned nervously.

'Ja, it was great, man. Good to see you again. See you later, hey.'

I wanted him to go away. I didn't want the Commissar to see him with me. I didn't want him to see me with the Commissar, either.

Who knew what role the Commissar had played in the area these past few years? Had he led assaults on MDC activists? He was well known enough to have been waved through the police roadblock we had passed on the other side of the pass.

I glanced over at the pharmacy and was horrified to see the Commissar striding purposefully back to the car. I turned to tell the activist to disappear and was surprised to find him already gone, halfway down the street, swallowed up in the crowd on the pavement and the tired queue outside the CABS bank.

Good man, I said to myself, *good man*.

Gracie sat in the back and said nothing. I wondered if she knew what it was about.

To get to the path up the Commissar's hill we took a road through Fairbridge Park, another now forlorn and decrepit suburb of Mutare. It was the road we used to take to the drive-in on the western outskirts of town. Though the drive-in was long gone, bulldozed to make way for housing, childhood memories returned effortlessly to me. Mom and Dad would always put Helen and me in the boot of the Peugeot 404 so they only had to pay entrance for two kids. They would park, hook up the metal speaker box to the window, rest the FN rifle between the seats – we still used to go during the war – then open a carton of box wine and start drinking it out of plastic cups. Twenty minutes into the film, once they were sure the night manger wasn't snooping around, they would let us out to join Stof and Zaan on the sticky leather back seat and eat the juicy hamburgers Mom made that always steamed up the windows. What movies we saw there! The child catcher in *Chitty Chitty Bang Bang* gave me nightmares. The albino in *Foul Play* did, too. Mom and Dad loved Peter Sellers – we must have seen every *Pink Panther* movie three times. Woody Allen, too, although as a kid I never got the point of that funny-looking man. One of the first things I did when I moved to New York, though, was go see Woody play clarinet at the Café Carlyle on a Monday night; I wanted to tell him how he helped my parents laugh their way through a war. Best of all was Clint Eastwood. We all loved Clint – Dad and me especially – and as we watched him ride into view above the hazy fields of blonde grass on the horizon of our town, it was easy to imagine he was our sheriff, our outlaw, looking out for us.

We arrived at a rusty park gate on the right side of the road. I pulled the car over in front of the gate. An entry fee was posted, but there was no one from the Parks Department around, and it looked as though a parks official hadn't been here in years. We managed to pry open the rusty gate, but it was hard to see any pathway. The bush along the fence was thick as jungle.

'I thought you said you came here all the time,' I complained to the Commissar.

He was wrestling with a green vine as if it were a snake.

'Many times, to pay respects to the ancestors,' he muttered.

'So where's the path, then?'

'It's here. Somewhere.'

Eventually we found a vague track under the branches, as faded as a distant memory. I looked at the granite boulders towering over us from the top of the hill.

'How long will it take to get there?' I asked.

'One hour, maybe two,' he said.

I doubted it. You could tell the path became bush again a few metres ahead. It would take much longer than that. I gave out the bottles of water I had brought.

'You going to climb the mountain with your briefcase?' I asked the Commissar.

'Not at all,' he said.

He handed it to Tweed Jacket. Then he took off his trench coat and gave that to him, too. The old man was weighed down, and for the first time he didn't smile.

'He may be the elder,' the Commissar reminded me, 'but in our culture the nephew is still the junior.'

We set off, but we didn't get far. The path petered out into a thicket of thorns twenty metres in. We tried to go under but got scratched and retreated. We tried to go around but ran into a high boulder. It stank of baboon shit. Flies swarmed us. We turned back to look for another way.

And then a terrifying thing happened.

To the right of us the grass and bush started shaking wildly and a loud grunting noise came from within. It sounded like a pair of bush pigs or a wounded baboon stuck in there. For a second I thought it might even have been a leopard, one of those that had scared my friend David and me off this mountain when we were kids.

Suddenly, crashing out of the undergrowth, hunched like trolls, their arms filled with pieces of wood, came two wild-haired white tramps, a man and a woman, their clothes torn rags, their eyes a methyl-alcohol blue. They had bulbous red noses and scabbed faces, and they grunted like Neanderthals as they barrelled toward us.

I leapt off the path; Gracie and Tweed Jacket did the same. The Commissar, though, ponderous as a drugged elephant, stood perfectly still and calmly watched them scurry past him and disappear into the corridor of bush that ran along the side of the road.

My heart was racing. Gracie's eyes were saucers. But the Commissar was utterly calm.

'They are just collecting firewood,' he said drowsily.

We gave up the hike after ten minutes. The bush was too thick. There was no way to get up the mountain anymore. I wondered whether the Commissar had actually been up there at all.

'So when did you say you were last here?' I asked.

'I am going to call the Parks Department,' he said to himself, shaking his head. 'This is simply no good. They have to keep this place maintained.'

'As soon as you pay the fine you owe them for the eland,' I muttered under my breath, not loud enough for him to hear.

The Commissar and his nephew stayed in town; I dropped them at ZANU-PF headquarters on Robert Mugabe Avenue, just off the main street. Gracie drove back over the pass with me. She needed to visit settlers on a farm in the eastern part of the valley to carry out the Commissar's instructions for finding a headman. She also wanted to get back to her fields. I could tell she was annoyed with the Commissar.

'I don't have time to waste like this,' she moaned about the aborted trip. 'Farming is hard work. This was just so much time wasted.'

I had mentioned Gracie to Mom – how she'd said she looked after me as a child – and we figured out that she was the daughter of the Russells' nanny. I asked Gracie how she'd come to be a settler on Frank's land. In a high-pitched voice laced with anger and bitterness, she recounted how for nineteen years she had been a housekeeper for a Mrs Baker.

'My father worked for Mrs Baker for twenty-five years. Mrs Baker gave my father a piece of land on her farm. She said that my father is going to stay there, and when he dies Gracie can have this piece of land. She write it down on a piece of paper.'

'What happened?'

'But then, when my father died, Mrs Baker fired me. She said this is not my land and I must go. I said, 'I want my benefit for nineteen years!' Mrs Baker said to me, 'No – you support ZANU-PF. I am not giving you land.' So nineteen years I am without benefit. How can this be right?'

This had happened in 2003, the height of the land invasions. I hadn't heard of Mrs Baker, but it seemed likely that she had since lost her farm; according to Gracie, she was now living in South Africa. Then Gracie had heard about the Commissar's moving into the valley, and she went to see him about getting a plot on Frank's place.

'I go see him and he let me stay there.'

I recalled the Commissar's words about the land reform programme: *Believe you me, there are advantages and disadvantages.* Personally, I hadn't seen any advantages, but it seemed that in

Gracie, perhaps, there was one. I was pleased she had land, and I could tell by how frustrated she was at the time we wasted in town that she worked hard on it. She was gutsy, determined.

We took a right turn at the bottom of the pass and drove east. We motored past once thriving fields now overgrown with bush. Gracie directed me down a bumpy dirt track, and after a while we came to a tumbledown red-roofed farmhouse on a hill. The farm used to belong to a family called Palmer; clearly it had been taken years ago. The house was in worse condition than Frank's, and the fields around it were desolate. A barefoot woman with a baby on her back appeared in the doorway of the house. Gracie spoke to her in Shona. The woman pointed to a barn a hundred metres away. Milling in front of it were half a dozen young men, no different in age or appearance from the listless, defeated settlers on Frank's place. We sat silently in the car for a while, looking at them. They looked at us.

After a time Gracie said: 'Okay, I am going now.'

'How are you going to get back, Gracie?'

'By foot.'

It was at least sixteen kilometres to our part of the valley. It would take her forever to get home. I gave her a brick of notes, everything I had left in my bag.

'Here, take this. Maybe you can catch a bus home.'

She took the money with urgency and thanked me. Then she scurried off to tell the settlers on this farm to choose headmen to report to their new leader, the Political Commissar.

Good luck, Gracie, I said to myself as I watched her go. *Good luck.*

It was just two o'clock. As I was pulling away I realised I was only ten minutes' drive from the chicken farm where we had lived. I hadn't been back there in twelve years. I didn't know what I would find, but I decided to go and see it. I turned onto a gravel road up into the mountains, and then onto a bumpier, rockier track forged into the cliffs of the slopes.

I felt I was going back to more than just the old house; I was going back to the first bright bone of consciousness, my very earliest memory. My father had carved this road out of the cliffs, just as he had the road at Drifters, but it had seen better times, and I made sure to hug the side of the mountain. Below, to the left, was a steep drop to a roof of dense jungle in a deep ravine. For some reason I pictured a gleaming silver spaceship. Then I remembered: Skylab, the American space station.

Stephanie was a voracious reader and a news junkie, but she'd been a tormentor, too.

'Skylab is going to fall out of the sky and land on us,' she'd told me.

'No, it isn't!'

'It is. It's going to fall on the house and probably kill us all.'

'Waaaaaaahhhhh!'

For weeks on end I'd looked up at the sky and waited for it. I prayed it would land gently in the ravine below the road. When we moved to the grape farm in late 1978 I actually thought it was to avoid Skylab.

I pulled up to the house – or at least what was left of it. The stone walls still stood, but the roof was mostly gone.

In my mind's eye it was a mansion on a high cliff overlooking a vast estate. It turned out to be no more than a small stone cottage on a few hectares of gently undulating ground. The 'cliff' was a brief slope down to a grassy vlei, now wildly overgrown, I could see no trace of the chicken sheds that used to stand below or the cold-storage freezers in the hills behind, where Mom would slaughter, pack and freeze a thousand grade-A broilers a week. The orange groves and apple orchard were gone, too. I remember Lawrence, our Shona gardener, peeling oranges for me in the shade of those trees and telling me magical tales of Manyika kings and Shona princesses as he stirred a pot of sadza on a wood fire during breaks from slashing the grass. Lawrence left my parents' employ in 1975 to join the Rhodesian police force. My father next ran into him twenty-five years later. Older, greyer, he was still a policeman but had never risen above the rank of sergeant. It is one thing to be white and on the losing side in a race war, but to be black and to have served on the side of the white regime, as tens of thousands of black Rhodesians did, is to carry a mark of shame in Mugabe's Zimbabwe – and little chance of promotion.

The jacaranda tree in front of the house was still there, bigger than ever. The branch our dog Ruff would violently gnaw on, honing his jaws, still bore the scars of his rage. If I cut it open, I thought, I might find one of his teeth.

My parents had sold the house to the Rhodesian government in 1978, and because the war was raging around us, no one moved in. But now, it appeared, a black family had, and a pretty young girl in a dirty red dress carrying a romance novel came out to greet me. She said her name was Grace and that her father, a bus driver, had moved the family in here in 2002.

'Hi, Grace. That's my wife's name. I used to live here – can I go inside?'

'Yes, it's okay.'

I started in the living room, walking through the hole in the wall that used to frame sliding glass doors opening onto the slate-stone veranda. Some of the fleur-de-lys-shaped clay tiles laid by Dad's builder, Lekan Mukwamba, were still there, but most had been uprooted. Dad always hired black contractors from rural districts, and Lekan had helped build Drifters, too. 'They're cheaper and they give you less shit,' Dad reckoned.

I climbed the stairs to the landing that used to be the dining room. I remembered aiming a pellet gun at the head of my mother's bridge friend, Libby Bentley, before Dad, looking up from the *Time* magazine he was reading on the couch, leapt up in a rage and ran over to give me a good hiding. 'Do not point a gun at *anyone*. Do you understand?'

Gracie had the room Helen and I had shared, so small I could barely swing my arms. I found the bathroom and shower stall, all the fittings looted. Dad used to sing 'We All Live in a Yellow Submarine' to me when I showered with him in the mornings, his Barlow-Wadley radio on the towel rail, always tuned to some crackling foreign news station.

Stephanie used to give me our weekly sports quiz while I sat on the toilet in here. One day in 1978 she asked me, 'Who won the Grand National?'

'Red Rum.'

'Who scored a perfect ten in Montreal?'

'Nadia Comaneci.'

'Who's the heavyweight champion of the world?'

'Ali.'

'Incorrect.'

'He is!'

'He's not!'

She'd showed me the back page of the *Rhodesia Herald*. I couldn't believe it. Ali had been beaten by some loser called Leon Spinks. I was upset for weeks.

A goat and some chickens had claimed what used to be Stephanie's room, and the walls of the passageway had concertinaed, giving a clear view of the front lawn.

Sandra's room, in the middle of the house, was still intact. I remembered we'd taken shelter in there one terrifying night in 1978. Helen and I were woken up by Mom and Dad arguing loudly in their bedroom next door. It was raining outside. The frogs in the fish pond were silent, but for some reason the weaverbirds were screaming. Through the curtains I could see our tree house, in the fork of the fig tree at the bottom of the garden, light up with each crack of lightning. Suddenly the house shook with an almighty explosion.

'Christ,' screamed Dad. 'You're fucking right! It's not a thunderstorm – it's an attack!'

ZANLA guerrillas had begun mortar-bombing Umtali from the top of the mountain behind us, as they often did. The Rhodesian artillery were firing back from the Vumba, on the far side of Umtali's valley. The problem was, they were overshooting, and their salvos were sailing over their target and landing around *us*. We were being shelled by our own side! The house shuddered again. Stof, Zaan, Hel and I blocked our ears and wept under our Basotho blankets. Our dog Flossy's litter of puppies squirmed in our hands. Mom and Dad cursed the bright light on top of the rigging of a gold mine that had recently begun drilling operations on the western edge of our land. The light lit up our house like a beacon.

'We might as well have a fucking bull's-eye on the roof!' Dad screamed.

There was another explosion.

'We should have built a bunker,' Sandra wept.

Bunkers were all the rage in Umtali. Our friends' fathers were digging up their front lawns and turning them into underground bomb shelters.

'The Gobles have a bunker,' I said.

Mom rolled her eyes. 'I'm not digging up our lawn for a bloody hole in ground,' she swore. There was another explosion.

'That's it,' said Dad, grabbing the FN. 'I'm going to shoot out the mine light.'

My mother was incredulous.

'No, you are bloody not,' she said. 'You're staying right here.'

But my father had made his mind up. He couldn't keep still.

'Rosalind, they can see us down here. I have to shoot out the light.'

And with that he was gone, out the door with the gun, into the night.

Seconds later we heard the biggest explosion yet. The windows shook; it seemed the ceiling might cave in. We looked at each other and we knew: our Dad was dead. Blown up by a 25-pounder on our front lawn. Just then the front door opened, we heard cursing and Dad was back, diving for cover into Sandy's bedroom. 'Okay, okay' he muttered. 'Maybe that wasn't such a bright idea.'

The firing lasted for about an hour, and in the end we survived, shaken but intact. We thought we would get the day off from school, but of course we didn't. I didn't mind. Michael Russell and I found lots of shrapnel on the roof of Dad's office on the main street. Another friend let us hold the tail end of a mortar his brother had picked up on Hillside Golf Course. It had Chinese writing on it. I wished it was mine.

We left the chicken farm soon after that attack. Most people would have moved to a town by then. My parents bought the grape farm, in an even more dangerous area.

But it was walking out onto the lawn that the most powerful memory returned to me again, with an intensity that overwhelmed me. It was a dusky evening in November 1977. Mom and Dad were drinking gin and tonics on the veranda. I was hitting cricket balls against the front wall of the house. Stof, Zaan and Hel were pretending to be horses, jumping over imaginary hurdles on the lawn. Our cousins Neil and Barbara, champion show jumpers, had recently come down to compete in the Umtali Agricultural Show. They'd won all the events, and Stof insisted we learn to ride ourselves, even though we didn't have horses.

We heard them first: a low, rumbling *thwack-thwack-thwack* like an electric saw blade wheeling in the air, coming in from the twilight of Mozambique. The noise built to a crescendo. Then we saw them. One, three, ten, twenty – finally more than thirty.

They were Rhodesian Air Force helicopters, green-camouflaged, flying through the valley, almost eye level to us on this high promontory, and close enough for us to see the helmeted pilots and the gunners with their weapons in their arms. Dusk was falling, and the choppers' red warning lights glowed like burning coals as they moved slowly west, toward Salisbury. We all stopped what we were doing and walked silently to the edge of the lawn, hearts racing, eyes on the sky. For several minutes the entire formation was framed in front of us, close enough for us to wave to them and for them to see us waving. It was beautiful. Then my father yelled at me: 'Douglas! Go get the radio! Hurry!'

I ran to get his Barlow-Wadley shortwave.

We knew something big had happened – a raid in Mozambique. We tuned in to all the stations to find out. The attack is known in Zimbabwe today as the Chimoio Massacre. It was known to us Rhodesians at the time as Operation Dingo. It was a surprise dawn raid on a chain of ZANLA guerrilla training camps at Chimoio, eighty kilometres into Mozambique, involving Selous Scouts, ground troops, helicopters, fighter jets and vintage 1940s transport planes. The intention was to kill the ZANLA leadership based in the camps, including Robert Mugabe and the Top Man. It turned out the leaders were all away at a meeting in Maputo. More than twelve hundred people were killed in the daylong assault, and more than three thousand were injured. European radio stations said the dead were mostly refugees, women and children. Our station said they were terrorists.

I knew what to believe. I ran around the garden, my heart beating madly, my hands in the air. 'We've killed twelve hundred, we're going to win the war! We've killed twelve hundred, we're going to win the war!'

I was nine years old.

I drove home and started packing for our Kariba trip. We would be leaving for Harare at six o'clock the following morning, where we would meet Grace at the airport. Back in New York she would be getting ready to fly out of JFK. I was excited about her visit, and nervous. A rat had died under the floorboards in my bedroom, and I set up my mattress on the floor of the living room because of the terrible smell. I hoped it would be gone by the time Grace got here.

The power had gone out, and Mom padded softly through with a gas lantern to get the coffee ready for the morning while I set up my bed. She came and stood in the living room when she was done, and we spoke for a while in the dim glow of the gaslight.

'Ma, was it the mortar attack in seventy-eight that made us leave the chicken farm?'

'No, darling. It was the mine. It made so much bloody noise we couldn't sleep at night.'

'Wasn't the grape farm in a more dangerous area?'

'Oh, we didn't think of that. There was a war on. Land was cheap.'

She reached over to pull out a box of cigarettes from the chess table drawer and lit one.

I propped myself up on the mattress. 'How cheap?'

'Well,' she said after a while, 'they said the grape farmhouse was cursed ...'

I loved the way my mother told a story. She spoke slowly, with exaggerated drama, often pausing to look up, as if at the balcony of a theatre, to find the right words.

'The original owner died after being poisoned by her dentist. The next owner had seven children. She found out her husband was having an affair with a socialite in Salisbury. She gathered her seven kids and drove to Mozambique. In Beira she walked out into the sea and drowned herself.'

She took a deep drag and exhaled an elegant plume. 'As for the lady we bought it from, she wanted out. She had just seen her neighbour get blown sky high by a land mine while driving a tractor in his fields. She watched it from the living room.'

'Weren't you afraid to move us there? Helen was only eight. I was ten.'

She paused again and her mind drifted back to that time. 'A little. But I spoke to that house. For days I sat in the living room before we moved in, sewing the curtains, and I said to it, "Be good to us. Be good to us."'

'We were never attacked.'

'No,' she smiled. 'But close. Neil Barry's place was shot up in the middle of the day once. Don't you remember? Dad was away on army call-up. We were all in the swimming pool except Helen, who was riding her bike on the road outside. I had to run and get her while the attack was under way. We found out the gooks had camped the night before beside our fence right by the pool. Their fires were still warm.'

'You must have been mad to move us there,' I said.

She took a last, deep drag. 'That's what our friends said. And then, two years later, the war was over and we owned a wine farm. That's when our friends said, "Those Rogerses – lucky bastards."'

I soon fell asleep. I dreamed my parents were sitting on the veranda of a beautiful gabled Cape Dutch farmhouse. They were drinking homemade wine out of plastic cups. Helicopters clattered overhead. The view was not of a lawn or maize fields or vineyards, it was of ocean. A woman was walking out into the sea. She turned to wave goodbye to her children on the shore.

Dad shook me awake. It was still dark outside. It seemed too early to be leaving already.

'Joyce is on the phone,' he said.

It was 4:00 am.

'Joyce?'

'Grace's sister.'

'What? Why's she calling?'

'She's on the phone. She needs to talk to you.'

Why would Grace's sister be calling me in Zimbabwe from New Jersey at 4:00 am?

I picked up the phone and heard sobbing.

'Joycey?'

Joyce said: 'Our mom's died. You have to get Grace.'

For six years now I had been waiting for a call from Zimbabwe telling me one of my parents was dead. I never expected to be in Zimbabwe getting a call from America telling me that a parent of Grace's had died. Barbara had come home from work on the afternoon of 15 June feeling tired. She had had chest pains. She lay down on the back porch of their beautiful home in Upper Saddle River, New Jersey, while Ed made her tea in the kitchen. Ed heard her moaning. An ambulance rushed her to the hospital. She died at 7:08 pm in Valley Hospital, Ridgewood, from a massive heart attack.

Grace had no idea. Her flight had left at the same time her mother was being rushed to the hospital. She was in the air right now, likely somewhere over Senegal, en route to Johannesburg, where I would have to meet her and tell her the news as she stepped off the plane. We would fly straight to New York.

I packed up my bags. Dad drove us in near-silence to Harare, where I was to catch the emergency flight to Johannesburg. It was more than an hour before any of us spoke.

'I'll never forget going to see *Faust* with her at Lincoln Center,' said Mom. 'She was such a lovely lady.'

'I'll tell Grace that, Mom.'

'She looked so young,' said Dad.

'She was. She did everything.'

Barbara was seventy years old. Yet she worked full-time as an environmental chemist, and part-time for a dentist doing his books. And she still found time for opera, bridge, a book club, a garden club and tennis. She left the world like she lived life: with gusto, no half measures.

FOURTEEN
Entering the Castle

IN JULY 2006 my parents discovered they no longer owned the farm.

The Top Man didn't deliver the news. The Political Commissar, who'd become strangely subdued, even polite, since my visit, was nowhere in sight. Neither was there a mob of chanting war veterans rattling their gates.

Dad found out through an amiable estate agent in Mutare whom he went to see in a moment of rare triumph: his subdivision had come through. Six months earlier he had applied to the Department of Physical Planning in Mutare to legally separate the lodge and chalets from the rest of his land. Not only would two properties be harder to take than one, he reckoned, but if he managed to get a subdivision, he could try to sell the lodge. Now, incredibly, his man in Physical Planning had called to tell him the application had been approved. He would soon have his papers. That thousand-rand bribe had been well worth it.

'I feel as if we've won the lottery!' he told Mom jubilantly after he got off the phone. 'It's freed us up. Now, if we can only find a buyer for Drifters with some cash out of the country, that will be our security, our retirement fund.'

Mom smiled but said little.

Ever the optimist, imbued now with a vision of new worlds opening up for them, Dad immediately went to see an estate agent in Mutare about putting Drifters on the market. He knew he wouldn't get a fair price for it. This was Zimbabwe, after all. People were getting farms for free; buying one was hardly a secure investment. But the approval of the subdivision meant he now owned *two* separate pieces of land. He was convinced someone would want to buy the lodge. Hell, maybe even one of those businessmen who came out with their hookers might put in an offer. True, the only work they really wanted to do out there was on a mattress, but who couldn't see the potential in a rustic budget tourist resort with a dozen chalets, a swimming pool, a restaurant and a bar?

The estate agent, a laid-back fellow by the name of George Moyo, leaned back in his chair in his office off Herbert Chitepo Road, listening to Dad's request.

'Of course we can look for a buyer for you, Mr Rogers,' he said, 'but are you sure you own the land?'

'Excuse me?'

'Are you sure you own the property in question?'

Dad laughed.

'I bought it. I've lived there for sixteen years. It's mine.'

'Yes, but wasn't your title deed cancelled?'

'Come again?'

'Wasn't your title deed rescinded last year?'

Moyo was starting to annoy my father. What was he talking about?

'What do you know about my title deed? I have the original, the government has a copy. Nothing's changed. I own the bloody place.'

The estate agent stopped rocking in his chair. He leaned

forward and spoke in a low, serious tone, like a doctor about to inform a patient of a terminal illness – cancer, perhaps.

'I am not sure how to tell you this, Mr Rogers, but in August 2005 the government passed an amendment cancelling the title deeds on all existing farms and stripping the owners of the right to appeal expropriations.'

My father's heart did a somersault and landed near his feet. What? Had he not gotten the memo? Perhaps he'd not read the *Herald* on the day in question. The government passed new land laws all the time and never informed the people affected by them. Farmers literally discovered that their homes had been designated for resettlement by reading it in the small print in the *Herald* on a Friday while scanning the newspaper for Premiership soccer results. Mom and Dad only found out Drifters had been listed in 2003 because Stephanie phoned them from Harare when she saw they had made the papers. That was one phone call he wanted to forget. But then, with a surge of relief, Dad remembered the amendment. It had been pretty big news at the time.

'Oh, that!' he said. 'No, no. That was for farms that had been *designated*. Our designation never went through. We objected. The land inspectors came and saw that it wasn't suitable for farming. It was taken off the list. It's basically a hotel. No, that law only applied to farms that were designated.' But then his voice rose an involuntary octave. 'Didn't it?' he added.

The estate agent sighed sympathetically.

'I'm sorry, Mr Rogers, but I think you'll find that the law applied to everyone. There are hundreds of people in this country who have no idea they no longer own their homes. Before we proceed, may I suggest you check with the Registrar of Deeds in Harare that they've not rescinded your title?'

Dad felt a shiver run from his neck to the base of his spine. The word *rescinded* made his skin crawl. So did the words *Registrar of Deeds*. They called to mind tall, grey, windowless cement buildings filled with faceless bureaucrats who sat at empty desks and put official stamps on pieces of paper that ruined people's lives forever. The sheer banality of it chilled him.

Now he started to panic. What if the amendment *did* apply to him? How had he missed that? He was a lawyer, constantly planning ahead, always on the lookout for the next series of hurdles the government put in his way. He thought he had stayed one step ahead of their relentless game.

He phoned the Physical Planning official who had gotten him the subdivision.

'Listen, Mr Maranga, there might be a problem here. Can you get me a copy of my title deed from the registrar in Harare? I'm sure it's nothing, but someone here is saying the government may have, well, cancelled it.'

David Maranga sat at an empty desk deep in the bowels of Physical Planning behind the OK Bazaars department store on Robert Mugabe Avenue. He was a vaguely competent man with a permanent half smile who always wore a neatly pressed suit and tie. He had started to complain to my father these past few months as he massaged the subdivision through that if it ever became known in the Ministry of Lands that he was helping a white man, he could lose his job.

But he was very helpful this morning.

'Yes, Mr Rogers, I can get them to fax me a copy.'

The fax came through a couple of days later and Dad went to see him.

'It's here,' said Mr Maranga, handing him the document with the half smile.

It was an exact replica of the original my father had in his safe.

But there had been an addition to it.

A large, official-looking stamp had been planted smack in the centre. It read: *In terms of Section 168(4) of the Constitution of*

Zimbabwe, this Property now vests in the President of Zimbabwe.

It was dated November 2005. The government had owned my parents' farm for eight months already.

My father wanted to vomit. Gradually the reality of their situation began to sink in. They no longer owned their own home.

They were still on it, but they had now joined the legions of dispossessed waiting for the new owner to claim it.

He thought back to all the schemes he had adopted over the years to ward off the war veterans, the settlers, the Top Man, the Commissar. He'd hauled out the shotgun. Grown the bush wild. Erected an electric fence around the house. Shot at baboons and the poachers' dogs just to let the settlers in the valley know that he had a gun. Spoken to Chief Mutasa. Contested the Section Five. Met the lands inspectors – three times – and seen them delist the property, agreeing that it wasn't suitable for farming. Leased cottages to black tenants. Leased the camp bar to a black farmer. Given lifts to the Commissar and probed his motives. Even avoided the interests of the Top Man himself, a man with a voracious appetite for property, a man with five farms of his own. All the while the bush grew taller, the shotgun stayed loaded, and Muranda kept him abreast of the latest goings-on with the war vets and visitors to the camp.

And for what? Nothing! Now they were sitting ducks. He envisioned how it would happen. The Ministry of Lands had what was called 'the list'.

It was a list of all farms now 'vested in the president'. Ones that had not already been swept up by ministers, generals, brigadiers and senior party officials were now being handed out to ordinary applicants, those A2 farmers. An applicant simply had to go to the ministry and say he wanted to farm. He wouldn't have to pay anything. He wouldn't even have to *be* a farmer. He could be an accountant, a doctor, a hamburger flipper. All he had to prove was that he was a supporter of the ruling party and claim that he could run a farm. He might have a particular farm in mind – one he'd driven past and liked the look of – or he would simply be allocated one.

Dad pictured how the meeting would go. The Ministry of Lands official would scroll down the list with his forefinger. Would Drifters be under *D* or under *R*? He presumed *R*, alphabetically lower. If it had been under *D*, they would have lost it months ago.

'What about this one?' the official would say, as if offering ice cream.

'What is it?'

'Seven hundred and fifty acres. On some hills near Mutare. Not good farmland. Signs of a river. Apparently lots of buildings. Chalets. A tourist lodge with a bar.'

'Like a hotel? Excellent – I'll take that.'

The applicant would then be given an offer letter.

An offer letter gave him the rights to the farm. (It was supposed to be followed by a 99-year lease, although these rarely came.) He would drive onto the farm and hand the farmer the letter. The farmer would then have to vacate the premises.

Dad pictured his A2, some city twerp in a slick suit, driving through his front gate in a BMW or Land Cruiser or Toyota Camry and presenting him with his letter. He suddenly wished he was back to worrying about the Commissar. At least there he knew what he was dealing with.

The news of the loss of the title deed spread to the cottage residents like wildfire – before he had even told any of them. It was as if the tenants just *sensed* something was wrong.

Confidence dropped, like a crash in the markets, and the mood darkened. A rumour soon spread that by 20 December, every white farm in the country would be passed on to new owners. Or was it a rumour? It was hard to keep up with the new laws; fact merged easily with fantasy. Some said it was true but that farmers had forty-five days to vacate from that date or be prosecuted. Either way, a deadline appeared to be looming.

Unita Herrer and Lady Charlotte left for South Africa at this point. They were joined on their way out the gate by Danie and Hanli Slabbert, an Afrikaner couple who'd briefly found refuge in Cottage 15 after losing their farm to the Top Man. Hanli was a famous Afrikaans gospel singer who had won music awards, performed in concerts in America, Brazil and Israel, and sung for crowds of forty thousand people at Christian festivals in South Africa. Hanli was a church minister as well as a gospel singer, and she preached to congregations throughout the valley. She said she became a born-again Christian one night in July 1978 during the war, when she and Danie were attacked in their home with RPG-7 rockets, AK-47s and mortars by ZANLA guerrillas. I could see why that might have done it. The thought that they were all about to lose their homes for a second time helped ease the sadness of their departure.

But then, out of the blue, Dave Burnett, a veteran stalwart of the cottages who had lived in number 10 since 1998 and been something of a talisman for the community – helping to maintain levies, hosting Sunday afternoon braais and sundowners at his cottage, the highest on the hill – suddenly upped and left, too.

Mom took the fatalist view.

'Everyone has to look after themselves,' she said.

But Dad was annoyed.

'First sign of real trouble and Dave's out of here? Fuck me. Not the kind of guy you want in the trenches when the shit goes down.'

'It's hardly the first sign of trouble, Lyn,' she told him. 'Really, I'm amazed some of these people have stuck it out this long.'

My mother had stopped worrying about the title deed at this point. She'd come to the conclusion that there was nothing they could do. Their future was in the laps of the gods, and the gods were faceless bureaucrats in those grey, windowless buildings. They would deal with an A2 when he turned up.

But then the atmosphere at the camp bar got nasty, and she did worry. Dawson had found work at a Western-funded aid organisation that was training rural farmers to grow crops for export – exactly what he'd been doing at Kondozi for a Zimbabwean company – and he rarely opened the bar now, but one Sunday afternoon Mom and Dad were up at the house when a blast of music louder than anything they'd heard in Sydney's hip-hop heyday rent the still air, scattering the loeries from the sycamores.

'It sounded like a bloody nightclub,' she explained to me later. 'Dad and I went to get them to turn it down. The bar wasn't open at all, but on the back deck there were a dozen buggers and their girlfriends or *mahures* having a party, several crates of beer open, and this huge ghetto-blaster on.

'Your dad loses his temper in these situations, so I walked upstairs to speak to them while he stood back with Muranda by the chalets. I told them, very politely, "Excuse me, gentlemen, you're very welcome to drink here and listen to music, but please keep it down as other people live on the property."

'One of them was sitting on a garden chair, shirt off, sunglasses on, in military trousers. He sneered at me: "Do you know who you're talking to?"

'I said, "No, and frankly I don't care. I don't mind you listening to music, but please respect the rights of the other people living on this property."

'Then he said, "Do you know that I am a guerrilla? Do you know that you white people are only allowed to stay here because we are letting you stay?"

'Well, I just laughed. He was about thirty years old! I said, "Oh, please. Come, come, young man! You're far too young to have ever been in the war."

255

'His friends started laughing. I didn't know if it was at him or me, but the stereo was next to him and he made an exaggerated show of turning it down.

'But then, as I was walking away, one of the women on deck shouted after me: "Go back to Britain! Go back to Blair!"

'Well, your dad heard that and he stormed over from the chalets. I wanted to turn around and tell her to shut up, but I ran down the stairs to stop your father and calm him down. But what could we do? Who knows who they were? You don't know whom to trust anymore, and in the back of your mind you know they could very well make things very difficult for you.'

Dawson's lease ended a few weeks later in the controversial aftermath of a near-riot down at the camp. Mom and Dad had arrived back from a trip to town one Saturday to discover a dozen vehicles in their driveway and a long line of cars queuing up outside Drifters' gate. It looked like a crowd for a rock concert.

Dad stopped to ask the man in the lead car what they were doing here.

'Where is the AIDS party?' the driver asked.

'AIDS party?'

'I've bought a ticket for an AIDS party at this Drifters place. There is a band. Free food. Free drink. Some discussions on AIDS.'

He showed Dad his ticket, which he said had cost Z$15 000. It had Drifters' address, that day's date, a lineup of speakers and bands, and the time: *3pm to late*. It had even been advertised in the *Manica Post*.

Dad was pleasantly surprised. Dawson had hit on a scheme to drum up some trade. Perhaps he wanted to keep the lease after all, give it another go, the old college try. My father loved an entrepreneur, anyone with an eye for business, and he thought all that Drifters needed to thrive again was a young man with a few innovative ideas. An AIDS party – that was just the ticket!

They were about to direct the ticket holders to the camp entrance when Dawson himself appeared, scampering up from the camp through the tall grass and avocado trees, looking terrified, as if pursued by a pride of lions.

'It's crazy, Mr Rogers!' he bellowed. 'It's crazy!'

'What's the matter, Dawson?' Dad asked.

'I have a hundred people at the camp saying they've bought tickets for a party here. There is no party! No music! No discussions on AIDS!'

The man in the car produced his ticket and waved it in Dawson's face.

'I know – but it's a trick! I didn't write that. It's a trick!'

Which, of course, it was.

Drifters had fallen prey to an elaborate con. Someone somewhere was running around with a lot of cash from selling fake tickets to an AIDS benefit. It was exactly the kind of publicity they didn't need.

But it wasn't my parents' problem. Dad locked the gate and left Dawson to sort it out. The ticket holders came close to burning down the joint that afternoon. Somehow Dawson managed to quell a riot.

Now my parents were looking for a new tenant.

At this point it might have been wise to lie low, to stay under the radar. For every farmer who thought it best to confront the regime, there were many more who deemed it wiser to keep a low profile; not draw attention to oneself.

But it wasn't in my father's DNA to sit and wait. In the middle of that mortar attack on the chicken farm in 1978 he had run out onto the lawn with the FN rifle, shells pounding the earth around him, to try to shoot out the mine light that made our house so visible. So he decided to go back to work. He would become a lawyer again. Not for a client this time, but for himself. For thirty

years he'd worked at solving other people's legal problems; now he had to solve his own. He set himself the goal of either getting his title deed back or getting an offer letter for his own farm, and in so doing getting off the list.

Mom thought this was about as likely as Hammy's getting his farm back and Piet's having his cattle returned. 'It'll never happen, darling. No one has ever got their deed back and no white person has ever received an offer letter.'

In fact, she thought trying to do so would only make things worse. They argued about it up at the house for nights on end.

'The more noise we make, the more attention we get,' she protested.

'Rosalind, we need to be prepared for them if they come.'

'We didn't own the property for the whole past year and no one came.'

'But if they had come, we wouldn't have been prepared.'

'Maybe they haven't come because they don't know we exist. Doing this will alert them to our existence.'

'But we do exist! I'm not going to sit back and take a chance we don't.'

They began to sound like African existentialists.

And so, sixteen years after he had retired from the law, my father swung into action, an imaginary *Rocky* soundtrack in the background. It was what got him up in the morning, and in a strange way it invigorated him, made him feel more alive.

He drew up a list of officials he needed to see and started to make calls. His argument was simple and legally accurate, even by the government's own laws: Drifters was not suitable for re-settlement and should not be on the list.

He went to see Didymus Matongo, Margaret's husband, their black neighbours. He knew Didymus was a friend of the provincial governor, and he asked him to arrange a meeting. But the governor said to see the provincial administrator. The provincial administrator referred him to the local land resettlement officer.

Incredibly, the land resettlement officer agreed there had been a terrible mistake.

'I can see the property was delisted,' the man said, paging through a file. 'And I don't know why you had your title deed cancelled.'

Dad was relieved, even excited. 'So can you restore it?'

'I can give you a guarantee you will not be moved,' he said.

'So give me a guarantee.'

'I just did.'

'Not a *verbal* guarantee – I want something in writing.'

There was a long silence.

'Sorry, I can't do that.'

No one wanted to put anything in writing.

Dad wrote to the provincial land resettlement officer and his predecessor, the district administrator, and got no replies. He then met members of the Provincial Land Resettlement Committee that Chief Mutasa sat on – or, rather, used to sit on. He was shocked to discover that Chief Mutasa had had his own farm listed. Black farmers who didn't belong to the ruling party were losing their homes, too. If a legitimate chief wasn't safe, what chance did he have? Several weeks later a committee member finally told him that he would have to go to the Registrar of Deeds or the Ministry of Lands in Harare. Lands was the Top Man's department. Dad called their respective offices. The lines rarely worked, and when he did get through, his calls were never returned.

Where was the Top Man when he actually needed him?

Then, at Mom's suggestion, they changed tack and tried the tourism route. Zimbabwe has one of the biggest civil services in the world, and there are three tourism departments: the Tourism Ministry, the Tourist Authority and the Tourism Council. There were far more tourism officials than tourists.

Drifters wasn't suitable for farming, which is why it had originally been delisted, but it was also a tourist business, and hotels and guesthouses were supposed to be exempt, too. He set up a meeting at the annual Travel Expo in Harare with the top honcho of the Zimbabwe Tourist Authority (ZTA), who was due to speak there. The official was a no-show.

'This wasn't such a surprise,' he wrote to me, 'because everyone in the country knows the head of the ZTA is a famous fucking asshole.'

It wasn't hard to meet people, my father discovered, but it was hard to meet the top people. You had to *earn* the right to meet the chefs.

He described the process as being 'like entering a tall building'.

'You start at the ground floor and are told to see the person on the first floor. Sometimes he's in, sometimes he's not. It's best to arrive soon after the start of work, before they can start running around. At each floor, if you are lucky, you see the person you want to see, only to be told that you should speak to the person on the floor above. And so on, until you get to the top floor, when you are told to see the person on the floor below. And down you go again. It is a race against time – except you can't see the person you are racing against. Is he in front of you or behind? Is he in the race at all? You don't know.'

The Mutare stand at the Travel Expo was vacant, but my parents were surprised to find a pile of Drifters brochures they had printed out in its 1990s heyday. They stole a bunch of them since it would make them look more official.

Dad then contacted the Tourism Ministry. Weeks later he got to speak to a friendly-sounding woman, a Mrs Masinga, who said she was fourth in charge.

'I feel I'm clutching at straws with the ZTA,' Dad told her.

'Mr Rogers. Why are you clutching at a straw that has already sunk? Come and see us – we are a straw that is still floating!'

At last, he thought, a human being. Mom and Dad drove together to Harare again and met her at the ministry. Mom described the meeting to me in a long e-mail.

'It's a run-down Lubyanka in the centre of town, badly in need of paint or demolition. The power was off when we entered the lobby, but it came on as we approached the lift, which was just as well, since the lady's office is on the twelfth floor. We waited at reception for half an hour while a very sweet secretary painted her nails and read the *Herald* behind an empty desk. Then we were summoned into a plush office filled with carpets and sumptuous leather armchairs and with a magnificent view of the streets and jacaranda trees below. If this was her office, I wondered what the minister's office must look like. You can see where all our tourism levy money goes.'

This time Mom did the talking, explaining their predicament. They had decided on the drive up that since she would likely start crying when she spoke, it might elicit more sympathy from Mrs Masinga.

'Mrs Masinga,' Mom began, 'Drifters was a thriving tourist business and a great boon for the region and in fact all the country. It was made famous around the world in the pages of *Lonely Planet*. Here – have one of the brochures we've printed up for our new season.' She handed her one of the 1998 flyers they had nicked. 'Yet now we've discovered we are on the verge of losing it because our title deed has been cancelled. This is a terrible mistake, because as a tourist business we are supposed to be –'

Then the tears came. She couldn't help it. They ran down her face like rain and she choked up. 'We are supposed to be exempt. And besides, isn't it the policy of the country to attract people for the World Cup?'

South Africa had been awarded the 2010 World Cup. The biggest sports event on earth was going to be held to the south of them, and tourist officials in Zimbabwe saw this as a potential cash cow. Mom and Dad thought it would help their case, too. Soccer fans might visit Drifters, bring in some cash.

Mrs Masinga looked at Mom with sad brown eyes. It appeared she might cry, too. 'Mrs Rogers,' she said, 'we are not all cruel and greedy people.'

Mom suddenly felt terrible for making a scene. 'So can you get our deed back?' she sobbed.

Mrs Masinga sighed. 'For that you are going to have to see the Ministry of Lands.'

'But they don't answer calls and don't write anything down!' said Dad.

'No, they don't,' she agreed.

'What – you are aware of this?' he blurted out.

'Oh, yes. It's their policy. They only have "conversations". No minutes or notes. Please understand. They don't want any written evidence of their deliberations during the land reform process to ever come out afterward.'

It was a startling admission; they were stunned by her candour. Mrs Masinga said she would try to help.

'Mr and Mrs Rogers, I will investigate this matter and write to the Ministry of Lands about your problem. I do not want you to lose your livelihood. But please understand, there is very little I can do with them.'

They thanked her profusely and invited her to come and stay at Drifters, free of charge.

As they were entering the lift Mom said: 'Christ, I hope she doesn't come. She'll find out our livelihood comes from prostitution.'

None of the officials my father met took minutes of their meetings, but he did. When he got home, and after every phone call, he meticulously wrote down in letter form everything that had been discussed, made a copy for himself, and then posted the letter to the person he had met.

'This becomes a minute,' he explained to me. 'A record of what has been said and agreed. As they do not reply and dispute any of the facts, this letter becomes the agreed record. If our problem ever has to get to court, I will produce my letters as proof of what they said and agreed to.'

Six months after he began his quest, he had a file as thick as a telephone directory. It would be his legal case for the future. It didn't help him in the present, though. And so they waited.

They had been paying so much attention to their legal situation at this point that they had lost track of all the comings and goings in the cottages. The demographics were changing fast.

What had been an all-white enclave six years ago was now filled with black Zimbabweans. The only whites left were the De Klerks, the Hammies and a new refugee, a tiny eighty-two-year-old widow named Joy Wolf whose husband had died soon after they'd been assaulted and tied up in their home one night by war vets in the north of the valley. Dad said there were only six white farms left in the valley and only 350 left in the country, from a high of 4 500.

The four engineers and technicians from ZESA had arrived to join Mr Mhlanga. They needed them. Power cuts were so frequent now that my father found he was writing up his minutes late at night on his desktop computer since it was the only time the electricity worked. That was when he would e-mail me, too. I would wake up in Brooklyn to long essays sent from the front lines of another world, detailing his daily struggle, his meetings, the impossible tedium of it all. Dad wanted a record for himself, but I also came to realise he wanted me to have a record in case anything happened to them. He had his file, and I had hundreds of e-mails he had sent me about what was going on.

And yet my parents were rather pleased with their new community. The new tenants brought down the average age and added a certain vigour.

Florence and Ernest Muzorewa had moved back to their farm across the road, but their twenty-four-year-old family friend, Macdonald, moved into number 4. Soon, two of Margaret Matongo's sons, Trevor and Stephen, cool young hipsters in baggy jeans and sneakers, iPods permanently playing hip-hop, moved in with their partners, Zondile and Tsitsi. 'Steve and Trevor remind me a bit of you at that age,' Mom wrote. 'They work on the farm for Margaret, and I suspect they can't wait to get away. I told them you live in Brooklyn and they are excited to meet you. They want to know if you know someone called Jay-Z who lives there and another person called Mos Def. Funny names.'

The last person they expected to find living in the cottages however, was a relative of the Top Man.

They were doing their ritual walk one afternoon when they passed Cottage 12A. (My father, always superstitious, didn't want a Cottage 13.) There, sitting on the veranda, shaping an elephant from a plaster moulding – a technique used in bronze sculpting – was a tall, slim black man in his early thirties. The green lawn of the cottage was filled with beautiful bronze sculptures of twisted baobab trees, antelopes and hippos.

They introduced themselves.

'Hi, I am Simbarashe ____. I am the new tenant.'

Mom was delighted. An artist! She loved bronze work. She far preferred it to the generic soapstone carvings churned out by so many local artists, and she had a number of bronze pieces she had collected over the years. She asked if he wouldn't mind coming up to the house one afternoon to show her his work.

But my father, permanently on guard, noticed something else.

'What did you say your name was again?'

'Simbarashe. Simbarashe ___'

He recognised the surname.

'Where are you from, Simbarashe?'

'Rusape.'

His heart skipped a beat.

'You're not related to the minister, are you?'

The sculptor smiled.

'Yes, he is my uncle.'

Dad steadied himself against a fence post.

He had the distinct feeling the world was closing in on them again.

But what could he say except 'Welcome'?

At this point, unable to make headway, he decided to try acting. Mom was the actress, of course, but Dad practised a set piece, channelling all the cheesy Hollywood cop movies and TV shows he so loved – *Beverly Hills Cop*, *Starsky & Hutch*, low-budget police and legal dramas he liked to watch on satellite TV. He acted out what he would say to the suited upstart he was sure would one day drive up to the house in a fancy car and present him with his offer letter.

He rehearsed it so often Mom saw him talking to himself in the shed and thought he was going crazy. In the end, though, he had it down quite well.

He told me how it would go.

'"Gosh, what a surprise," I'll say. "So you have a letter, too! My goodness. Someone was here a week ago with the exact same kind of letter! This is very strange. What did you say your name was? Okay, Mr __, I will have to speak to the minister and ask him how this mistake came about. Which minister, you ask? Oh, the Top Man, of course. Tell me, where is your letter? Here – give it to me. As you probably already know,

I am a lawyer. I will have to make a copy of it and show the minister when I see him. I think you should come back next month and then we can talk again."'

He knew he would tell any A2 who arrived at Drifters he was a lawyer. That was paramount.

It was something he had come to learn: people were afraid of lawyers. The reason no one in any ministry wanted to put anything in writing was because they didn't want a paper trail leading to them. This meant that either they knew they were breaking a law or perhaps they were guilty of something else. He reckoned that if he told the A2 he was a lawyer, this would make them even more wary. A lawyer was as good as a shaman out here. A lawyer might know the law better than any of them, and it might come back to haunt them one day.

On 11 September 2006, two days before my father turned seventy, he received a surprise gift, a bolt from the blue. Actually, he got two gifts.

Grace and I phoned to wish him a happy birthday and to give my parents our news: Grace was pregnant. The baby was due in April.

The second gift, however, was more pressing. It came in the towering form of Oom Piet, who strode up to the house that morning looking younger than he had in years, eating up the metres in giant strides, as if he was still tearing for the goal line, fifteen All Blacks on his heels.

'Lyn,' he said excitedly, 'Lyn – I got my cattle back!'

Dad was writing up minutes in his study. He wasn't sure he had heard correctly.

'What's that, Piet?'

'I got my cattle back, Lyn!'

Dad was stunned.

They moved onto the veranda.

'Jeez, Piet, well done. What, all of them?'

'No, not all. Only seventy-nine. Plus a hundred sheep, a hundred goats. Oh, and the horses and Stripey the zebra. All infested with ticks and in terrible condition, of course. I've put them on Droppie's place. Can you believe the war vets on Kondozi want to charge me for grazing and upkeep these past three years? They gave me a bill for almost two billion Zim dollars! No way I'm paying anything. But at least I got them back, Lyn. Better than nothing.'

My father was elated for him, and completely surprised.

'So how did you manage it, Piet?'

'I went to see the Top Man, Lyn. He sorted it out.'

Dad looked at Oom Piet as if he had lost his mind.

'The Top Man? Jeez, Piet, how did you get to meet him, and why on earth would he be helping you?'

Dad had been engaged in an elusive dance with the Top Man. For years he had tried to avoid him; now he was trying desperately to meet with him.

'Well, that's why I came to see you. The soldier I told you about, the sergeant – he's the uncle of one of our old Kondozi farm managers. He knows the Top Man. He had a word with him and took me to see him. The soldier sorted it out.'

'But I thought you told me he's just a lowly staff sergeant, Piet.'

'I know, Lyn, he is, but it's all very strange. He says he's a staff sergeant but I think he's something more than that. He's a ZANLA war veteran. Told me some interesting stories about his time in the war, and he's very close to the Top Man. He took me to the Top Man's house in Harare. That was when the Top Man sent a letter to the war vets to give me back my livestock. Listen, this soldier worked for me, Lyn. I think he can maybe help you with your deeds.'

My father didn't know what to think.

'Jeez, Piet, *baie dankie*. So how do I get hold of him, this soldier?'

'I already told him about you. He's going to give you a call.'

They wondered about this gift, Mom and Dad. Was it really the silver bullet they had been waiting for? Or was it a curse? They were wary of entering into an 'arrangement'.

The government functioned as a Mafia now, and the worse the economy was, the more of a racket it became. I had written an article for the *Guardian* once mentioning a Prince Edward school friend of mine who had entered into an 'arrangement'. His name was Simon and he was still on the tobacco farm he'd bought outside Harare in 1995, but he no longer owned the farm. It was 'owned' by a brigadier who lived in Harare and to whom Simon paid rent and a share of profits come harvest time. In that way he was allowed to stay.

'But that's how the Cosa Nostra worked,' I had told him.

'I'm a farmer, Doug,' he said. 'It's what I do. What choice do I have?'

Now my parents had to make a decision: were they going to enter into an arrangement, too?

In the end they decided on fate: if the soldier called, they would meet up with him; if he didn't, they wouldn't pursue it any further with Piet.

Sure enough, though, as Piet said, the soldier did call. Dad spoke to him and told him to come out to the house to meet with them one Sunday morning, and a few weeks later they were face-to-face with a Zimbabwe National Army staff sergeant, a veteran of the liberation war and a close confidant of the man they believed was the most evil man in the valley.

His name was Walter Sebenza. He was forty-eight years old, married with one child, and, according to Mom, he was 'the size of a buffalo and the colour of burnt toast'.

They sat on the Adirondack chairs on the veranda, drinking lemon tea that Mom had brewed, making small talk at first about family and religion. Small talk suited my parents. They didn't want things to get political. They were wary enough of having a national army soldier in their home; a supposed close aide to the Top Man in their house put them on edge.

'Mr Rogers, are you a Christian man?' the soldier asked straight up.

Dad smiled. 'These days, I have to say, I find myself praying a lot. I don't know if God exists or anything, but I would rather be safe than sorry.'

The soldier nodded. 'I am a Christian man, Mr Rogers. My wife is a religious woman. I did theology. I have a diploma in it, so when I am doing this military job sometimes God makes me understand and I don't use a pistol.'

Dad was relieved. 'It's good that you don't carry a pistol, Mr Sebenza,' he said.

'Oh, no,' boomed the soldier, leaping out of his chair. 'Of course I carry a pistol!'

He reached into the belt of his khaki trousers, pulled out a gleaming military-issue revolver, and started waving it around like a table-tennis paddle.

'I said I don't *use* a pistol!'

Dad's eyes bulged.

Mom calmly got up from her chair. 'More tea, Sergeant Sebenza?'

'Thank you, Mrs Rogers,' he said, sitting down again, holstering the weapon.

'I think you were talking about religion,' she reminded him.

'Eh, yes. Let me be certain with you. I went to school to learn the Bible, so one day I want to quit this job and simply start a church. I will just resign from the army. I want to become a full-time churchgoer.'

He had a deep baritone voice, deeper than John Muranda's, and he spoke English with a thick African accent, flattening the vowels, as if with a shovel.

'What denomination are you, Mr Sebenza?' asked Dad, getting his eyes back.

'Call me Walter, Mr Rogers. No denomination. Just a Christian man.'

Dad suddenly hit on a way to perhaps bond with him: his favourite new subject – witchcraft – and his promise to Miss Moneypenny about revenge.

'Tell me, Walter, does your religion perhaps include traditional healing?' He knew it would. Zimbabwe might be a deeply Christian country, but traditional healers still play a dominant role in Shona culture, even for the most westernised black family. An official association of traditional healers represents thousands of licenced *n'angas* in the country and is, unsurprisingly, a powerful political lobby given the widespread belief that its members have the power to heal, bless, protect, read the future and even kill.

The soldier's eyes lit up. 'Of course, Mr Rogers. In our culture everyone has a traditional healer.'

'In that case, do you happen to know of a *n'anga* called the Destroyer?'

Walter, I discovered when I met him, had two catchphrases: 'Let me be certain,' said in the sonorous baritone; and 'Don't tell me!', uttered in a surprised-sounding high-pitched squeal, like an American teenager saying 'Omigod!'

'Don't tell me!' shrieked Walter. 'How do you know the Destroyer?'

'Have you heard of him?' said Dad excitedly.

'Of course, Mr Rogers. Let me be certain. He is the greatest *n'anga* of them all. He lives in the mountains near Mozambique. I know him very, very well. He is very powerful. Some time ago at our military barracks some weapons went missing. We called in the Destroyer. He nominated who the thieves were. Now there is no more stealing! Why do you ask about the Destroyer?'

'I have a friend who needs to hire this Destroyer. There might be good money in it for you if he can solve a problem that she has.'

The soldier nodded seriously.

'It is okay, Mr Rogers. It is okay. We can discuss.'

The conversation soon turned to my parents' property problem and the possibility of meeting the Top Man and getting his title deed back or an offer letter. Could he help them out?

The soldier had come prepared. He gave Dad a phone number.

'I've already apprised the minister of your situation, Mr Rogers. Phone him and make an appointment.'

Dad was surprised. Was that all it took to get to the Top Man, to the top floor of the tallest tall building? The correct phone number?

'Thank you, Walter. I will try to make an appointment, but will you not come with me? I believe you accompanied Mr de Klerk to see the minister.' My father was nervous. He knew too much about the Top Man.

There was an ominous pause.

'Mr Rogers, it is better you see the minister on your own,' said the soldier.

Dad had expected it. He and Mom had both got to know and like Simbarashe the sculptor in the last few weeks, and once, in passing, they had asked him if there was any possibility of *his* taking them to see his uncle. The sculptor said, 'It is better you see my uncle on your own.' They had come to the conclusion that even the Top Man's own family was terrified of him.

The soldier didn't stay much longer that morning, and Dad

resisted the temptation to ask him how he knew the Top Man, but they did make an 'arrangement'. Dad promised him that if he got his title deed back or an official offer letter, he would buy the soldier a secondhand truck. He didn't know how he could afford one, but that was the deal. That way there was an incentive for the soldier to work for him.

He was even pleased when the soldier cautioned him not to get too excited.

'Mr Rogers. Please understand. With our government, these land issues can take time. Sometimes many months. But let me be certain with you. The channels are now open. I know many people. Failing the minister, I am ready to speak with my other contacts. I have many contacts. Many friends in government.'

And then, as he got up to leave, the soldier did a strange thing. He gave Dad a business card. It read *Staff Sergeant: ZNA*. Then he showed him an ID card. It read: *State Security.* State Security was Central Intelligence – the CIO, the Top Man's other department. The soldier was a spy!

Dad had wondered how a mere staff sergeant could be so connected, and this was it. Oom Piet was right. The chefs were all paranoid now. If there was going to be any change in government, it was increasingly likely that it would come from a military coup rather than an election. Dad reckoned the army must be full of spies checking up on other soldiers and officers – who was on whose side, who was saying what. And suddenly another ghastly realisation came to him: he had crossed a line. There was no going back. It was like jumping a border without a passport or a visa: you would never know if you could ever get out again. Everyone was corrupted in the end, he now realised. He was no different.

The Top Man's secretary answered the phone. She had been expecting Dad's call. He made an appointment and drove out to see the minister in his hometown, 96 kilometres west, on the Harare road.

It was a hot, bright, weekday morning in November 2006. Dad was nervous, and his mouth was parched. Halfway there, in the village of Odzi, he pulled over to buy a Coke. He paid Z$400 000 for it. *That's ten times what my entire pension was worth!* he thought. He realised that, despite everything that had happened, cashing in his pension a dozen years ago to build the cottages had actually been one of the best decisions he had ever made in his life. Z$40 000 could not buy you an onion now.

He drove on, passing Odzi Sports Club on the left. He remembered watching a rugby game there one Saturday afternoon in the 1970s and playing squash matches in the cement-block courts next to the clubhouse. The sports club was in tatters now. It had long since been taken over by war veterans.

Forty-eight kilometres on he arrived in the Top Man's town and turned right onto a potholed, jacaranda-lined street. He came to a small, double-storey colonial house surrounded by a high wire fence. Two armed guards at the gate asked his name and let him through.

It was a beautiful home. It had a steeply pitched tile roof, a wide veranda and a green front lawn that was being drenched by water sprinklers. The receptionist met him at the front steps and told him to take a seat on one of a dozen chairs neatly arranged on the veranda. He wasn't alone. Four people were already there, including an old white woman in a faded floral dress, her grey hair tied in a bun, her lips pursed and wrinkled. She didn't look at him.

He soon realised this was an audience with a chief. By the time the Top Man stepped onto the veranda half an hour later, more than twenty people were waiting. My father recognised him instantly from that time in the bar. He was plump, bald and not much more than four foot nine, but there was no denying he had presence. Wearing an immaculate charcoal suit and wire-rimmed glasses, he moved slowly through the rows, warmly welcoming everyone and shaking hands. My father was struck by how polite he was, charming even. But it occurred to him that almost every senior official he had managed to meet or speak to while trying to get his deed back was the same way. Some of them even had similarly posh British-sounding accents, picked up, he knew, in the country's colonial-era mission schools. He was always reminded of Unita Herrer at moments like that, and what the war veterans had done to her. He wasn't fooled. *They have the power to completely destroy us,* he said to himself, *especially this man.*

The Top Man took a seat at a table in front of the chairs. His secretary sat to the side, a notebook on her lap. My father was fifth in line. First up was a youngish man in a suit jacket, an A2 farmer, complaining, in English, that a man named Neil Moolman was not vacating his farm to make way for him. Fuck me, thought Dad. *I know Neil Moolman. He used to drink at Drifters. A huge Afrikaans guy. He's still on his farm? How did he manage that?*

The Top Man said: 'Don't worry, I will sort it out.'

Dad muttered: 'There goes Neil Moolman.'

Then the white woman stood up. She introduced herself. My father vaguely recognised the name. *Where do I know her from?* She had a heavy Afrikaans accent and spoke in a high-pitched voice that reminded him of Unita Herrer's. She started off normally enough. She said that her husband wanted his farm back. That he was a good man, with a good history in Zimbabwe. The farm was all he owned in the world.

The minister listened politely, nodding.

Then she said something that almost made my father fall off his chair.

'I want you to know that God has spoken to me,

Minister,' she said, her voice rising several octaves. 'God has spoken to me. He is very displeased with what is happening in this country. He is very displeased with what has happened on my husband's farm.'

Her arms were flailing about now. She pointed a bony finger up at the ceiling, the sky, the minister. 'God has spoken to me, Minister! God has spoken to me! There is going to be a lot of trouble if you don't mend your ways. Oh yes, Minister. A lot of trouble!'

My father was shocked, and suddenly he realised who she was: a South African woman who moved to Zimbabwe at the height of the land invasions to marry a local farmer after answering his ad in 'The Hitching Post', the lonely hearts section of *Farmer's Weekly* magazine. The woman was a born-again Christian, a religious firebrand. Within months of her arrival, they were booted off the farm. She hadn't taken kindly to it. She hadn't left South Africa to live in penury in Zimbabwe, she told people. She was going to get the farm back!

She railed on. Someone at the back sniggered. Dad, full of admiration, had to hold himself back from cheering her on. But then he looked at the minister. He sat perfectly still, nodding politely, completely untroubled by anything she was saying.

When she finished he said: 'Good to see you again, madam. I'll see what I can do.'

Dad realised she likely came to rail at the minister like that every week.

Soon it was his turn. He introduced himself and explained the situation. It was his one shot, and he tried everything. His land was a tourist business, he told the minister, totally unsuitable for agriculture. It had no water on it. No flat ground. Totally unsuitable for resettlement, too. 'Even the land inspectors have come to my place,' he pleaded. 'Three times! Even they say it's unsuitable.'

The minister shrugged.

'I agree,' he said.

My father didn't know if he had heard right.

'What's that?'

'I agree. I've been to your place. I had a look around. It's not suitable for resettlement.'

Dad's heart leapt – in a good way for a change.

'Does that mean you will give me an offer letter?'

'Yes, you can have an offer letter.'

He was stunned.

'So will you write one up for me?'

'No. For that you will have to go to the Ministry of Lands in Harare.'

My father's heart sank again. But he wasn't letting his one chance slip.

'I'm sorry, Minister, but I have tried to go there. They do not answer or return calls. They never write anything down. How will I get an offer letter from them?'

The Top Man shrugged.

'Don't worry. Call the permanent secretary in one week. I will inform him.'

My father was thrilled, ecstatic. He couldn't believe his luck. He thanked the Top Man, shook his hand, said goodbye. On the way back he bought another Coke in Odzi. This time he left a big tip.

A week later he called the permanent secretary. He knew nothing about any letter. Dad called the week after that. No word had come from the Top Man. He phoned a dozen times over the next month. He either couldn't get through or the secretary wouldn't call back. Eventually he called the Top Man again. His secretary answered the phone.

'He is busy,' she said. 'You shouldn't bother him at this time.'

And so it was happening again. A few weeks before Christmas, in a long Skype conversation, my father updated me on the drama.

'Now I've heard that the Top Man has told *other* white farmers that he would give them offer letters, and not one of them has got one. I think he was bullshitting me. It's just something he said to get rid of me.'

'So what did the soldier say when you reported back to him?'

'I've met up with him a few times now. He told me things take time, that the wheels move slowly. I wanted to say that if he wants a truck, they'd better move faster, or I'm downgrading him to an ox-cart. Anyway, he now says he'll go personally to the Lands ministry in Harare and sort it out. He says he knows the man. He also knows the Registrar of Deeds.'

'Do you believe him?'

'Well, I keep wondering: Am I making a deal with the devil here? Is he helping us or is he using us? I mean, it's occurred to me that he could be checking out our place and planning to get an offer letter for himself. Who knows? But I did eventually ask him how he knew the Top Man, and guess what? He says he was a guerrilla leader operating in our valley during the war. Some kind of war hero. He's got wounds all over his body. He showed me. He said that during the war he answered to the Top Man, who was his ZANLA commander back in Mozambique. That's how he's close to him. I mean, who knows what the soldier got up to in the war? I don't even want to go there. I tell you what, though, I think you should ask him when you come out.'

As 2006 moved into 2007 my father was no nearer to getting his letter. He sounded exhausted, spent. Indeed, he was so caught up in his relationship with the soldier, what the soldier was going to do for him – or to him – that he hadn't had time to find a tenant to run the Drifters bar. It had barely opened in months. It was running into the ground.

But he and my mother were eating dinner one Sunday evening just before Christmas when the telephone rang. It was strange to get calls at that hour.

Dad answered.

'Is that Mr Rogers?' the caller asked.

It was a rich deep voice, smooth as chocolate.

'Yes, who is this?'

'Mr Rogers. My name is Tendai. I am living in number Twelve A.'

The voice was confident, slow, self-assured, with a strong African accent.

'Twelve A? But isn't that the sculptor?'

'Simbarashe is my cousin, Mr Rogers,' purred the voice. 'His father has passed away. He has left the premises. I have moved here.'

Dad rolled his eyes. He couldn't keep up with the tenants, with who was staying on his land. It wouldn't have surprised him if Kofi Annan had turned up.

'Yes, so what is the problem?'

'I am a bachelor, Mr Rogers,' went the voice, 'and I want to know why I can't get a meal or a drink at your restaurant. The place is simply not open.'

It was a legitimate complaint, but still, it annoyed my father. Did this guy not know the circumstances in the country? What they were all going through? Who on earth did he think he was, calling late on a Sunday to complain?

'What did you say your name was?' Dad snapped.

'Tendai, Mr Rogers,' said the voice. 'My name is Tendai.'

'Well, Tendai, let me tell you something. In case you are unaware, there are a lot of shortages in this country. Shortages of beer, of food, of staff, even of electricity. If you think you can do any better, why don't you try running it?'

He said it to shut him up. It wasn't a business offer.

'Okay, Mr Rogers,' said the voice. 'Let me run it. I think I can turn the place around.'

My father spluttered. He looked at the handset. He couldn't believe his ears. Who was this guy? But there was something in his confident manner my dad suddenly liked.

'Um, well, okay then,' he gulped. 'Come up to the house to-morrow and we can discuss it with my wife. What did you say your name was again?'

'I am Tendai, Mr Rogers. The cousin of Simbarashe.'

My father should have made the connection right then, but he was suddenly so thrilled at the idea of someone's taking over the bar, paying rent and cleaning up the place that he didn't think of it. Neither did Mom. Indeed, it was only after they met him, instantly liked him, showed him around the bar, got him to sign a one-year lease and handed over the keys to their once beloved backpacker lodge that they realised that if he was a cousin of the sculptor, then likely he, too, was a relative of the Top Man. Did they really want to be handing over the keys to their flagship property to the relative of the most dangerous man in the valley? But by then it was too late. And besides, how could they have known that one day the stranger in 12A would change every-thing? Absolutely everything.

One Saturday evening they were sitting on the veranda reading when a car drove up in the rapidly advancing gloom. It was a Toyota Land Cruiser, not a vehicle that belonged to any of the tenants. It pulled up outside their locked front gate, headlights on full beam. Then it started hooting. They took a deep breath and ignored it. It hooted again. They looked at each other nervously. It hooted again.

'Shit,' said Dad.

For some reason – perhaps because it was getting dark, he

had the December deadline in his mind, and the vehicle was the typical kind a chef drove – he forgot his offer letter act. Instead, their plan from all those years before sprang into action. Dad got the shotgun from the cabinet next to the bed. He loaded it in the kitchen and took up a position behind a curtain from where he could see the front gate. It was the same window from which they had watched the Top Man drive by three years earlier.

Mom walked down to the car. Dad's mind was racing. He thought of the Top Man. And he suddenly thought of the new tenant, the stranger in 12A. The headlights were on bright, but if she shielded her eyes Mom could vaguely make out two figures in the front seat. The driver's door opened. Her pulse quickened. She felt the flutter in her stomach. The headlights went off. For some reason she could see even less. She felt momentarily blind, dizzy. She could make out the burly figure of a man exiting the vehicle. Then a booming voice rang out with a Scottish accent.

'Come on, Ros, we know yer bloody hoom! Just driving past an' thought we'd pop in for a wee drink.'

It was Jim and Jill – Rob's parents, Stephanie's in-laws. Mom had never been so happy to see them before.

'Jesus, Jim,' she gasped, hugging him when she opened the gate. 'Don't do that to us!'

Back in the kitchen, Dad heard Jim's booming brogue. He quickly ran to put the shotgun away and turned on the television in the living room. A rugby match was on. When Jim came in he pretended to have been watching it all along.

FIFTEEN
The Soldier

By 2007 ZIMBABWE was hurtling straight for the abyss.

It was hard to believe the economy could get any worse, but then one underestimates the mutant power of rampant inflation. It reached 6 000 percent in January, then 10 000 percent in June. It would only climb higher: 1 million, 100 million, 231 million percent! Higher than Weimar Germany's in the 1930s! Eventually it would be estimated in the sextillions. In 2005, the government's solution to the fiscal crisis had been to clip three zeroes off the banknotes. But those zeroes came rolling back and brought friends with them: a Z$1 million note was introduced. Then a Z$1 billion – nine zeroes. And finally the Z$100 trillion, with fifteen zeroes – the highest-denomination banknote in human history. Miss Moneypenny and other dealers were buying US$1 for Z$1 million in 2007. Had it really been only twenty years ago that the Zimbabwe dollar was equal to the greenback? The official bank rate, meanwhile, was a paltry Z$30 000 to US$1. This suited the chefs more than ever. Those with access to that rate could now buy a Mercedes-Benz in a few swift moves. Prices for food and basic goods surged by the hour. A friend of my mother's needed to buy a gas burner for cooking. It cost Z$5 million. She went to draw the money. When she returned to the store, the price had doubled to Z$10 million.

There didn't seem to be a political solution in sight, either. If you spoke to wise hands in Harare, the opposition was divided. Tsvangirai's MDC was unable to rally mass protests and street demonstrations. Many bemoaned the MDC's inability to rouse the people to action, but the commentators were usually speaking from exile. Of course, all protests were crushed. The international community found this out when images of Tsvangirai's bruised and battered face were broadcast around the world. Inside Zimbabwe the beating only confirmed what everyone already knew: the impotence of the people in the face of the ruthless state machinery.

As the country went, so went Drifters. Down at the camp you could gauge the national calamity in the changing methods of prostitution.

I visited again in February 2007 and caught up with the two Johns at lunch on the cement picnic table next to the swimming pool. The pool was empty now, drained of water. My parents couldn't afford the chemicals to keep it clean, and besides, the pump rarely worked because of the power cuts. Flies buzzed around the swamp of mud and leaves at the deep end. Gone was that luminous blue glow I'd found so alluring on dark nights.

'It's a dirty game now, Douglas,' Muranda told me from behind his red cash box, gazing at the swamp. He was talking about the brothel business.

'You know, these days a husband is dropping his wife or girlfriend here. He will say, "I will be back." Wife waits in a chalet for another mens. Then another mens. Then another. Then husband is coming later to pick her. In this way people survive. Flesh for cesh. It's a dirty game now. A dirty game.'

Agoneka stroked his dusty beard and nodded grimly as the

older John spoke. His orange overalls were as drained of colour as the swimming pool; the life seemed to have gone out of his eyes.

'This year, Douglas,' he told me, 'I am no longer in the middle class.'

I was surprised for a moment that he had ever considered himself middle-class, but then why not? He was educated, had worked in a successful tourist resort as a safari guide, earned a good salary, had food to eat, a place to live.

'Why this year, John?'

'For the first time this year I was unable to provide school uniforms for my kids. I could not buy textbooks or satchels. The gap between rich and poor has become too great now. We have become a nation of dealers. Even here at this place, as Muranda says, a man is dealing his own wife to survive. Only the dealers can make money, but the majority of us – aish – we are suffering.'

It broke *my* heart to hear those words. I couldn't imagine what it was doing to him. I knew all about John's respect for education and his dreams for his two children, Tariro and Confidence. And I recalled, too, the fever that would grip Zimbabwe on a Monday in January before the start of a new school year, when hundreds of thousands of parents hit department stores across the country to buy their children neat little uniforms, shiny brown lace-ups and tiny coffee-coloured cardboard satchels that would then be filled with new books, crayons, pencils, erasers, rulers, sharpeners and blue ballpoint pens.

I recalled how excited I was on my first day at Chancellor Junior School, age six, with my new satchel, my name stencilled on it in bold white letters, a pencil case zipped safely inside, and an apple and peanut butter sandwich Mom made in my Tupperware lunchbox. I felt as proud as my father taking his briefcase to work every day. But now? What was once the best education system in

Africa had fallen apart. School fees were too expensive for many parents; teachers often were not paid at all. Patricia Jombe, Dawson's wife, still taught at Dangamvura, but it cost her more to get to work now than her actual salary. 'I go in because of the children,' she told me. 'Teachers are more like social workers now.'

Muranda even talked wistfully about the colonial days.

'I remember 1963 I was going by bus from Honde Valley to Mutare with five bob in pocket – fifty cents. Bus fare cost two cents each way. I buy bread and two months' groceries to take back to Honde Valley. I drink some beer and still have money left in pocket! Now one million dollars is for a loaf of bread? Aish – we can't.'

My parents often paid the two Johns in food parcels now, since their salaries would be worthless in a few days. What cash they did get they would spend immediately before it lost value. I was amused to discover that the Johns often bought maize from a settler on Frank's place. According to Agoneka, against all the odds, 'one woman farmer is doing okay there, selling maize by the bucket'. I thought of Gracie Basket and knew it must be her. The Commissar was quiet, though. He was either lying low or basing himself at his town house. As for Saddam and Becks, I would never see them again.

I have to say I never witnessed a man drop off his wife or girlfriend at Drifters at any point, but I did discover Muranda had become something of a dealer in his own right, establishing a neat little sideline in, well, aphrodisiacs.

We were chatting outside his house one evening when a man checked into number 5 with a young woman. A few minutes later the man emerged and walked toward us. Muranda leapt up and met him by the empty pool. They spoke for a while in low tones. Then I saw John hand him something from a plastic packet in his pocket and collect a thick brick of notes in return.

'What did he just give him?' I asked Agoneka.

The younger John chuckled, his beautiful smile briefly returning.

'Juju,' he told me.

'Juju?'

'Many customers now, they come say to John, "Old man, I am off my game, do you have anything?" So he gives them something to perform.'

'To perform? What, in the bedroom?'

John beamed. 'Exactly!'

'What kind of things does he give them?'

'Just traditional medicines.'

Muranda made his way back to us, and he smiled sheepishly when he realised we were talking about his deal. I asked him what juju he'd just sold, but he was too shy to explain.

'Actually, Douglas, we can say just some roots from a pertinent tree,' said Agoneka. 'He soaks it in water. But at other times he visits the kraals in the valley where the experienced traditional healers reside, and he can purchase medicine from them to sell for the purpose of performance.'

He pointed to Naomi and grinned again.

'Mrs John – I can say she is also selling juju. In our Shona culture it is the elders who have the skills to advise on these medicines.'

The four of us laughed, Mrs John slapping her thighs. It was like old times again.

Was the soldier just another dealer, too, scamming my father? I met him on that same visit. It had been three months since Dad had been to see the Top Man, and there was still no sign of an offer letter, but Walter was telling him not to worry.

'Mr Rogers, let me be certain with you. With our government, these things can take time. Sometimes many months. But the channels are open. I am ready again to speak with my contacts in Harare. They are waiting.'

He had already made one trip to meet with a Ministry of Lands official he said he knew. Dad paid for his transport, food and accommodation. No letter resulted. Now he was going to meet with someone he said was more senior – 'a director'. He would spend the night at Drifters before taking a bus to Harare. Dad was starting to wonder whether it was not all an elaborate con, whether he was stringing him along, selling power and contacts he didn't have.

I joined the soldier in number 7 and we spoke at a pine table next to the narrow twin bed. The chalet smelled of sweet perfume and damp straw; the thatch leaked a little from the heavy summer rains. As night fell Muranda arrived with matches and lit a candle on the table, while outside a thunderstorm cracked and the sky spat with sparks.

Mom was right. The soldier was built like a buffalo: a full-grown bison with flared nostrils, skin as dark as hide leather, and enormous bovine eyes that were glassy black holes, set so far back in his head that it was impossible to tell what colour they were. His large head was shaved bald and was as smooth as a polished soapstone carving. But he had a kind moon face that was as innocent as a child's and he was surprisingly quick with a smile, despite the dead eyes.

I thought I might get an idea of who he was – and if he was really helping my father – if I asked him about the war. He claimed to have been a ZANLA guerrilla operating in our valley in the 1970s. The instant I mentioned the word *war* his dead eyes came alive, lit up like the yellow flames of a bush fire.

'You want to know about *whoe*, Rogers junior?' he said excitedly, speaking in a frantic staccato, as if he'd swallowed a gram of speed. 'I know everything about whoe! I can tell you many things!'

286

He pronounced *war* 'whoe', with a rush of breath on the 'w' like a gust of wind, and I immediately sensed that he wasn't bullshitting.

'I was thirteen years old when I went to whoe. In 1975 the Rhodesians came to my parents' village. They beat me and my brother very thorough. They were asking where the guerrillas were. It was then that I decided to go and fight for my country. I went to whoe to free my mother and father from the whites.'

He rubbed the flat of his palm over his polished head as he spoke, and in the flickering shadows of the candlelight, thunder broiling around us and a hard rain lashing the thatch, it gave him a monumental glow – like a black version of Brando's demented Kurtz in *Apocalypse Now*.

'I walked to Mozambique. We were four: my brother and my two cousins. It took us two weeks. We hid in the forest in the day and walked at night. We would sing *"Ishe Komberera Africa"* – "God Bless Africa", an African anthem – as we went.'

It was a journey taken by thousands of black Zimbabweans in the 1970s, including the president, the Top Man and most senior members of the current government. Some of them would have walked right past our chicken farm on the Mozambique border. Once in Mozambique they trained at guerrilla camps armed and funded by China and North Korea. (The Matabele-dominated liberation movement, the Zimbabwe African People's Union [ZAPU], was based in Zambia, and supported by the Soviets.)

'When we crossed a big river we were in Mozambique. I said *bom dia* to some black people. They did not answer, and I knew they were Zimbabweans also there to fight for our freedom. They directed us to Chikwekwete Camp. I became a commander for a Political Commissariat teaching history. I was fourteen.

'In 1977 I was chosen to go to training at Chimoio, Takawira Number Two camp, where our leaders were based – the top leaders of ZANLA. There was no food there, but I didn't bother.

My aim was to come back and fight this minority government to liberate our mother and father.'

The soldier fell silent for a minute, eyes down.

Then he looked up, and I knew exactly what he was going to say next.

'And on November 23, 1977,' he whispered, 'the Rhodesians came. It was early morning. We were three thousand of us in the camps, but they were fast: they came with ground forces, Selous Scouts, fighter planes, helicopters.'

He suddenly leapt off the chair in the dark room and began firing an imaginary machine gun at the thatch. He was grinning, his eyes like coals.

'We fought like lions, Rogers junior! But they were many! Helicopters shooting, jets bombing, explosions! Bodies were flying everywhere! So many people dying in front of me. I caught a bullet in my leg, shrapnel in my arm here. See, I have fragments.' He lifted his khaki trousers to show me a deep purple scar on his shin, and another on his arm, below the shoulder. 'They attacked for three days. The next day they dropped shells. I found shelter in the bush. I was bleeding. Many of my comrades were killed that time. You want to know about whoe, Rogers junior? This was whoe!'

The soldier sat down again, breathing heavily, and took a sip from a glass of water Muranda had left on the table. I didn't know what to say. Finally I told him that I remembered the helicopters, too, although from a slightly different vantage point: that I was a nine-year-old boy and had watched them fly right past our farmhouse one evening, returning from that same attack. I didn't tell him I'd cheered them on, that I was leaping up and down on our lawn at the exact time he was bleeding in a bush in Mozambique. It didn't seem appropriate, particularly since I hoped he was now helping us.

He returned to Rhodesia in 1978, a sixteen-year-old guerrilla, fighting under the *nom de guerre* Aaron Baya Mabhunu – Aaron Kill the White People. He was posted to this valley and became a detachment commander in 1979, leading seventy-two guerrillas, sending information about the state of the war back to the Top Man in Mozambique. He had been tied to the Top Man ever since.

When the war ended in 1980 he was eighteen years old. He joined a personal security team for the president, and on 18 April 1980, was at the stadium in Harare when Zimbabwe celebrated its independence from Britain. Bob Marley and the Wailers performed at the ceremony.

'I will never forget that day, Rogers junior. It was huge! I was thirteen when I went to war – now I was eighteen. We had achieved! Can you believe it?'

We spoke for another hour as the rain lashed down. I asked him about the mortar attacks on Umtali and told him how, as kids, my friend Michael and I would collect shrapnel in town. I told him how jealous I was in 1978 when the brother of a school friend found the tail of a mortar bomb with Chinese writing on it.

The soldier's eyes lit up again.

'Don't tell me, Rogers junior! I was commanding! I was sending those bombs on the top of that hill by the aerial: 'Two shells down. Up!' We were only ten because we were afraid of the helicopters. We came over three days through Imbeza Valley near La Rochelle. In Imbeza we used the forest fields, hiding there, eating mushrooms without salts. We would disassemble our weapons and carry them in sacks, and then assemble them at the GP.'

'What's the GP?'

'Ground point, Rogers junior, ground point.'

I couldn't believe what he was telling me. He had led the attack on our town, the one when the Rhodesian artillery almost shelled our house. Then he laughed.

'I am happy you two chickens picked up that shell I fired.'

I asked him if he had ever been involved in the attack on another farm one bright afternoon in 1979, right next to a grape farm near the Methodist mission in Old Mutare, and he grinned again.

'You are talking of Mr Neil Barry? No, that was my comrade, Garikayi. I was not there. But let me be certain: my detachment laid a land mine for Mr de Klerk. They planted a land mine there on his farm and he came and stamped on it in his vehicle. But he survived. I told Mr de Klerk this when I helped him recover his cattle, and he was laughing. He has very luck, that old man, Mr de Klerk. Very luck.'

So this was one of the 'interesting' stories Oom Piet had said he'd heard from the soldier about the war. I pictured the two of them laughing in Piet's car about how his vehicle had once been blown sky-high by one of the soldier's mines, and I thought of Mom's words to me: *There are lots of stories out here, lots of stories.* She didn't know how right she was.

Finally the rain subsided, the thunder became a dying rumble. I had to go. I said I would give him a ride to the bus the following morning, but as I got up to leave he told me something that sent a sudden electric surge down my spine, like a delayed shock from the lightning outside.

'Rogers junior,' he said, 'tonight we have spoken of whoe. Let me be certain with you. There are three political parties in this country, but only one party has a *history*. Only one party went to whoe: ZANU-PF. How can you feel if some puppet party comes that has no history of whoe and wants to rule? How can you feel? We fought for this country, we cannot just give it.'

It was something I often lost sight of. When one saw the failure of the regime, the corruption and cruelty of its leaders, it was easy to believe that their constant invocation of the liberation war was an act – a diversion from the fact that they had lost control and simply wanted power for the sake of it; for money, for riches, for protection from the crimes they had committed. But listening to Walter that evening, I realised it was no act at all. They were *believers*. To them, having fought in the war gave them rights. They had suffered, sacrificed, seen comrades killed; they had survived the bullets and bombs, and unleashed their share of the same in fighting back. But in winning the war and ending white rule, they had earned a privilege that those who never fought – Morgan Tsvangirai, for example – could never have: the *right* to rule. The war might have ended twenty-seven years before, but to men such as Walter it was still very much alive. And I realised right then that there could be no easy solution. The collapse of the nation was inevitable, an unstoppable force, but the ruling party was also an immovable object. There would one day come a terrible reckoning, that much I now knew.

The following morning I drove the soldier to a bus stop thirty-two kilometres west, and he pointed out the domed granite hills that rose out of the shimmering grassy fields around us. It was in those hills, he said, that he had fought the war.

'Rogers junior,' he said wistfully, his eyes glazed, as if he were talking about some old love, 'when I drive through this terrain, all I can think of is whoe. Next time you come I want to take you to the places I fought. I will tell you all the people I killed: the white farmers; the Rhodesian soldiers. I want to tell you our tactics. How I prepared my men for battle. Perhaps, when you return, we can even write a book together. My story. I can take you everywhere.'

It was happening again: everyone wanted their story told. I wondered whether it was something mystical in those eastern mountains that made storytellers of us all. I was intrigued, too. It sounded like a business proposal. I had one of my own, more open-ended.

'That's a great idea, Walter,' I said, 'but there's only one problem. What if my parents are not here anymore? If they lose their home, I won't come back and I won't write your story. That will be the end.'

The soldier nodded grimly, but he said nothing.

We came to the bus stop, a gravel shoulder on the side of the road, bush and trees all around, and we sat and waited. I wasn't sure how much money my father had given Walter for this latest mission, but I had US$20 on me and I gave it to him. I still had no idea whether he was helping my father or scamming him, but US$20 seemed worth the chance. He took it and thanked me profusely – so profusely, in fact, that he took my hand and kissed it. I felt embarrassed.

And still we waited. Half an hour. An hour. No bus. By now more than a hundred people had gathered by the roadside, ragged villagers, sapped by the humidity of the bush noon, waiting endlessly for a bus to take them away, to take them anywhere. They wanted out. But where to?

I'm not sure whether it was the sight of these bedraggled people or perhaps the thought that here he was, a war hero twenty-seven years after the fact, sitting in the car of a white man and accepting paltry handouts from him, but the soldier turned to me then and – doubt written over his face, all the bravado of war gone – said: 'I could have been *somebody*.'

I wasn't sure what he meant, but it sounded like a line from a movie.

'Sorry, Walter?'

'I could have been somebody, Rogers junior, but I didn't get an *education*. Instead I went to whoe. I went to whoe at age thirteen. Can you believe it? I was but a child. Thirteen years. I had no schooling. But today, these ministers, they have many houses, many cars, much money, and what do I have? Still I am just a simple soldier.'

He was shaking his head; he seemed close to tears.

I tried to console him.

'You have your honour, Walter,' I said. 'You fought for your country and you won. You are a good Christian man. You have not stolen from the people like all these ministers. Many of them are educated, intellectuals, but they have become thieves. I think God will reward you one day.'

He looked at me and shrugged. He didn't seem convinced. Neither was I. What did I know of God and his plans?

A bus finally pulled up, belching black fumes, its roof piled high with bags and baskets. It teetered dangerously to the left, as if the wheels on that side had come off. The soldier shook my hand, stepped out of the car and walked toward the bus. But then, as if forgetting something, he stopped, turned back, and leaned his head through the open passenger-side window. He said something that literally took my breath away:

'Don't worry, Rogers junior. I will protect your mother and father.'

I was stunned.

Was it an acknowledgment of an 'arrangement' between us? Or was he telling me that he'd known all along that I had wanted to meet him and ask about the war in order to find out if he was going to help my father? He walked to the bus, and I watched him go. A couple of kids ran to beg from him, but he scattered them in his wake like a buffalo swatting flies with its tail, and was gone. I loved the soldier at that minute. He was monumental to me. A hero.

I was about to drive off myself when my car was suddenly swarmed by a dozen skinny kids, barefooted, mud-stained urchins, none more than sixteen years old, all pushing their hands through the driver's-side window, all trying to sell me something. In their open palms I saw tiny bits of stone.

'Diamonds, sa!' they were shouting. 'Diamonds! Buy diamonds, sa!'

They were desperate, frantic, as if I was their last chance. Diamonds? That was ludicrous. This was farmland. I looked at the pieces. One resembled molten lava, another the glass of a Coke bottle. One was a small clump of soil.

It had come to this in Zimbabwe: children were trying to pass off bits of rock and detritus as precious gems.

If the soldier was a mystery to me, then so was the stranger in Cottage 12A.

I met him a few days later, slashing the tall grass around the wall of the lodge. He had brought some new staff on board, four teenage boys with grand-sounding names – Wilbur, Lancelot, Freedom and Reagan – and they were all slashing the grass together. To my parents, this would have been a good sign: the new tenant was a guy prepared to get his hands dirty.

If he was going to turn the business around, though, he was taking his time. The lodge had barely seen a customer since he took over six weeks earlier. Although he was maintaining the grounds and cleaning the kitchen and had installed a new colour television set and DVD player in the bar upstairs, I didn't hold out much hope for him. Liquor was expensive and food hard to come by, and even the few 'customers' who spent time in the chalets these days rarely popped in for a beer, as they had other priorities: *cesh for flesh*.

I could see why my parents were charmed by Tendai, though. Twenty-six years old, over 6 foot 5 inches tall, with the slim build of a middle-distance runner, he was without doubt one of the best-looking men I have ever met. He had caramel-coloured skin, thick black eyelashes and sleepy, hooded eyes that gave him an almost feminine look. He wore loose-fitting slacks, sandals and floral shirts, and moved in a graceful, upright manner that carried the calm breath of confidence. He spoke in a voice as deep and smoky as a late-night radio DJ.

'So you are Dougie,' he purred, smiling gently, leaning on his scythe.

'Hi, yes. You're Tendai, the new man in charge.'

I soaked in the sweet wet smell of freshly cut grass, and it gave me butterflies. It reminded me of cross-country racing season at school, feeling nervous before a race.

'Yes, Dougie. Your mom tells me you once lived in London?'

'Ja, for about eight years. Harare North. You?'

'No, but my sister was there for some time. I managed to buy a London bus through her. I imported it back here and sold it for a seven-ton truck.'

'You bought a London bus?'

'Yes, I sold it for a truck to start a transport company.'

'You have a transport company?'

'Not yet, but soon. I have strategies.'

I suspected right then that he was a bullshitter, another scam artist.

'So this is the first time you've run a restaurant and bar?'

'Yes. I think I can make it a success. I have plans. New strategies.'

'How is business?'

'At the moment it's quiet. But in a few months we'll be thriving.'

I doubted it. The economy was going south fast. I had to say I even felt sorry for Tendai at that point. Back at the house Mom and Dad thought the same.

'He keeps talking about "strategies",' chuckled Dad. 'I mean, at least he's enthusiastic, and he's cleaning the place up, but poor guy. The place will never get going again as things stand. He'll have to pack it in, just like Dawson.'

They'd come to the conclusion that he wasn't even close to the Top Man, which was a relief. They were simply glad to have a little money for the rent. I didn't think much more about Tendai on that visit, and neither did my parents. But then we all underestimated the stranger in number 12A back then. None of us knew what he was capable of at all.

My daughter, Madeline Barbara Rogers, was born at Lenox Hill Hospital, in Manhattan, on the seventeenth of April, 2007. If she had arrived twelve hours later, she and I would have scored a unique double: Zimbabwe's independence day is 18 April, and I was born on 11 November, the anniversary of Rhodesia's infamous Unilateral Declaration of Independence from Britain. Five years earlier my parents had practically given up hope of ever having grandchildren; now, in the past three years, Sandra had given birth to two boys in Johannesburg, and in London, Helen was pregnant, too. Soon my parents would have four grandkids.

Three months after she was born, Madeline's American passport arrived in the post, her gorgeous face with its cheeky lopsided smile lighting up the back page alongside the wonderful words *Birthplace: New York City*. Having been born in the United States, she will probably never have to worry about a civil war, and she will always be an American citizen. I couldn't say the same for my mother's birthright back then.

It was at this exact time that she became a stateless person, a woman without a country. In June 2007 her passport ran out of pages – all those visa stamps for food and fuel trips to Mozambique and South Africa – but when she went to renew it, she was told by a Home Affairs official that under a new law passed in 2001, in order to 'restitute' her Zimbabwean citizenship, she would have to renounce her rights to British and South African citizenship. She was horrified.

'But I have no rights to British or South African citizenship,' she told the official. 'I'm a Zimbabwean. I was born here. I've never lived anywhere else and I have no intention of doing so.'

'But your father was born in South Africa, your mother in Britain.'

'Yes, but I was born here. I want a passport – it's my right.'

'First you must renounce.'

'I renounce.'

'You need proof of doing so.'

She was back in the tall grey windowless building, having to prove a negative.

The Citizenship Act of March 2001 was used to disenfranchise white Zimbabweans, most of whom had European ancestry, and who the government knew supported the opposition party. But it was also used to disenfranchise hundreds of thousands of black Zimbabweans, many of them farmworkers, whose ancestors were born in Zambia, Mozambique and Malawi and had come to work on farms and mines in Rhodesia as far back as the 1920s. I recalled what Lady Charlotte had told me about her father farming in the valley in 1929: 'The population was so small back then we had to import people from Malawi and Mozambique to work.'

Zimbabwe specialised in queues at this point, but there were few as long or depressing as those outside the nation's passport offices as shocked and bewildered black Zimbabweans, the descendents of those migrants, discovered they were no longer citizens of their own country.

My mother was in the same boat, and she was now forced to get official letters from the British consulate and the South African embassy confirming what she already knew: that she had no rights to their nationality. Eventually she got that documentation. But when she discovered that it might still take two years to actually get a new passport and that the citizenship process would require her having to swear allegiance to the president, she put her foot down.

'I refuse. There's a limit to how much I'll humiliate myself,' she said.

There was one other way to get a passport, though: through a dealer. As with other Orwellian decrees the state passed, the effect of the citizenship amendment was to create a black market, a criminal commercial sideline in which dealers with connections to those working in the passport office could get you a passport, bypassing the red tape and the two-year wait.

A friend told Mom about one such dealer, a twenty-one-year-old woman named Sandra, the daughter of that friend's black maid. My mother met up with Sandra one morning on Herbert Chitepo Road outside the passport office. They sat in Mom's car and talked over the deal, how it would work.

'I felt dirty, like a criminal, bribing someone to get my own citizenship,' she told me later, 'but this Sandra was wonderful. She had all the documents ready to fill out, very efficient, her own little business going. We agreed to a fee of US$200, to be paid when my passport was done. I was so relieved.'

A month later Sandra called. The first stage, citizenship, was complete. But now she needed money up front to process the passport fee.

'She wanted another US$100 – in addition to the US$200 I would pay her when I actually got my new passport. But I trusted her and I paid it.' When Mom asked how long it would take, Sandra told her one more month, no longer than that.

A month later Mom got another call. Sandra asked to meet her downtown, at the lower end of Herbert Chitepo Road, near the Indian quarter. My mother was excited. At last she was going to get her passport! She arrived at the address, a little disturbed to discover that it was directly opposite a police station. Sandra was waiting for her on the curb and climbed into the car.

'The price has gone up,' she said calmly. 'I need an extra US$100 before they can process the document.'

My mother was stunned.

'What? I'm sorry, Sandra, but we had a deal. You told me it

would cost US$200 in total. I've already paid you US$100 extra. I will pay you the US$200 when I get my passport. That's all.'

A policemen walked past. Two other cops stood at the doorway to the station. Was she just being paranoid, or were they watching her? Sandra suddenly flew into a rage.

'It has gone up! You need to give me US$100 more. You must pay!'

My mother suddenly felt annoyed – as much with herself as with Sandra. What had she been thinking, going down this route? She was sixty-six years old and being forced to fence for her birthright with a woman younger than her own daughters. But she tried to stay calm.

'No, Sandra. I'm not giving you US$100. I don't know what's happened and why you're doing this to me now, but I'm not paying any more money.'

'Then you will not get your passport!' Sandra snapped.

'Fine. Forget my fucking passport – you won't get your money.'

'But you have to pay me for the work I have done. The time I have spent!'

'Sandra, I have already given you US$100!'

'That was for the processing! That was not for me. If you do not pay me for the work I have done, I will report you inside.' She pointed to the police station. 'I will tell them you are stealing from me. They are my friends.'

So this was why Sandra had wanted to meet there – to intimidate Mom.

My mother suddenly wondered how things had gone downhill so fast. The early cordiality of their relationship had disappeared. Only a minute ago she had liked Sandra, even admired her. But now a line was drawn: they were enemies. And for the first time, my mother was genuinely frightened. She felt a pit in her stomach, the same hollow fear she always experienced when a strange car appeared in the driveway, the same feeling she'd had down at the camp when the drunk man in the dark glasses told her that he was a guerrilla and they were only on the farm because he was allowing them to stay. *I'm too old for all this,* she thought. *And who is this Sandra? Did she really know the police? Or is she bluffing, trying to frighten me?* She was struck, too, by a desperate irony that almost made her laugh: this twenty-one-year-old woman blackmailing her had the same name as her own daughter, whose passport she had once gotten from the same office forty years ago – in two days. What had happened to her once orderly and law-abiding hometown?

My mother weighed her options and decided on the only feasible one.

'Okay, Sandra, what do you want for this supposed *work* you've done?'

'US$50.'

My mother thought it outrageous. But at that point she just wanted to get away. Hell, for the first time she even wanted to leave the godforsaken country. Maybe it *was* time to get out, to go to Mozambique, South Africa. But then it hit her: she couldn't! She had no passport! She was stuck – a prisoner.

'Okay, Sandra,' she said. 'I will pay you US$50 and then I never want to see you again. I think you have lied to me here. You've gone against your word.' She had two crisp US$100 notes in her handbag to pay for the passport. 'I have US$100 on me – you need to give me change.'

'Give me the US$100 and I will go and get change,' said Sandra.

'No, no, no, young lady! I don't trust you to bring me my change. You wait here and *I* will go and get change.'

She had decided she would go see Miss Moneypenny, but there was no way she was going to take Sandra with her and expose Moneypenny's hideout.

'I don't trust you, either,' scoffed Sandra. '*You* will not come back.'

My mother was furious. 'You don't trust *me*? I'm not the one who broke her word!'

'I did not break my word – the price went up!'

They were getting nowhere.

'We can change on the street,' said Sandra.

She pointed to some dealers on the pavement, those same streetwise teenagers fencing fuel, cooking oil, sugar, bread and flour. Mom was struck by how much commercial activity still seemed to go on in town despite the economic morass: where did people find the money? She and Dad had wondered about it in recent months. There seemed to be a wild energy – new cars on the streets, more dealers. Did remittances fuel all this trade? But she knew one thing and told Sandra as much: no mere street dealer in Mutare was possibly rich enough to carry change for US$100 – it was a small fortune.

Sandra looked at her, incredulous.

'They have! They all have! Come, we can change.'

Though my mother doubted it, she said, 'Okay, but not here. Not by *your* police station.'

They drove into the centre of town, several blocks north, where they parked outside the Dairy Den, a popular ice cream and burger shack with outdoor seating right next to Dad's old law firm. Dairy Den was where Mutare schoolkids used to hang out – our own mall. Helen and I had drunk brown cows (Coke floats) here with our friends, waiting for Dad to finish work and take us home. No longer frequented by schoolkids, its red tables were filled with street dealers sporting baseball caps and baggy jeans.

And then my mother witnessed something extraordinary.

Sandra went to ask the four dealers at the first table if they had change for US$100, and they all casually pulled out thick bundles of cash from their pockets. Not Zimbabwe dollars – greenbacks! Huge wads of crisp $20, $50 and $100 bills. My mother's eyes were wide as saucers. She had never seen so much cash in her life. How was this possible? How had they gotten it?

Getting change was easy after that. She handed over US$100, got two US$50 bills back, and gave Sandra one. Their deal was over. There was no warm goodbye. No 'see you later'. No love lost at all. My mother walked back to her car, shaking, on the verge of tears. She no longer understood her town, the town where she had been born sixty-six years before.

If the catastrophic economic consequences of the land invasions were entirely predictable back in 2000, in July 2007 the government came close to surpassing that policy for stupidity. With inflation nearing 20 000 per cent and prices surging by the hour, they came up with a new law: they ordered shop owners to slash prices by fifty per cent. The brain trust behind the policy, the National Incomes and Pricing Commission, was headed by a convicted criminal. As for the president, he maintained that it wasn't corruption, mismanagement or the arbitrary printing of vast amounts of cash that created hyperinflation and high costs; rather, it was unscrupulous businessmen 'in collusion with the West' who charged too much in order to drive the desperate population to drag down his government.

And so, in an urban reenactment of the land invasions, in the second week of July 2007, soldiers, policemen, war veterans and youth militia – the inflation Taliban – raided shops and businesses across the country and forced them to cut prices. Prices were to be set back to mid-June levels, when inflation was around 10 000 percent, half the July rate. The result was state-sanctioned theft. In an insane, week-long shopping orgy, supermarket shelves were emptied within hours as militiamen hovered over checkout counters and called out new prices as they saw fit, and their friends and family members rampaged down the aisles. Bakeries, bottle stores and the few remaining butcheries were cleaned out. Thousands of horrified shop owners who didn't comply were arrested for 'profiteering'.

It wasn't only food prices that were slashed, but luxury goods, too: computers and flat-screen televisions were snapped up for a few black-market dollars; the Bata shoe company lost its entire inventory in two days; motorcars were rolled out of showrooms by militia youths who could barely afford bread weeks earlier. Meikles, the most famous hotel in Harare, lost a celebrated wine collection in one sitting as diners discovered prized bottles of French Bordeaux now cost the equivalent of US$5. The country had no bread, but Harare street vendors suddenly discovered they could actually afford high tea in Meikles's sumptuous Edwardian lobby, and they swarmed the salon for cream scones.

'I thought we had reached the bottom, but the lift keeps going down,' Mom wrote to me. 'We are passing the basement now. Nevertheless, it is quite exciting to watch. You never know what a new day will bring.'

My father compared the regime's thinking at this point to King Canute. 'Canute commanded the tide to recede, but the sea and tides don't listen to the commandments of men. Basic economic laws do not, either. The consequences of this will be even greater disaster,' he wrote me. And of course, they were.

Shop owners who lost everything overnight could no longer afford to buy new stock. Manufacturers, unpaid by shop owners, could no longer afford to produce. Plants and factories shut down. The government tried to pass a law *forcing* them to produce, but the tides didn't obey. By August, virtually every supermarket in the country was bare, and surreal film footage of endless empty aisles was broadcast around the world. Then, in September, for the first time in its history, Zimbabwe ran out of beer. Breweries closed down, and taverns, beer halls and restaurants ran dry. Five-star hotels where chefs and CEOs drank had only the cheapest lager. Some wags speculated that this was it: the shortage of booze would finally rouse the population to rebellion and bring down the regime.

Every bar in the country had run out of beer except one, that is, and that one had lots of it.

On a bright morning in early September a seven-ton truck pulled up at Drifters. The truck belonged to Tendai. It was the one he had bought with the proceeds from the sale of an imported London bus. Tendai, it turned out, was no bullshitter. He was very much for real. Four boys sat in the back atop a cargo of wooden crates piled high. The crates were filled with beer, a complete menu of it: Castle Lager, emerald-green bottles of golden Zambezi, tall amber quarts of crisp Black Label. Tendai was there to greet his crew and help them carry the cargo upstairs into a new refrigerator he'd installed. Drifters even had regular power at this point (one of the ZESA tenants informed my mother that a government minister had taken a farm in the valley on the same feeder as Drifters), and so not only did Tendai have beer, but it was cold. The seven-ton truck left. It returned the following day with more beer. Then it left and returned with food: goat, lamb, pork chops, chicken, beef, maize meal and hamburgers.

My parents realised something odd was up when the phone started ringing. They hadn't received inquiries about Drifters for a year.

'We hear you have beer!' a caller would say. 'Is this really true?'

'We hear you have *cold* beer!' exclaimed another. 'Is this possible?'

They even got a call from La Rochelle, the hotel and botanical garden in the east of the valley: could they come and buy beer from them? By this time Muranda had run up to deliver even more remarkable news.

'Madam,' he said, wide-eyed in astonishment. 'We have customers! Very many customers!'

And so they did.

My parents walked down to the lodge and laid eyes on a remarkable sight: a line of motorcars stretched all the way to the gate. Four acolytes slashed at the bush by the camp to make way for more parking. Up in the bar, meanwhile, it appeared that the entire beer-starved population of Mutare was quenching its thirst, knocking back the golden nectar faster than they could order it, and feasting on chicken, chips, stew, *sadza*, lamb chops and hamburgers from the kitchen.

My parents looked on in wonder. Drifters had not been this busy since the millennium – and that seemed about a thousand years ago. As for Tendai, they now saw him in an entirely new light.

'He calmly glides above the fray of rowdy young drunks, making notes in his black accounts book on the couch at the back of the bar, and even instructs his barmen not to play the music too loud so it won't disturb the neighbours,' wrote Mom. 'I have to say, he's rather impressive.'

Dad asked Tendai how it had happened. He replied calmly: 'My strategies are paying off, Mr Rogers.'

Mom jokingly complained to Tendai that the telephone hadn't stopped ringing.

'I'm very sorry, Mrs Rogers,' he apologised. 'Perhaps you can just leave a message on the machine: "This is Drifters, we have beer – plenty plus!"'

My parents didn't ask him where he'd gotten that beer. They didn't want to know. But it dawned on them that he must really be connected to the Top Man, and they weren't quite sure what to make of it at that point. What surprised them even more, though, was the clientele. They were mostly men and women in their twenties and thirties – a generation younger than the usual well-connected fat cats who frequented the place. How did these young people have so much money? Tendai was charging five times the usual price for beer and much more for food – there were no inflation Taliban out in the bush – and yet his customers happily ponied up the bucks. Even the fleet of chariots surprised my parents. There were Mercedes-Benzes, BMWs, gleaming Opels and several neat little Nissan Suns, one with a private licence plate that read *007*. Often, standing beside the cars and drinking beer or flirting with a girl from the bar, would be a guard, taking his turn while his friends partied inside.

But who were my parents to wonder? Drifters had miraculously reinvented itself again. And their chalet business, their main source of income, was thriving once more. For the first time in years some of the customers were even genuine guests. They would get too drunk and choose to spend the night, or they would phone to book a chalet for a weekend of nonstop liquor. The lodge had become an oasis of alcohol in the bush, and the good times rolled.

And yet, if Drifters was a drink-fuelled oasis, it was on an island. For just beyond the gates of the farm, the valley was in disarray and as dangerous as ever. My parents had long since lost their fence and animals to poachers and had their cottages and toolshed burgled. But now the last three commercial farmers in the area – the black farmers Ernest Muzorewa, Margaret Matongo and Dr John Pfumojena – were becoming victims of crime, too. Their farms were raided for irrigation equipment, feedstock, fuel supplies, fencing, cables and even telephone wires as bandits ran rampant. Which was why Ernest Muzorewa came to see Dad at the house one afternoon with a proposition. He and the other farmers wanted to get policemen to run permanent security patrols in the area. If they could find good policemen, would it be possible to base these men at Drifters? Dad listened to his request. He quietly wished Ernest had suggested it six years ago, when Drifters was first under siege. But he still thought it a good idea. Actually, he considered it a brilliant idea, and he knew just the man to help them find the right kind of policemen: Walter the soldier.

My father had gotten closer to Walter these past nine months. Walter still hadn't procured him an offer letter, but he often came to stay the night at Drifters before trips to Harare on Dad's behalf. He phoned regularly to update him, and even apologised for the slow progress. Dad still wasn't sure whether to trust him, but he'd worked out that if the soldier had been going to take Drifters for himself, he would have done so by now. Besides, there were those strange words the soldier had said at the bus stop, which I had duly reported back to them: *Don't worry, Rogers junior, I will protect your mother and father.*

By now Dad had even introduced Walter to Miss Moneypenny (not at her lair, of course), and she had agreed to pay him a small fortune if he would take her to meet the Destroyer, that famous *n'anga*, in the hope that he might be able to exact her revenge on the slimebag who'd stolen her money and house. A drive to the mountains to visit a world-ranked witch? Dad wanted in on that trip. In the meantime, he phoned Walter about security.

'Walter, can you help me?' he asked. 'There is lots of crime around this area right now. Muzorewa, Matongo, and I are thinking of getting some policemen in to stay here at Drifters and do patrols of the area. Some good men.'

There was a long silence.

Usually my father practised the pregnant pause, not Walter.

Finally the soldier spoke.

'Mr Rogers,' he said softly, 'I don't think that will be a wise idea.'

Dad was surprised.

'Why is that, Walter?'

'Mr Rogers, you are prospering at this time. I have seen your place. It is very busy. This is good. Why do you want to change that situation?'

'Why will it change, Walter? It might make it better. Safer for the customers. They won't even have to worry about having to guard their cars.'

'Mr Rogers, I don't think you understand. The young people who come to drink at your place – they do not want my police friends to be watching them.'

'Ah, Walter, I understand. It's because these customers bring prostitutes out here. Yes, I can see why that would be difficult.'

'No, Mr Rogers,' said Walter. 'That is not the reason. The people who frequent your place are diamond dealers. Illegal diamond dealers.'

SIXTEEN
Diamonds

THE DIAMOND FIELD had been discovered in the Marange communal lands of southeastern Zimbabwe in September 2006, right next to the now barren and derelict Kondozi farm and adjacent to Speros Landos's old place. It was a mere 24 kilometres over the camel-humped hills at the back of Drifters.

'So near to riches and yet so far!' wailed my mother.

'I knew it!' cried Speros. 'For years I was telling Piet de Klerk Jr, "There are diamonds in our area. It's the right geology for it. Let's forget this farming game and try out mining." But of course, we didn't.'

Mienkie de Klerk just grinned.

'It's not the first time. My parents sold the farm I grew up on in South Africa, and the new owner found *gold* on it a year later. That's how it goes.'

Everyone knew about the discovery of the field, but few knew what effect it was going to have.

Rumours spread fast and wild: It was richer than the great mine at Kimberley! Marange's dusty earth shimmered with emeralds the size of marula berries! The area was the site of biblical

Ophir, that great city of treasures, the very legend of which had first attracted so many white settlers to the country a century ago! One rumour, less breathless, sounded more plausible: the field had been mapped out decades earlier by De Beers, which had sat on it, biding their time, not wanting to flood the world diamond market, which they already controlled, with 40-carat gems.

The facts, however, were that in September 2006, a ten-hectare field of alluvial gem and industrial diamonds was disclosed by a British-registered mining company, Africa Consolidated Resources, who had the concession to operate it. But in December 2007, in yet another echo of the land invasions, the state-owned Zimbabwe Mining Development Corporation revoked the licence and seized the property for itself.

A fence was erected around the field, and soldiers and police were sent in to guard it. Vice President Joice Mujuru (who had failed to get Hammy's farm back for him) claimed a section for herself. The mining company took the government to court, but what could they do? When the regime smelled easy pickings, they descended like vultures. And yet the Zimbabwe of 2007 was a far cry from that of 2000. In 2000 the country at least had a semblance of a functional society. Now it was bankrupt, and eighty percent of the population was unemployed; people were starving, desperate. There was no way a mere fence in a remote rural area patrolled by poorly paid soldiers and policemen would keep out the masses.

And so began the great Manica diamond rush of 2007.

Tens of thousands of Zimbabweans converged on Marange, pockets empty but heads full of dreams – much like those white pioneers of yesteryear. They included teachers, nurses, bus drivers, farmworkers, goat herders, schoolchildren and street kids. The panners hid in the bush during the day and burrowed under the fence at night, and from dusk to dawn they moved in ghostly columns through the field, hunched as pilgrims, sifting the sand for the precious gem that could change their lives forever. To the rural people of Marange, thousands of whom had lost their livelihoods when the De Klerks' farm was seized, the discovery of diamonds literally under the soles of their feet seemed like a gift from the ancestral gods, just reward for their long suffering.

News of the find spread around the world, and soon buyers from Belgium, Lebanon, Israel, Nigeria, South Africa, Russia and China descended on Mutare. They lay low in the hotels and suburban guesthouses of town since, as foreigners, they were easy for local intelligence agents to spot. Indeed, by February 2007 the Reserve Bank estimated the state was losing US$50 million a month in smuggled stones, so soldiers and spies – Walter among them – were sent out to make arrests. 'We must protect the nation's riches from crooks and scoundrels!' railed one minister. But a fish rots from the head: in March 2007, William Nhara, an official in the president's office, was arrested at Harare's airport with a Lebanese associate in possession of 10 700 carats of diamonds. Soldiers sent in to guard the field, meanwhile, made merry with the loot. A newspaper quoted an unnamed officer: 'You don't stand in a pool of water and go thirsty!'

The real engine of the trade, the fuel behind it, were the diamond dealers: young black middlemen from Mutare, many of them the same desperate street dealers from whom my parents had often bought sugar and flour. Now they had a new trade, and it made them wildly rich overnight. Every morning they would drive 48 kilometres out to Marange, bribe their way through security checkpoints, purchase stones from those dusty, dishevelled panners, known locally as *gwejas*, then race back to sell to the foreign buyers at their hideouts in town. Within months, unbeknown to much of polite Mutare society, the town was transformed. Flush with easy money, pockets bulging with fat wads of American dollars, young men and women were suddenly buying houses, cars, cellphones, suits and designer shoes. They splurged on imported food and drink – the kind of luxuries they had watched the chefs gorge themselves on for years. There was a lurid democratic justice to it all: brick houses started springing up beside straw huts in Marange; men who had only ever ridden donkey carts turned up in their rural villages in Toyota twin-cabs; peasants tramped the bush with the latest Nokia cellphones (phone camera flashes were used to distinguish real gems from fool's diamonds). It was of course diamond dealers to whom Sandra, the passport lady, had taken my mother to change her US$100 note that day; and it was diamond dealers who, thirsty during the great beer crisis and food shortages that followed the price control debacle, fell upon Drifters and made it their playground, their hideaway. Those men who took turns guarding the cars parked on the lawns of the lodge? They were protecting the suitcases and backpacks laden with the stacks of American dollars in their possession.

My father couldn't believe what the soldier was telling him in that phone call: 'Come on, Walter, what do you mean they're diamond dealers?'

'Mr Rogers, let me be certain: our town is overrun! There are thousands! I have arrested many! Some are drunk, and when I ask from where they are coming they all say that secret place, that place in the bush where they have beer, that place they call Drifters!'

Dad felt a flush of outlaw pride – followed by something approximating panic. The last thing he needed was Walter and his CIO comrades raiding his lodge. But Walter must have sensed his concern.

'Don't worry, Mr Rogers,' he said quietly and conspiratorially. 'I instruct them to keep very quiet about your place. Very quiet...'

It wasn't hard to meet a diamond dealer at Drifters. You just had to walk into the bar.

I took a corner stool next to a tall thirty-something black guy in a red Liverpool Football Club shirt. He had on brand-new Timberlands the size of cement slabs and a Fidel Castro-style military cap worn jauntily to the side.

It was 27 December 2007, and although it was the Christmas holiday and beer was back in the bars of Mutare, Drifters was on the map now and doing brisk business. There were about twenty customers at the bar, drinking beer, smoking cheap cigarettes and talking loudly over a hip-hop DVD playing on the new colour TV Tendai had installed. Kanye West was performing 'Diamonds from Sierra Leone' – an improvement on the president's fist. I ordered a Zambezi from Freedom and cigarettes from Lancelot, who were manning the bar.

Was it really only four years ago that I had sat on this exact stool, ordered a beer from a handsome stranger named Sydney and been propositioned by a leggy hooker in skintight jeans? I'd felt nervous here, then, a little out of place. But now the camp was like a second home to me, an extension of my parents' house on the hill and the land around us.

Up at the house, meanwhile, my wife, Grace, and baby Madeline were fast asleep. We had flown in from New York four days earlier, spent Christmas with Stephanie, Rob, Mom and Dad in Harare, and then driven down to the valley. Stof's beautiful home had been the perfect African introduction for Grace, the lulled luxury before the storm of my parents' life. I worried how Grace would react to it: the fruit bats, frogs and bugs in the bathroom. Our friends had been horrified we were taking our eight-month-old to Zimbabwe for Christmas, and Grace had made sure we took out life insurance before we left, but more than anything I wanted my parents to meet their granddaughter in their home, on their farm, in their country, before it was too late, before they lost it forever. So far Maddy seemed to have adjusted well: slathered in mosquito repellent and wrapped in netting, she grinned and gurgled from her Pack 'n Play travel cot and dreamed milky dreams.

Drifters was warm and cozy, and down at the camp we huddled close to the counter, as if to a life raft, for outside it rained ferociously, hammering the thatch with a thudding percussion. It had rained across the country for two weeks now and it would do so well into the New Year: not the short, sharp thunderstorms that I recalled from my childhood and previous visits but something much bigger – a continuous downpour so relentless that it seemed to seep through the skin, drench the bones, turn everything to damp and mud. It was as if the Zimbabwean earth itself needed to be cleansed.

I'd come down to speak to Tendai, but Lancelot told me he wasn't around that night.

I put my notebook on the counter, lit a Madison, and sipped my beer. The man in the Liverpool shirt introduced himself.

'My name is Fatso,' he said.

We shook hands.

'Howzit, I'm Douglas. You're not that fat.'

He patted his small potbelly and laughed.

'I'm getting there, my brother.'

He had a friendly round face and spoke in a fast, articulate, scattershot style with some American slang; I guessed he either watched a lot of TV or had gone to a good school. He introduced his friend, who sat drunk and wobbly on the stool to his right.

'This is No Matter, my business partner.'

No Matter raised his head from the pine counter and smiled lazily at me, revealing a single neat gap in the middle of a handsome row of perfect white teeth.

He was a bullet of a guy, stocky as a boxer, dangerously good-looking.

'His name's No Matter?'

'Yes, nothing matters to him!' Fatso laughed.

There were only two women in the bar, and they were with Fatso and No Matter: pretty twenty-somethings, all lip gloss, perfume and curls, arms draped over their men. They swigged beers and texted on Nokia cellphones the whole time. I wondered whether they were girlfriends, prostitutes, mistresses or small houses. Fatso said they were their wives.

He saw my notebook.

'Are you a writer?'

'Yes. I'm writing a book about this bar, this farm. My parents own it.'

He seemed intrigued.

'So if you're a writer, have you seen a film called *Blood Diamond*?'

'Of course. I liked it. DiCaprio did a great Zimbabwean accent.'

Fatso shrugged.

'Maybe – but he knew fuck-all about diamonds.'

I knew then that he must be a *ngoda* – a diamond dealer. I wondered how many others around the bar were dealers. Everyone was in the right twenty- or thirty-something demographic except for one middle-aged man in horn-rimmed glasses who sat hunched, tortoiselike. and alone against the wall. He drank his beer quietly and occasionally glanced over at us.

'Why do you say that?'

'Because I have a much better film to write,' he told me.

'About what?'

He leaned in close. I smelled beer and sweat. A black moth flapped in my face, and I slapped it away.

'About our business,' he said softly. 'The game we're in.'

'What game are you in?'

He smiled, and the red seemed to clear from his bloodshot eyes.

'Stones,' he whispered. 'Stones. Only stones.'

'You mean diamonds?'

'Of course. It's what we do. Everyone in town is doing it. Making good money.'

'So what's your film going to be called, then?'

He took my notebook and scribbled six words on the back page: *Filthy Way to Riches in Marange*.

'It's a good title. Better than *Blood Diamond*. So, are you from Marange?'

He was. His parents still lived in the area, which was how he was able to get past the tight security cordons set up on the road to the field: he could tell them he was simply visiting his family. He had worked at a timber company for many years, lost his job in 2002, and moved to Johannesburg. But he didn't like South Africa. 'Too much crime there,' he said. He returned to Mutare in 2006, and a friend who knew that he was from Marange asked him to drive him out there soon after the diamond rumours started.

'It was hard for outsiders to get in, but I knew the area. I watched him buy a pile of stones and sell them to a Nigerian at the Wise Owl Motel. To me they looked like sand and rocks. But they were industrials. He got lots of cash. I was just watching, learning.'

He learned quickly. He started buying stones from the *gwejas* who dug them up, sifting through everything he could get hold of. And he watched the buyers – 'Jewish guys, Lebanese, Belgians. I learned what they wanted. I saw how they looked at a stone. Every day I learned.'

He met No Matter, who had been a *gweja* at the start of the rush and had graduated to dealing, and together they had formed a syndicate with an Indian in Mutare, who knew the foreign buyers, and a retired National Army soldier who had some security connections.

Now they spoke like geologists: about flaws, cut, cloud, clarity, light, weight. He said he paid on average about US$50 a carat to *gwejas* and got twice that, sometimes more, from buyers.

'What's the most you've made on a stone?' I asked.

'We sold a twenty-four-carat to a Lebanese for US$75 000. For the buyer it's still below market value, but it made us guys rich – very rich!'

Fatso grinned, and he and No Matter clinked beer bottles at the memory of that sale.

'*Zhulas!*' they toasted, over the music.

'*Zhulas?*' I asked. 'What's *zhulas?*'

Suddenly the power went out. The bar turned black. A collective groan went up. The rain became our soundtrack – like the rhythmic percussion of a samba band. Freedom started lighting candles set in empty beer bottles lined up along the counter, and soon a flickering yellow glow returned to the bar, bringing us all back to life at a lower volume. Fatso moved his stool closer to mine, picking up one of the candles as he did so and casting a glance over my shoulder at the tortoise-man in the glasses sitting hunched and alone against the wall in the dark. Did Fatso think he was CIO? A plainclothes cop? The regime was lashing out at the dealers, trying to plug the dyke.

He held the candle just below the counter and tapped my arm. And for the first time I saw that between his thumb and forefinger, just above the flame, was a tiny off-white stone.

'A *zhula* is a gem, my brother,' he whispered. 'A pure gem. Clear and clean. No flaws.' He twirled it, and it glinted in the candlelight. 'I can tell just by looking at it how many carats. I don't need a loupe. Just my bare eyes. I have trained myself. One day I want to get a licence, but now I am freelance. Stones. That's our game.'

My mind was racing. I wished I had met him years earlier: it was a much bigger rock than the engagement ring I'd bought for Grace in New York's diamond district.

'How much for that?' I asked.

'I have a buyer from China. I can get maybe US$6 000.'

It was cheaper than Grace's, too.

I was horrified to realise that it also looked a lot like one of the pieces those desperate young dealers had offered me when I dropped Walter off at the bus stop earlier in the year. Had I turned down a genuine gem back then? Fatso calmly slipped the diamond back in his pocket and went back to his beer.

'So, Fatso,' I said. 'I have an idea. I told you about my book. I am writing about this place and the people who drink here. Can I mention you in it? Maybe if you introduce me to your syndicate and the other dealers in town and take me out to the fields to meet the *gwejas*, someone will read what I write and help you make your film.'

Fatso grinned widely.

'We can! Of course! Let's meet in the New Year. I will take you in.'

He gave me two cellphone numbers.

'Let me tell you,' he said, 'we are the most feared syndicate in town.'

And still it rained.

Grey clouds gathered like cavalry over Mozambique at dawn, turned to dark infantry battalions above the valley at noon, and let loose in the early afternoon, drenching our world. The bush on the property, already dense, turned to jungle before our eyes – a vivid monsoon green of twisted vines and creepers. With it came mutant life-forms: creepy scarlet beetles exploding against the veranda walls, flying ants rising in dark clouds from the front lawn. The albino frog returned to the copper coffeepot in the kitchen after a six-month absence. Mom was delighted: 'He's back! He's back! I missed the little guy!' I had grown rather fond of him myself. I had once thought him so odd and out of place, but I saw now how he adapted, blended in. The house would have felt empty without him.

Dad showed Grace and me where he'd shot an eight-foot-long black mamba on the roof under a branch of the giant fig tree a month earlier: its blood was still splattered on the wall. I shuddered and quietly suggested to him that he not tell Grace about the scorpion he said he'd squashed in the passage outside our bedroom a week ago.

And yet, apart from a few scares – a giant hawk moth dive-bombing her at dinner; stepping on a pile of fruit-bat droppings in the pantry – Grace took to local conditions like a frontiers-woman, while Madeline continued to sleep and grin and gurgle, very much at home. Perhaps the pioneering gene skips a genera-tion: she had it like her grandparents.

Just as my parents had adapted to the outside political world, the house had adapted to internal realities. The kitchen now re-sembled a museum of medieval implements. Since electricity worked for only a few hours a day by this point, my father had built a sawdust stove out of a cylindrical tin can and a rusty pipe. Sawdust burns for much longer than firewood and is good for slow cooking. 'You'll find we do a lot of slow cooking because the meat we get hold of is so poor now it's only good for stews,' Mom explained to Grace as she seasoned a beef casserole sim-mering on the rusty device. Grace blanched, but the dish was as delicious as ever, and good enough for *Recipes for Disaster* (which Mom had nearly finished writing). Dad cooked us a spicy prawn Thai curry one night on a wok placed over his gas grill, the grill fashioned from an old car part. At the age of seventy-two my father could still make a canoe out of a crocodile.

The living room had also taken on a life of its own. The

electrical outlets were all plugged with flashing digital boxes and cables that whirred and winked when the power was on; there was a mini-generator to operate the television during blackouts, and battery chargers to power the flashlights and halogen lamps my parents used whenever the house went dark. Frogs still hopped through the house from the veranda to the backyard, and fruit bats that resembled domesticated Stealth fighters made frequent flyovers.

'I feel like we're camping,' Grace whispered to me during one blackout as a flying ant roasted itself on the gas lamp beside the piano. 'Camping *inside* a house.'

I know my sisters would have been mortified by it all, but to me there was something heroic about the way my parents made do. 'We'll make a plan,' said Mom and Dad – an expression all Zimbabweans used at this point. When crops failed, shops ran out of food or hospitals were emptied of medicine, an almost atavistic survival instinct kicked in. 'We'll make a plan,' people said, and somehow they did. Hundreds of thousands of Zimbabweans had starved to death or died of disease under Robert Mugabe; the more incredible story was how so many millions managed to survive. They refused to become victims.

Two days before New Year's, Mom hosted a dinner party for the cottage tenants, and Grace got to meet most of them in one sitting. Piet, Mienkie and the tough-as-nails farmer widow, Joy Wolf, eighty-four, represented the old guard; Dawson, Patricia, and the Matongo brothers and their wives were the new blood. The racial demographics of the farm had changed dramatically over the years, and yet a wonderful sense of community still existed, embodying new possibilities. It turned out Madeline wasn't the only baby around, either. Dawson and Patricia had a daughter now, whom they'd named Nicole, and Stephen and Tsitsi also had a little one, Donelle. The veranda became a nursery that night: two black babies and one white one rolling around together on the carpet in front of us while we ate chicken and rice that John Muranda, called into action from brothel duty, had prepared on the gas burner in the kitchen. He'd lost none of his touch as a chef.

I thought Tendai might not show up, but he duly arrived. He floated soundlessly onto the veranda from the dark wet night and without a word to any of us lifted Madeline off the carpet, took a seat on the low veranda wall with her on his lap, and said to her in that deep, caramel-smooth voice: 'So, you are the next generation.'

Then he kissed her on the top of the head and said hello to the rest of us.

I noticed he called my dad 'Mr Rog' now; Dad called him 'Mr Cool.'

'So, Mr Cool, how are your dealers?' my father asked.

Tendai, it turned out, had yet more strategies, new plans. He wanted to expand.

'Listen, Mr Rog,' he told him. 'These diamond guys, we must take advantage. They want the life. They want the luxury. We must upgrade the chalets. Get TVs. Satin sheets.'

Dad guffawed.

'Mr Cool, how can I afford televisions and new sheets for the chalets?'

'We need to invest, Mr Rog! These guys, they can afford. Now is the time. Before it's too late.'

'Why will it be too late?'

'These dealers are not investing their money, Mr Rog. They are not planning for their futures or their families. They just spend: Z$150 million on beer and food and girls in one night! One year ago these guys were nothing – nobodies on the street selling bread and sugar. Now they are millionaires! We need to capitalise, Mr Rog, give them the taste of luxury and enjoyment that they desire, before the diamonds run out or the military removes them.'

I had never before seen anyone more enthusiastic or innovative about business than my father, but Tendai was that man. His long-term strategy was the 2010 World Cup.

'Listen, Mr Rog, I am going to import a big-screen TV for the event. I will set it up outside. I want to get the DJ Tich Mataz down here from Harare, put his sound system on my seven-ton, and he can play to the customers on the grounds. I saw on TV all the big parties they had in the parks in Germany for the last World Cup. We can do the same!'

But Dad couldn't think that far ahead. He was worried about the day-to-day. Hell, he was worried about Mr Cool's ruthless relative up the road. He had actually been to see the Top Man again two months earlier. With no sign of the promised offer letter, he'd called the number Walter gave him and arranged another appointment, but when he got to the house the security guards said the Top Man was away. Annoyed, he phoned again when he got back and was told by the secretary that the Top Man had been waiting for him all along, and why hadn't he arrived? He knew he was being played; there was nothing he could do.

'Mr Cool,' he told Tendai, 'if I ever get a guarantee from your uncle that he will leave my property alone, we can talk satin sheets.'

Tendai smiled and said nothing. Madeline had fallen fast asleep on his lap.

New Year's Eve was another party, an even bigger bash for my parents' friends.

'You'll meet the survivors!' Mom said.

'And the jailbirds!' Dad added.

Dad bought a full-grown pig from Margaret Matongo, and on the morning of 31 December, next to the garage where his fuel had been stolen years earlier, we trussed and dressed the swine and wired it to a gurney. I say 'we', but Dad and Muranda did the work; Agoneka and I stood back, trying not to get in the way. My father would just have shouted at us for dropping the pliers or for not tying the twine properly. We did help dig a pit for the coals, though, and we spent much of the afternoon turning and basting the pig until it was dripping in juices, its skin crisp, golden, crackling. Muranda seemed to do most of the work again, and the smoke got in his eyes so much that I fetched him a pair of plastic swimming goggles I had found in an old box of childhood toys in my bedroom. Agoneka and I doubled over in laughter as we watched Muranda work, his face squashed like a fish in a tank, his nasally voice ordering us to stop teasing him.

Agoneka considered the rain.

'It has never been this hard, Douglas. I can't remember so much water.'

'It's the La Niña effect,' I told him, turning into Cliffie from Cheers. 'It's replaced the El Niño current. Cooler water in the Pacific Ocean has a ripple effect, and it's bringing more rain here.'

He looked at me like I was an idiot, then went back to staring into the burning coals.

'I think it means there will be a change this year,' he said.

Ah, *change*. That word. The MDC slogan. The next election was only three months away, a presidential and parliamentary poll in one. It was the most important ballot since 2002. But change? I doubted it. In Harare over Christmas all the whites I had met were in agreement: it would be more of the same. The opposition was still divided, they said, and Tsvangirai had no stomach for battle; any change would have to come from within the ruling party. My father hated hearing this. He reckoned whites in Harare were living in a bubble, a rich and corrupt cocoon. They didn't know what was happening in the heartland of the country. My father was convinced the MDC was going to produce an electoral upset.

More than twenty guests came for New Year's Eve – my parents' last remaining white friends, many of whom had lost their farms in the valley in the past eight years and been forced to reinvent themselves. One farmer, Pete, had found work with a Western NGO, handing out imported maize seed to 'new farmers' across the country.

'So, Pete,' I said, 'you must miss your farm.'

He shrugged.

'Not really. Listen, for twenty years I ran a tobacco farm. I woke up at five in the morning six days a week, spent an entire day in the fields, employed four hundred people and dealt with poor soil, drought, frost, broken tractors and sick workers. Now? Now I drive around in a white Land Cruiser handing out shitty imported maize seed to poor buggers who don't know how to farm it. Then I collect a salary in US dollars. It's not very moral and it doesn't make me feel very good, but it's easier than farming.'

Everyone bought their own drink to the party, as well as side dishes and desserts. It was the way of things: no one could afford to cater a whole party anymore. I had imagined chronic food shortages would have led to the urge to hoard, a certain selfishness, and yet the opposite was true: my parents were going to as many parties now as they had in their twenties. Friends would call and say, 'We've got hold of a side of beef, bring potatoes,' or 'So-and-so has a crate of Mozambique prawns, make some homemade bread.' The same happened this night. The banquet table filled with cheese, bread, fresh fruit, salads, garden vegetables – all of it either homegrown or saved for months for this very night.

Brian and Sheelagh James were there, Sheelagh beautiful as ever in a skintight evening dress. I hadn't seen Brian since he took me to the rally in Buhera. I asked him about the elections.

He said the MDC had been campaigning hard, not so much in the cities, where they had overwhelming support already, but in rural areas – ZANU-PF territory.

'Ag, we're drawing much bigger crowds now. Our structures are all in place; we've got so many organisers and activists. The difference this time is that the results will have to be counted and announced at each polling station at the end of the day. If that happens, we win. They can't rig it like before. We'll have all the evidence we need.'

He sounded as confident as my father. I wasn't so sure. I remembered 2002 and how confident we'd all been then.

Speros and Wendy Landos were there, too. It was their swan song. They were about to leave to farm in Zambia, joining the De Klerk sons and hundreds of other white Zimbabwean farmers. I asked Speros for more stories about prison, and he told me that former cellmates still came up to him on the street. 'They remember how I brought books and magazines into the cells. It's amazing to meet these guys. They looked after me in there.'

But wasn't he bitter about losing his farm and now having to leave the country? He looked at Wendy, and she smiled.

'I can honestly say no,' he said. 'We learnt so much in that time of tribulation. We learnt the true meaning of what we often say by rote, 'Forgive us our trespasses as we forgive those who trespass against us.' Forgiveness is so important, whether it is forgiving another person for a trivial matter or for hurting you to the core of your being. Unless you forgive, you'll always harbour bitterness and you won't be able to move on with your life.'

At one point Dad put his arm around Wendy and said in his ironic tone: 'Wends, I know you're leaving, but remember, I've booked you. We have a piano here. I don't want a record playing. I don't trust these others to get it right.'

'Yes, Lyn, don't worry, I'll make it,' she sighed.

'Booked her for what?' I asked.

Dad smiled sheepishly.

'Wends was the last pianist left in town,' he told me. 'She's been playing funerals. A lot of us nearly deads are dropping off now. I'm just making my booking early.'

I almost dropped my drink. Still, at least I no longer worried that he might do himself in. Had it really been only five years ago, on this same lawn, that Mom, tears rolling down her face, told me she feared he was going to shoot himself? It felt like another lifetime.

The best story I heard that night, though, was Miss Moneypenny's. Loud and magnetic as ever, she spun a cracking tale about her trip with Walter six months earlier to meet the Destroyer, the country's most famous traditional healer. Sadly, Dad had had to miss the trip, but he loved hearing Moneypenny talk about it, and if I hadn't known better, I would have said that my father had a newfound belief in the power of witchcraft. After all, hadn't a traditional healer, at the insistence of their first manager, Mrs Magondweni, come to bless and protect this property fourteen years ago? What else could explain the fact that they were still on it? That despite everything it was still theirs?

'He lives way up there in the mountains, past Chipinge and the tea estates overlooking Mozambique,' Moneypenny began. 'Not in a hut or anything. A fancy double-storey with a sat dish on the roof. The lounge is full of televisions and stereos people have given him. His yard is lined with cars. People come from as far away as Namibia to see this guy.'

'Did he know Walter?' I asked.

'He did. But even on the way up there, at the police roadblocks, the cops all knew Walter. The Destroyer is an old man, stooped, wrinkled, like a wizard. He sat on a wood stool in a dark room dealing one by one with all the visitors. Finally it was my turn. I told him my situation. He said I had to pay him a bit of money – it wasn't much – and then he did some chanting, threw a few bones around and just said: "Yes, we can fix this fellow."'

As Moneypenny spoke, a white moon weaved through clouds hanging over the valley, and the fruit bats streaked between the fig trees.

'Anyway, he gave me these three little balls of a hard red pasty substance, and I'm thinking, *Oh, hell, now I gotta eat this or something?* But no, not that at all. He tells me to take the balls home, light a fire in my house, take all my clothes off and dance around the fire naked. Then I should throw the balls onto the fire and tell the spirits how I want this guy who stole my house sorted, how I want him "dirtied". Finally, in the morning I have to take the pile of ash that's left over and find a place "where two paths cross". I should scatter the ash there.'

I pictured Moneypenny getting ready for this transgressive act, closing the curtains of her suburban home. I hoped that her Charlie Tens might have been spying on her that night, that they might have seen the ceremony and been terrified she was casting a spell on them.

'So did you do it?' I asked.

She cackled.

'Of course! It was my last chance for revenge!'

'So where did you drop the ashes?'

'Just off the fairway of the thirteenth hole at Hillside, of course. Two paths intersect there: it's right outside my house.'

I expected that to be the end of the story, but then Dad jabbed me in the ribs and said, 'Wait, wait, there's more,' his eyes wide with excitement.

'And then,' said Moneypenny, 'an uncanny thing happened. A couple months later I'm playing golf at Hillside with a friend who lives next door to my brother's house. We came to the thirteenth hole, and I told my friend the big joke about the spell I had cast and how I came to scatter the ash here. She looks at me

in complete shock and says, 'Don't you know? The chappie's
been rushed to hospital – he's nearly dead!' I couldn't believe it.
I went white. I mean, I didn't want to kill the guy, but I did make
my wish into the fire that he get seriously ill!'

My heart was racing. Dad was laughing loudly.

'What happened to him?' I asked. 'Do you know if he died?'

'Well, that's the other uncanny thing. A few weeks later Faith
gets a phone call at the office. I wasn't in. It was a man's voice.
The voice just tells her: "You can tell your boss that everything
is okay with me now. I am better."'

'It was him?'

'I'm sure it was. He must have worked out I had cast a spell on
him. Maybe he went to the Destroyer for the antidote. I'll never
get my money back from him, but I know one thing: he no longer
lives in my brother's house. He's moved out. I think he's terrified of going back. His parents are living in it now. I don't mind.
That's good enough for me.'

On a grey morning two weeks later I met up with Fatso, the diamond dealer, in town. Grace and Madeline had flown home; I
wanted more time with Mom and Dad.

He was waiting for me in a parked car on Herbert Chitepo
Road, directly opposite the pharmacy where I'd taken the Political Commissar for headache pills two years earlier. I'd expected a
BMW, but he was in a battered Isuzu bakkie. The same gorgeous
girl he'd been with that night in the bar stepped out, and Fatso
pulled some money from his pocket. Not Zim dollars, but a thick
brick of greenbacks. He peeled off a crisp Ben Franklin and gave
it to her. She took it, saying nothing, and sauntered off in her
tight pink tracksuit and high heels. At nine in the morning, with
a thudding hangover, I found her a glorious sight.

'Okay,' said Fatso. 'Let's go meet the guys.'

We drove north up Herbert Chitepo Road, turning left at the

Central Police Station. It was an oddly beautiful colonial building, whitewashed, colonnaded, but with an air of the gallows. Speros and Brian James had both been detained here, and I wondered how Speros's old cellmates were doing, whether they still had books and magazines to read.

Four uniformed policemen crossed the street in front of us. Fatso hooted, and they ran over like eager puppies. He distributed paper – thick wads of Zimbabwe dollars this time.

'Friends of mine,' he said as we drove on. 'I know them all. I keep them happy.'

'So what's with the shitty car?' I said. 'I thought you would have a BMW or a Merc.'

'I do. I just bought this today. When I go out to the fields, if I hear of a stone, I will swap.'

'You'll swap the truck for a stone?'

'Of course. That's what we can do. If I hear of a *zhula,* a good gem, and I don't have the cash on me, I tell the *gweja* he can drive me back to town and take my car.'

'Have you ever done that before?'

He grinned. 'A lot of goat herders are driving my cars!'

I considered all that money in the pocket of his combat trousers.

'How many US dollars do you carry on you at a time?'

'Maybe US$4 000, US$5 000,' he shrugged.

'Aren't you worried you'll get mugged?'

'It's not so easy. Few people are going to do that. Everyone is making their money.'

For the next two hours I got a tour of my former hometown, and it was like stepping into a parallel universe. There were two worlds out on those streets, and it was remarkable how easy it had been for me to exist in one and know nothing about the other.

First we rounded the block and parked outside the Dairy Den. In the parking bays were Mercedes-Benzes, BMWs, Hyundais and several shiny Nissan sedans. Ragged street kids washed the cars while their owners, black guys in baseball caps and baggy jeans, spoke on cellphones. There were more than thirty of them, all diamond dealers, and the Dairy Den was their open-air office. I felt like the last person to be let in on a joke: how had I not noticed this before?

Fatso introduced me to some of the dealers. There was Haj, a ninety-kilo hulk in a 50 Cent T-shirt, his bulldog neck dripping gold chains. He gave me a fist bump. No Matter was there, chatting to a chubby Indian named Kapil, a porky bald guy in beige slacks and open-toed leather sandals. I wondered if he knew Salim. Kapil was the Indian in Fatso's syndicate. But there were other syndicates, too, and Fatso said they all helped one another.

'If we don't have money for a stone, we can ask other dealers. Or I can tell them about the stone. There is no jealousy. We don't have guns. There is riches for everyone.'

It was decided that Fatso, Kapil, and I would do the run to the field — if we could find fuel. At ten o'clock a call came through on Kapil's cell: there was some in Sakubva, the township past the Indian quarter. We left the ice cream parlour and sped off. Fatso crunched gears down potholed backstreets like he was grinding millet with a rock while Kapil straddled the stick shift between us and talked on two cellphones at once in fluent Shona.

'He's calling the guys in the fields!' Fatso shouted over the noise of the engine as he swerved to avoid a goat that had escaped from a broken-down passenger bus. 'He's updating the security situation. We know most of the cops out there but it's getting dangerous these days. They are beating *gwejas*, arresting dealers, stopping our cars.'

We came to the petrol station. There were only four vehicles ahead of us. I made a point to tell Mom and Dad about it. They were always looking for new places to score petrol. A tall, light-skinned black man in a leather jacket stood by the diesel pump.

'That man is a diamond buyer,' pointed Fatso.

'You know him?'

'Never seen him before. But I can tell by the way he looks and moves and dresses that he's not a Zimbabwean. See that cellphone and leather jacket? He's a buyer.'

We got out to buy Cokes. In a shiny SUV directly in front of us two beautiful girls sat smoking cigarettes. One had a towering Macy Gray Afro and gold hoop earrings, the other a perfectly round shaved head and Jackie O sunglasses. They looked like supermodels – or assassins. Fatso nodded to them as we walked by. Macy Gray blew smoke rings out the window and ignored him.

'A rival syndicate,' he muttered. 'Damn, those chicks are good.'

We filled up the car and returned to town, parking outside Meikles, once the elegant Harrods of Mutare, our flagship department store.

'We must wait for the Baron,' said Fatso.

'The Baron?' I asked.

'The Baron. He's the top dealer in town.'

'Why are we meeting him?'

'I bought this truck from him. He's bringing me the papers for it.'

And here the two worlds collided. The pavement and the road were full of activity, most of it illegal or desperate. Fatso pointed out dealers and buyers as they drove past, while half-naked street children came to the window to beg me for money or bread. They didn't want pens or pencils anymore; they needed the stuff of life. I had the distinct feeling of being in a country out of control, the wheels coming off the town.

The mannequins in Meikles's display windows were naked. Although Christmas had barely passed, there were no holiday lights or wrapped gifts on the shop-floor displays. I used to love Meikles at Christmas time – visiting Santa in his grotto, where he'd ho-ho-ho and give out Smarties and cotton candy and toffee apples. The tea-room where Mom used to take Stof, Zaan, Hel and me for brown cows on her Saturday-morning shopping trips had long since closed down.

I handed a brick of Zim notes to a street kid; he took it and scurried away.

'So how did all you guys end up drinking at Drifters?' I asked Fatso as we waited.

'When the town ran out of beer we found out about it. It became a place for the e-light.'

'The e-light?'

'Yes, the e-light.'

'Oh – the elite!'

'Yes, the e-light.'

'Do you do deals there?'

'We can. But it's usually just a place to relax. It's quiet, very secret. You can take your woman there, or if you are in a relationship with your friend's wife, that's where you go. In town everyone knows us guys, but out there it's like a holiday place, a place to get away.'

Mom and Dad would be pleased: *Like a holiday place...* Hadn't that been the intention?

A white Mercedes 300SL pulled up in front of us.

'The Baron,' said Fatso.

The Baron didn't move. All I could see was the back of his head through the tinted glass. Fatso went over to him while Kapil and I waited. I saw documents exchange hands through the driver's-side window.

Kapil said: 'The Baron was just a street guy two years ago. Selling bread. Now he is the biggest dealer in town, the godfather. He came into some cars last year. Some Nissan Suns. He told the *gwejas*, 'If you find me gems, I will give you cars.' That's why there are so many Nissan Suns now. He has lots of money, but he always looks after people.'

The Baron was thirty-eight years old, a self-made million-aire. I was thirty-nine.

Fatso hopped back into the car just as two glamorous women in tight tracksuits much like his wife's walked out of Meikles swinging shopping bags and hopped into the Baron's Merc. Price controls had long since been abandoned as a disaster; inflation was now over 50 000 percent, and what goods Meikles did stock only millionaires could afford – millionaires like the Baron.

Finally, we set off for the field, driving on the same road I had taken to the MDC rally with Brian James two years earlier. The sun briefly peeked through low clouds, then hid again, and a light rain began to fall, building up to the daily afternoon tempest.

I was excited to see the diamond field, but nervous, too. Fatso briefed me: 'We know most of the cops at the security check-points. Things should be okay. Just tell them you are with me, you are my friend, joining me to visit my family, understand?'

'I understand,' I said. My heart was racing.

But then, ten minutes out of town, a strange thing happened. Their cellphones started ringing simultaneously, like alarm clocks. Kapil answered as if he was drawing a brace of pistols, and Fatso, steering now with his knees, answered both of his. They began shouting down the line in Shona. Suddenly Fatso slammed on the brakes, swerved off the road and came to a halt in a cloud of dust. He did a screeching U-turn and headed straight back to town.

'What's up, man? Why are we going back?' I protested.

'It's not safe!' said Fatso. 'It's not safe! That was our secu-rity. They've changed the police on the roadblocks. Bought some CIOs in from Harare. We don't know them.'

'So we can't go in?'

'*We* can go in, but if they see you, a white guy, they will say you are a buyer. They can jail you, or beat you, or make you pay a very big bribe. It's not safe for you.'

I was suddenly disappointed. I wanted to see the field. Fatso dropped me at Dad's car, which I had parked at the back of the Holiday Inn.

'Call me tomorrow,' he said. 'We will know more then. We have to go.'

'Sure, man, I will.'

They sped off in the truck. It was just after midday, not too late. *What the hell?* I thought. What was to stop me from going to the field on my own? I was in a car with a local licence plate. I had no briefcase packed with foreign currency. I was an ordinary civilian. What harm could it do to try to get in?

And so, loaded with a tank of petrol and a fresh box of cigarettes, I drove out on my own. Sixteen kilometres out of town, still on the main road, I came to the first police checkpoint. It was not the normal kind of roadblock; this one had satellite dishes, sensors and electronic devices for searching cars. Dealers like Fatso hid diamonds in car tyres and air-conditioning units; they swallowed them or stuffed them in loaves of bread or fruit. The sensors picked up stones.

The cops searched my car and found nothing.

'What are you looking for?' I asked a policewoman.

She smiled. 'Diamonds.'

'There are diamonds here?'

'Actually, my dear, I can say we are standing on riches!'

They let me pass. I drove on, looking for the turn off-to Marange. The roadside alternated now between dense green bush, ghostly baobab trees and fields of brown mud. Suddenly, just before Nyanyadzi, a rural farming town my father had supplied with several liquor licences in the 1980s, dozens of dusty, dishevelled boys dressed in honeycomb rags leapt out of the bush or down from the branches of overhanging trees, forming a human gauntlet along the road. They held thumbs and forefingers of each hand together in the shape of a diamond and screamed as I drove past: 'Dah-mons! Emeralds! Gemstones!' They were desperate, almost feral.

I wanted to see a stone, and so I pulled over at a quieter section three kilometres up the road where one *gweja* stood alone under a baobab. But no sooner had I stopped than twenty screaming kids appeared out of nowhere, swarmed my car, and began shoving mud-stained hands through the open driver's-side window, shouting: 'Dah-mons! Emeralds! Buy dah-mons! Five hundred rand! Ten *usas*! Buy dah-mons!'

The car was surrounded. I couldn't tell a gem from a pebble but they were practically forcing them on me. They were knocking at the passenger window now. One tried to open the door; I leaned over and slammed it shut. I now wished I hadn't pulled over. *What an idiot. What was I thinking? They're either going to rob me or rip the clothes off my back.* The driver's door opened. 'Dah-mons!' they kept shouting, 'Buy dah-mons!' I slammed it shut again. One kid grabbed my right hand and tried to push a stone into it. They were begging me. Just to shut them up, I almost decided I would have to buy one. But then, just as suddenly as they had appeared, they fled. They raced off into the bush, leaping over tree stumps and running through muddy fields into the hills like terrified rabbits.

I looked down the road and saw why. My heart sank. Barrelling toward me was a police vehicle, a white bakkie with a radio aerial on the roof and a half-dozen uniformed officers in the back. I tried to start the car. The ignition failed. *Christ.* It had done that before. But where was I going to go? The police vehicle stopped beside me now, and six uniformed officers leapt out of the back and ran at me, pistols drawn. I froze. I wanted to take time back; I wanted it to be five minutes ago. I would have done everything so differently.

'Get out!' one policeman shouted.

I got out of the car. The grey of their pistols matched the grey of the sky and the gunmetal grey of their uniforms. I had never had anyone draw a pistol on me; now I had six.

'You are buying diamonds!' the lead cop shouted.

'No, I'm not,' I said, shaking my head.

'You are – open the boot!'

They began searching the car. They hauled out the spare tyre and flipped over the back seat. They rifled through the glove compartment and tried to take apart the air-conditioning unit. I had a small rucksack on the back seat with my tape recorder and notebook in it. They ploughed through it. *They'll discover I'm a journalist. They only have to read my notebook, listen to a tape. What's worse, being a suspected diamond buyer or a reporter?* But it seemed they weren't interested in my notes or tapes. They were after stones or money – foreign currency that would prove I was an illegal buyer, a smuggler. They found a few bricks of Zim notes in my bag and in the glove compartment. They weren't interested in them.

'Where is your ID?' the lead cop asked.

I gave him my American driver's licence. Would they ask why I had an American ID but was in a car with local plates?

'Where are the stones?' one asked again.

'I told you, sir. I don't have any.'

'You have!'

'Sorry, I don't.'

They searched again, looking under the passenger seat, behind the sun shades. Gradually I started to feel a calm wash over me. They had nothing.

'Listen,' I said, 'I am on my way to my parents' farm over the pass. My car was giving me trouble. I pulled over to check. Then all these guys ran out at me from the bush. I don't know who they are. They wanted to sell me stones. They said they had diamonds. I don't know anything about diamonds. I have never seen a diamond before. All I want is some help to start my car. Please, guys, can you give me a push?' They looked at me, stunned. 'I can show you – the ignition doesn't work,' I went on.

One of them shrugged, thoroughly disappointed.

'Please,' I pleaded. 'Please. Give me a push and I'll be on my way.'

The one with my driver's licence reluctantly returned it. And then they all slowly holstered their pistols. They waited for me to get into the car. Then they lined up, the six of them, at the back of the car. I took off the handbrake. They began to push me down the road. The vehicle gathered speed, and I slipped the clutch. The engine jumped to life the first time. I pulled over, revved hard and leaned out.

'Thanks, guys,' I shouted. 'I hope you catch the crooks!'

They looked on awkwardly as I drove away. One of them waved warily. My heart was pounding through my shirt. I couldn't wait to get home.

'Rogers junior – don't tell me! You have very luck, young man!'

It was the day after the diamond debacle and I was driving west through the valley with Walter the soldier to visit his old battle sites, the places where he had fought the war.

Dad had been trying to get hold of him for weeks, without success. Walter had finally called to say he had been in Zambia 'on military training'. I only had a few hours to spare, though; it was my last day, and I really wanted to spend it with Mom and Dad.

'Would they have put me in jail if they'd found me with a stone?' I asked.

'Maybe they will just shoot you, Rogers junior. Let me be certain: there was one policeman stoned to death by those dealers just some days before in Nyanyadzi. Our policemen shot and killed one of them right there. It's getting very dangerous at this time.'

'Two people were killed?'

'Right there – in Nyanyadzi!'

I didn't want to think about it, but then I did. And I thought about life insurance; I was glad Grace had made me get it.

We turned onto a muddy dirt track and drove through bush and tall wet grass for several kilometres, past mud huts and the ghostly ruins of old farmhouses overrun with vines. Giant domes of granite rose around us, and grey clouds rolled in and boiled above. Walter pointed out farmsteads he had attacked during the war, places he had laid ambushes. He was in war-story mode again, his eyes alive and excited. He reminded me of Mac the mercenary, the white soldier whose war stories I'd so loved hearing at the lodge and when I visited him in Mozambique as a young man. They were on opposite sides, but they were both monumental.

We parked at the foot of one of the granite domes and began a steep, twenty-minute climb to the top. At the peak, the view was spectacular. You could see the entire valley all the way to Mozambique – a perfect vantage point from which to plot war.

An eagle wheeled overhead, and a couple of vultures did, too. Walter raised his arms in the air, as if in triumph, and surveyed the scene.

'From here I used to plan,' he said. 'I gathered my soldiers before battle. I tell them: "Let's apply our tactics. I want brave comrades, not cowards!" I used to command with a Star pistol. And a bayonet. Sometimes we used to fight 6:00 am to 6:00 pm. One time we battled with Grey's Scouts, those Rhodesian soldiers on horseback. That battle consumed a whole day!'

He pointed out farms below that he had attacked in the 1970s, and he reeled off names: Moolman, Kok, Slabbert, De Klerk. I recognised most of them. Several had stayed at Drifters. Lady

Charlotte's surname was Kok; the gospel singer was Hanli Slabbert. And of course Oom Piet, who had hit that land mine.

'What about villagers, Walter? Did you kill any villagers?'

Twenty thousand Zimbabweans died in the liberation war from 1965 to 1980, mostly rural black civilians – the most abused and brutalised population in the country, then and now. As many were killed by the liberation fighters as by Rhodesian soldiers, although the fact is not much a part of the accepted discourse of the war in Zimbabwe. Walter fell silent. Then he nodded.

'There were many, Rogers junior. We killed many. The reason we killed them: they did not want us to liberate our country. They were sellouts – *mutengesi*. They would phone to the Rhodesians when we visited the villages, and the Rhodesians would come and bomb us.'

I remembered Agoneka's story about his village being strafed by helicopter fire. How he hadn't run away, and that had saved his life.

'It's very open up here, Walter. Couldn't the Rhodesian helicopters see you living here?'

He laughed.

'We would take cover under tree branches,' he said. 'And we used traditional spirits. We had a *n'anga*. The helicopters could not see us. We became just invisible.'

He pointed to a cave between two rocks on the fault line of a granite dome opposite.

'There we buried two comrades: Shingirai Hondo and Shingirai ma Guerrilla. I did not know their real names. We did not use our real names in the whoe. Only after 1980 did we come and collect their bodies and put them to Heroes Acre in Harare.'

I asked him if he had taken anyone else up here since the end of the war twenty-seven years ago.

'Only the minister. When the war was finished I brought the minister here.'

The minister. The Top Man. They were still fighting a war.

'There are lots of stories here, Walter,' I said. 'Lots of stories.'

Walter nodded. Then he smiled and said softly, 'After the election you are going to have – I don't know – more stories.'

'Like what, Walter? What's going to happen?'

I wondered if he meant what I hoped he meant. That the results were going to surprise everyone, and the MDC was going to win. That would be a story. Dad had told me that when he'd last met up with Walter he was shocked when Walter turned to him in the car and said: 'Tell me, Mr Rogers, what kind of president do you think Tsvangirai would make?'

But of course the soldier wasn't thinking along those lines at all.

'Rogers junior. We have spoken of this before. Only one party can win this. Only one party has a *history*. We are organising. If you want to see a big story you should wait until then.'

'What do you mean, Walter?'

I had an inkling of what he would say, yet my gut still twisted when I heard it. He turned to me and in a throaty whisper said, 'It is going to get very violent.'

Then we turned and walked down the hill, back to the car, and drove away.

The clouds had cleared by the time I got home, and the valley was bathed in a resplendent glow. Dad opened a farewell bottle of red, and I recognised the label. It was the same Oregon pinot noir Grace and I had served at our wedding in 2005. Dad had taken two bottles of it all the way back to Zimbabwe, opened one while Grace was here, and saved this for now. We sipped it on the veranda, Mom occasionally checking on dinner. By some miracle the power stayed on all night and she was able to prepare a roast beef she had saved for months. We moved to the dining room when it was ready and I raised a glass in a toast.

'To you guys. To getting through this. And to the election – let's hope.'

We clinked glasses.

And then my mother said, 'This time we're going to win.'

'You mean win the election?' I asked, surprised.

'Absolutely. This time. I have no doubt.'

Usually my father was the optimist; Mom kept her cards close to her chest. I had never seen her confident about an election – nor had she ever been wrong before, even back in 1980, when we all believed Bishop Muzorewa would win. It had been the same in 2002. Yet now she was convinced the MDC would triumph.

'You really think so?'

'Mark my words. Who is going to vote for these bastards this time?'

We didn't speak much more about politics that night. We didn't have to, for the pendulum had swung again. My parents looked exhilarated. Dad was back to his fighting weight; with his beard trimmed, he looked dashing. Mom seemed to have grown into the lines on her face; she had worn them as scars, and now they were part of her story. Only five years ago they had both seemed so old and frail. Now they looked invigorated.

And it occurred to me that something remarkable had happened here. The very predicament they had found themselves in, the very chaos engulfing them, had given them purpose, a reason to live. Every day for the past eight years they had woken up to plot and plan their survival, and yet, instead of being crushed by this struggle, beaten down, they had been buoyed by it. In fighting back they had found a rare energy, passion and lust for life that had kept them young, active and alive. And for the first time in eight years I allowed myself to wonder: Might they get through it after all? Might they come out the other side into the light?

Dad raised a glass.

'I just want to survive this thing,' he said. 'I want to see the end of these people who are responsible. I really do. I want to see their end. What could be more enjoyable than that?'

Mom smiled.

'We've come this far,' she said. 'There's not much longer to go.'

Outside the crickets chirped a ragged chorus. But it was the words of the soldier that whispered to me: *It is going to get very violent. Very violent.*

SEVENTEEN
Endgame

THE 29 MARCH 2008 election went according to plan. Actually, it went better than that, far better than even optimists like my father expected. The campaign of terror they all were braced for didn't happen. For the first time since its formation in 1999, the MDC held rallies free of intimidation. Tsvangirai drew massive crowds – not only in the cities, but in rural areas, ZANU-PF strongholds. A sophisticated ground operation swung into action that stunned those who claimed the party was weak and divided. Tens of thousands turned up at those rallies: onlookers saw waves of red cards in a sea of open hands. And on election day, a Saturday, they voted en masse. Turnout was only fifty percent of the official number of registered voters, but since an estimated one million names on the voters' rolls were either deceased or had left the country, it was a massive showing.

And then the masterstroke: the results were displayed at each polling station at the end of the voting day, as stipulated by new electoral rules. MDC monitors, prepared for this, made sure to take cellphone pictures of the ballots and to phone in the tallies. According to the MDC, the result was clear: they had won in a rout! ZANU ministers Joseph Made and Chris Mushowe, who had taken the Kondozi farm, both lost their seats. Rumours soon spread that the Top Man had been defeated; that Air Marshal Perence Shiri, who'd led the slaughter of twenty thousand Matabele by the North Korean-trained Fifth Brigade in southern Zimbabwe in the early 1980s, had committed suicide; that the president had fled to Malaysia.

My parents rode a wave of euphoria. Brian James was elected mayor of Mutare. It was extraordinary: a white farmer who'd lost his land had been voted in by a black constituency in Zimbabwe's third-largest city. On the Tuesday after the poll my parents received a surprise visit at the house from an elderly black gentleman. 'My name is Misheck Kagurabadza,' he told them. 'I am your newly elected MDC MP. Thank you for your support over these years. I'm honoured to represent you. Let's work together to fix our beautiful country.'

Mom and Dad stared at each other in amazement.

'It was like living in a normal country,' Mom said later. 'Your MP actually coming to visit you, to tell you that he's there to represent *you*? Now that's democracy.'

On April 2 the electoral commission confirmed that the MDC had won a majority in Parliament, but the presidential result was still not being released. What was happening? Why was it taking so long? Suspecting the regime was massaging the ballots at the counting offices in Harare, as they had done many times before, the MDC pre-empted the commission by producing their own result: they claimed they had evidence, those cellphone photos taken at polling booths, that Tsvangirai had won 50.3 percent of the vote – an outright majority. He would be the new president.

But the regime lashed out and accused the MDC of staging a coup. And slowly, as the days wore on, it dawned on everyone that it wasn't over at all. Not even close.

The Top Man, it turned out, had won his seat. Perence Shiri

344

was still very much alive. The president appeared in public; he hadn't fled the country at all. The regime was clearly stunned, but they conceded nothing and circled the wagons. A war veterans group marched menacingly through Harare: 'We will not allow the country to be returned to whites!' they raged. The *Herald* ludicrously reported that hundreds of white Rhodesian farmers were flooding back into Zimbabwe to reclaim land that had been returned to the masses. The president said, 'We are prepared to go to war.'

And go to war they did. It was called Operation Where Did You Put Your X? – a statewide wave of terror masterminded by Mugabe and his senior military leaders to punish those who had marked ballots for the MDC. Former ZANU-PF strongholds that had swung over to the opposition were singled out. That meant my parents' area – the valley. Air Marshal Shiri was not only alive but had checked into La Rochelle, the mansion and botanical garden built by two liberal British philanthropists in the 1950s, and in whose home the first ZANU constitution was signed. From there he conducted the mayhem in the east. A Chinese ship carrying thousands of tons of arms and ammunition for the regime soon docked in Durban. The South African dockworkers, in an extraordinary show of solidarity with Zimbabweans, refused to offload the cargo. Mbeki's government wanted it unloaded. The dockworkers won out.

By the time official presidential results were released, five weeks late, on 2 May, the terror was in full swing. MDC activists were abducted, beaten, tortured, murdered. Supporters in rural villages were burned with molten plastic, the soles of their feet clubbed until they could no longer walk. Hundreds of thousands were burned out of their homes. Tsvangirai had indeed won the 'official' poll, but his 47.8 percent over Mugabe's 43.2 percent wasn't an outright majority. There would have to be a runoff. Tsvangirai reluctantly agreed to compete in the runoff. It was

345

set for Friday, 27 June. Zimbabwe drew a collective breath. The country knew what was coming.

The terror campaign went into overdrive. Now the soldiers, war vets and militia weren't simply punishing those who had voted MDC but were instructing them to vote for Mugabe in the next round. 'Your vote is your bullet,' soldiers told terrified villagers in Rusape, in the west of the valley. I recalled Walter the soldier's words to me on top of the granite hill, barely thirty-two kilometres from Rusape: *It is going to get very violent*. And I realised now that Walter had known all along what was coming. Likely he was part of the planning. The regime was going to mete out punishment to those who had voted against it *even if they won the election*. Now that they had lost, the reprisals were simply more brutal.

So where was I for this big story? Where was I during my country's – and my parents' – darkest hour? In Zimbabwe? Not a chance. Six years on, I still wasn't the fearless foreign correspondent Zimbabwe clearly needed. I could say that I had a book to write, a deadline to meet, which was true. But who am I kidding? I was too *frightened* to go. I didn't have the stomach for it. And when I tucked Madeline into her cot at night and saw her beautiful face stare up at me with such love in the morning, I was glad not to be there. The United States was my home now.

Fortunately, many journalists, far braver souls than I, were there, and I followed the reports out of Zimbabwe with a dedication bordering on obsession. There was no shortage of sources. By April 2008 it had become one the biggest news stories in the world. I read the Zimbabwe reports in the *New York Times* on the F train on my way to work in my writers' space in Manhattan, then spent the morning downloading Zimbabwe news websites, blogs, British newspapers, radio reports. I joined chat rooms; I e-mailed and phoned friends who had contacts on the ground, in the government, in the MDC.

And, of course, I spoke to my parents.

It wasn't easy. Two days before the 29 March election, their telephone line was stolen. With the line gone, so went their Internet dial-up. They were isolated, alone. My father finally bought his first-ever cellphone, but he had to drive three kilometres up the road to get a decent signal, and it wasn't always safe to stand on an open road in the middle of a simmering war. We worked out a routine. I would call him every morning at 10:00 am New York time, 5:00 pm Zimbabwe time. Sometimes the signal worked; mostly it didn't. Sometimes he could get to the roadside; mostly he couldn't. When he didn't answer, I feared the worst. When he did answer and told me what was happening around them, I felt sick with anxiety.

The violence in the valley started slowly, then gathered strength, like a deadly virus working its way through the bloodstream. On Sunday, 6 April, a week after the euphoric election, my parents received their first 'visit'. Six young men appeared out of the blue at their back door in the middle of the day. Dad was in his study, Mom in the kitchen. 'They were here so quickly we didn't have time to be afraid,' Dad said later. 'They actually looked a little nervous themselves.'

'Yes, can I help you?' Dad asked.

The leader was a well-spoken dreadlocked man in his early twenties.

'We have information you are celebrating,' he told Dad, his eyes darting about the place.

'Celebrating what?'

'The election results.'

'I didn't know there were any election results. Why would we be celebrating?'

The youths muttered amongst themselves.

Dreadlocks held up his finger and pointed at each of them in turn.

'We are warning,' he said. Then he handed them a note.
Dad read it.

To: Rodgers [sic] – Drifters
If you are celebrating the outcome of the harmonised
elections partial results in unison with your brethren before the outcome of the final polls be advised that you risk
vacating that location unceremoniously forthwith within
10 hours from this moment.
By order of the National Homeland War Veterans

Christ, thought my father. *The National Homeland War Veterans?*
This guy wasn't even born during the war. He passed the note to
Mom. Her hands were trembling as she took it. After she read it
she tried to sound calm, but her voice quivered.

'No, gentlemen. As he says, we are not celebrating anything
at all. Just surviving.'

Dreadlocks jabbed his finger again.

'We are warning.'

And then, just as suddenly as they had appeared, they were
gone. Mom and Dad looked at each other, hearts pounding.

'Last kicks of a dying horse,' Mom said. 'Last kicks of a dying
horse …'

But the euphoria of the past week had already worn off.

At times my parents were literally living the stories I was
reading in New York. One morning in late April Dad answered
my call at the arranged time.

'It's hotting up here,' he told me from the roadside, trying
to sound chirpy. 'They've just burned out two hundred workers on a farm up the road. Ran through it at night torching huts,
beating people with iron bars. I've just been to see Brian at the
MDC offices in town. They've got two hundred people shelter-
ing there. Battered heads, broken legs. Half of them are just kids.

These guys from the US embassy came. They were taking pictures. Anyway, I've taken in three of the workers and given them jobs.'

'You've taken in the farmworkers?'

'Ja, they've got nowhere to go. Muranda's a bit nervous. He reckons if the war vets find out they're staying here, they're gonna come give *us* shit. I told him to keep quiet about it.'

I worried about that myself.

A few days later, on 28 April, I read about the same farm attack in the *New York Times* and about the US embassy officials coming to document the stories of the victims. 'At the time of our visit to the Mutare MDC office, there were 106 children under the age of 12 and 113 adults camped in the open at the office grounds,' an official was quoted as saying.

On 12 June, another story (by Celia Dugger) in the *Times* made my mouth fall open on the subway. 'Zimbabwean authorities confiscated a truck loaded with 20 tons of American food aid for poor schoolchildren,' it began. I shrugged. What was surprising about that? They did that all the time. Then the article went on to quote a man named Misheck Kagurabadza. I recognised the name instantly: my parents' new MP, the man who had come up to the house to introduce himself.

'Kagurabadza [is] one of many opposition leaders who have gone into hiding to avoid a sweeping crackdown by ZANU-PF,' the story explained.

My head was spinning. I called my father at the appointed time and got him.

'Jeez, Dad, are you okay? It sounds crazy there. I've just read about your guy Misheck. He's apparently had to go into hiding. Have you heard from him?'

A bus blew past. I heard the whistle of the wind down the line. My father's voice came to me from the other side of the world.

'Heard from him? Of course I've fucking heard from him.

Where do you think he's hiding?'

'Christ, don't tell me …'

'Yes, at the camp. And not just him. We've got two other guys. And sometimes their wives. They're on death lists. They can't go home at night. They're basically fugitives.'

I couldn't believe what I was hearing. Drifters had now become a safe house, a haven for opposition activists on the run.

My father told me Misheck had come a few times, but the other two were regulars. At first he only referred to them on the phone to me as 'the two Ps.' But he told me later their names were Pishai Muchauraya and Prosper Mutseyami. They had both won seats in ZANU-PF strongholds and Pishai was the MDC spokesman for Manicaland. I would soon read them quoted everywhere from the *Guardian* to *The New Yorker*.

I wondered how it worked, this arrangement. Weren't they being followed to the Drifters gates?

'They have a few safe houses around the area,' my father explained. 'I told them they can check in here whenever they want, just sign in under false names. They arrive at dusk and leave in the morning. John knows who they are. He puts them in the chalets near the back, in case they have to do a runner. The staff are in awe of them. They see them as heroes.'

'Is it safe?'

'Who knows? But you should meet these guys. They're about the same age as you, late thirties, and utterly fearless. They hide at night and go out and campaign during the day. They search for missing people, file reports on abductions, speak to torture victims, hold rallies. What's amazing is they're being hunted but they go out every day with these huge smiles on their faces. They're convinced they're going to win the runoff. They say the rural people are so pissed off now that they're still going to vote MDC no matter how much they get beaten up.'

I suddenly thought of the soldier.

'But what if Walter turns up and sees them with you? Then you're in the shit.'

'Fuck Walter. I've been trying to call him all month now and he doesn't answer. I've got the feeling he's probably involved in this. Probably leading some of these attacks.'

I had had that feeling, too, but I didn't tell him so.

Occasionally my father would warn his fugitives. He told me how one Saturday night Tendai had held a party in the bar. It sounded bizarre to me that there might be a party at Drifters in the midst of a terror campaign, but Tendai was a businessman. He hired a DJ from Harare and dancing girls from Bulawayo. It was advertised in town. He apologised in advance to my father about the noise. But Dad knew exactly the kind of clientele who would be coming to a party at a time like this. He immediately called the two Ps.

'Pishai, you mustn't come to night. There is going to be an event here and I'm sure there will be some government guys attending. It's not safe now.'

He could hear Pishai chuckle.

'Okay, Lyn, thanks for letting me know.'

I realised that in some way my father was now to Pishai and Prosper what Muranda was to him: keeping them informed, watching their back. But I also knew that Dad had crossed a line. He was a bigger target than ever.

For four straight days in early May I didn't speak to my father. He wasn't answering the phone. I feared the worst. Then, on 8 May, I got the message I had been dreading. I opened my inbox to find a note from a travel writer friend in London, a fellow Zimbabwean named Melissa Shales.

Dear Doug, it read. *I have just seen a blog about a Mr and Mrs Rogers being attacked on a farm in Zim – is this your family? I do hope and pray not. If it is, are they okay?*

I wanted to throw up. I knew it was them. How many white

farmers named Rogers were in Zimbabwe? There were fewer than three hundred white farmers left in the entire country. I found the story on Sokwanele.com, a pro-democracy website that catalogued the atrocities in Zimbabwe with appallingly graphic images. 'Mr and Mrs Rogers Viciously Assaulted,' read the headline. I scrolled down. A photograph of my father, his pale blue eyes staring out of a bloodied face, appeared on the screen. His nose was smashed in, his ear was torn, his thin grey hair was a mess. I scrolled down, my hands shaking. A picture of a woman came on the screen. She was in even worse shape. Her left eye was bruised shut. Her jaw was cracked. But she didn't look anything like my mother. I scrolled back up again. The man *did* look like my father. He had the same light blue eyes and thinning wisp of grey hair. But he was younger, and he had a moustache and no beard. He looked like my father ten years ago. And then I realised – with horrific elation – that there *was* another farming couple in Zimbabwe called Rogers. William and Annette Rogers lived near Chegutu, south of Harare. On 6 May, armed war veterans raided their home, and assaulted and tortured them for several hours. 'It's not them,' I replied to Melissa, my hands still trembling. Then I looked at the photographs of the couple again and wept.

In the middle of this mayhem, my parents suffered a body blow. On 30 May, Sheelagh James, Brian's wife, was killed in a car crash in Mutare. Everyone suspected an assassination attempt intended for Brian. It was, however, an accident. A motorist drove straight through a stop sign at high speed. My parents were devastated; I couldn't imagine how Brian felt. The funeral was held around the ninth hole of Hillside Golf Course. Two hundred people turned up, including fifty MDC activists and the MDC Ladies' Choir, who sang Shona hymns. The MDC had to get permission from the police to attend the funeral: the government still banned gatherings of more than three people.

My parents had become very friendly now with the young fugitives, the two Ps. They often hosted them up at the house for drinks and were awestruck not only by their courage but also by the stories they brought back about how resolute the supporters were in the devastated villages. Dad found out that Pishai had never owned his own suit, and he promised to buy him one if he survived the death squads and made it to Parliament one day. Dad was with him in town the day before Sheelagh's funeral when Pishai received a call from the leader of the MDC choral group due to sing at the funeral. They apparently had a problem. They had never attended the funeral of a white woman before and didn't know what to sing.

'What's that got to do with it?' Pishai said. 'Come on, man. Mrs James was an African, just like you. Sing what you normally sing.'

He snapped the phone closed and turned to apologise for the interruption. He didn't understand why my father had tears in his eyes.

The danger only grew closer. The squash courts at Odzi Sports Club, a few kilometres down the road from my parents', were burned down one night. Those were the same courts my father had once played on. The club had been taken over by war veterans years ago, and my parents assumed a wood fire had gotten out of control. A brave undercover reporter for the BBC, a man named Ian Pannell, however, revealed that the squash courts had been used by war veterans as torture chambers. Word had gotten out to the surrounding villages, and it was MDC supporters who burned the courts down.

By mid-June I hadn't spoken to my mother in six weeks. Dad said Mom didn't want to have a stilted conversation by the side of a road over a crackling connection. I didn't know it at the time, but she had in fact been badly shaken by the very first visit of the war veterans. She sneezed for days after their visit, a nervous reaction. She felt exhausted. The death of Sheelagh James knocked her even further. It followed hard on the death of Mary Ann Hamilton, Hammy's wife, from cancer a few months earlier. Mom's country was dying, but so were her friends. Time was running out.

By some miracle, in mid-June, ten days before the runoff, their land line was suddenly repaired. The electric power was out, of course – it had been gone for days – but I finally got to speak to my mother on 18 June. Her voice was soft and gentle, but it no longer contained any trace of a theatrical air.

She spoke clearly and plainly, and she said something to me I will never forget.

'Darling, I want you to know that your father and I have lived through a lot in our lives. We've seen some things. But nothing, nothing has ever come close to what is happening around us now. Not in my wildest dreams did I think that even this government could resort to what they are doing.' The line crackled. I pictured her sitting in the darkness. 'It's getting closer, darling. I can feel it. For the first time in my life I have to say I am genuinely scared.'

Then the line went dead.

In the end it was Mrs Muranda who delivered the news. It was a Saturday morning, 21 June 2008, less than a week before the presidential runoff, which now hung over the nation like a bloodied axe. So often it had been Mr Muranda who brought them word: 'Sa! An important man has moved into Mr Frank's place, a very important man!' 'Sa, that is the minister, sa!' 'Madam, we have customers – many customers!'

Now it was Naomi, and it caught Mom by surprise. Mrs Muranda rarely came up to the house, and certainly not on a weekend, when the staff tried to take it easy. Mom was standing in the living room flipping channels for television news. She had heard, through the two Ps, that there was a possibility Tsvangirai might pull out of the vote. More than eighty MDC agents had been killed now, and hundreds more were missing. Their structures were being decimated. MDC headquarters in Harare had turned into a hospital ward, filled with battered supporters fleeing the violence. To contest the election would mean certain death for hundreds if not thousands of voters.

Mrs Muranda was on the veranda, head down, hunched like a bird. Her hands were trembling, and when she spoke it was in a whisper, not out of politeness but out of terror.

'Madam,' she wheezed, 'you must to leave now. They are here!'

Mom put down the remote and smiled at her through the French doors.

'Hello, Mrs John,' she said. 'What's the problem?'

'They are here, madam. The war vets. They are looking for you and Mr Rogers. You must to leave now, madam, it is not safe.'

My mother wasn't sure she had heard correctly. Then she saw the whites of Naomi's eyes and her trembling hands.

'Lyn!' she screamed. 'Lyn!'

Dad had been fixing the coffee roaster at the back of the house, but he had already sensed something was wrong, for he came barrelling onto the veranda that very moment.

'Who are they, Mrs John? How many?'

Naomi rubbed her hands nervously in front of her, as if they held worry beads, and moved her weight from foot to foot, like a little girl jogging on the spot. She couldn't keep still.

'Many, sa! There are many!'

'How many, Mrs John? Six, eight, ten?'

'Twenty-five,' she said. 'They are looking for Mr Rogers.'

'Twenty-five? Fuck me. Do they have weapons?'

'Sticks, sa. Some sticks. Some slashers for cutting grass.'

'Are they from Frank's place? Is it the Commissar and his men?'

She shook her head. 'No, sa. I don't know these people. Mr John say he don't know these people. He tells me to come to house to tell you to leave. You must to go now.'

For eight years they had waited for this day, and now it had come on a glorious morning, the news delivered to them by a beautiful old woman in the voice of a terrified angel. The fact that she was here and John wasn't sent a shiver down Dad's spine. He wondered what was happening down at the camp, what the war vets might be doing to the two Johns. He thought of the three farmworkers he had taken in and his fugitives, the two Ps. Had they come for them?

And suddenly he remembered: the soldier. Dad had run into him four days ago on the road a kilometre or so from the entrance to the farm. He had been driving to the cellphone point, and a passenger in the back seat of a white Toyota Corolla speeding in the opposite direction had waved him down. It was Walter. They pulled over on opposite sides of the road and stood facing each other for a minute as a couple of cars clattered past. Then the soldier bounded over.

'Mr Rogers,' he boomed, patting Dad on the back. 'Good to see you again!'

'Hello, Walter,' said Dad, less enthusiastically. 'Good to see you.'

The soldier looked exhilarated. His eyes were alive. My father had never seen him so happy before.

'I saved you, you know,' said the soldier.

'What's that, Walter?'

'I saved you.'

'What do you mean, you saved me?'

'Your name came up in a security meeting. They said you were MDC.'

My father's stomach twisted into a knot. He felt an involuntary smile come to his face.

'Uh, come on, Walter,' he said, exasperated, throwing his hands in the air. 'Come on! You know that's not true.'

Walter stared at him impassively for several seconds, saying nothing. Then he smiled and said softly, 'I know. I told them that. I made sure they remove your name from the list.'

Dad didn't know what to say. He didn't know whether the soldier was bluffing or not. Part of him suspected that Walter wanted money from him and had simply made up the story. But he didn't want to give him money any more. Instead, there was just an awkward silence.

'So which way are you going, Mr Rogers?' the soldier eventually said.

'This way, Mr Sebenza. To make a phone call. You?'

'That way, Mr Rogers. Towards Rusape. I am working.'

And they said goodbye.

But now my father's mind was racing. Perhaps his name was on a list but the soldier had just been bullshitting about taking him *off* it. Was that why the war veterans were looking for him – they knew he was MDC?

He had to think fast. Were they going to go down fighting now, just when they were in sight of victory? Or would it be better to lie low in town for a few days, find a safe house of their own until things blew over? My parents were both still strangely convinced that the MDC was going to win the runoff. Spending time with the two Ps had convinced them of that. But in the end, it was something else that made Dad decide. It was more than just wanting to survive: for the first time in his life, for the first time in his seventy-two years in Africa, he knew that he was on the right side. In fact, it was bigger than that. For the first time in 350 years that his people had been on this tormented continent, they were – at last – on the right side of history.

It was easy in the end: they chose life.

'Rosalind, get a bag together and pack some clothes. I'll get all the documents.'

'You must to hurry, madam,' whispered Mrs Muranda. 'They are here!'

Mom packed a sports bag with clothes for both of them for three days.

Where will we go? she wondered. *To town? To Nyanga, to our friends Joe and Claire? Who knows, we might finally go to Mozambique, just as Douglas suggested all those years ago.* A familiar pit of fear hit her in the gut. She suddenly recalled something Unita Herrer had told her: that the war vets had smashed her family pictures. She ran to the passageway and took three framed photographs off the wall: Teo, Neo, Madeline and Barnaby, her grandchildren. She wanted more, but there was no space. She peered into the living room and saw the piano, the antique rocking chair, the shelves filled with her beloved books. Would they burn it all?

Dad was in his study. He got the title deed for the farm from the safe, along with the huge file of documents from his meetings. *It'll still come in handy,* he thought. *There's no official government right now. This invasion is definitely illegal.*

They ran together to Dad's twin-cab bakkie in the carport. They were about to get in when Dad remembered something.

'Shit, Rosalind, the shotgun!'

'The shotgun?'

'I have to get the fucking gun!'

'Why?'

'Because we might have to shoot our way out of this.'

She rolled her eyes.

'Well, hurry, Lyn.'

The gun was in the cabinet where he usually locked it during the day unless there was a baboon around or he heard the poachers' dogs. He ran to the study and fumbled for the key, missing the first time in his rush to slide it into the lock. He pulled out the weapon. It felt cold and heavy in his hands. He thought for a second of loading it. No time. Instead, he took a handful of cartridges from the ammo box and stuffed them into his pockets. He ran out again.

Mom was smoking furiously by the open car door as if her life depended on it, one eye on the front gate, waiting for the mob to appear, praying that they wouldn't.

Where has Mrs John disappeared to? she wondered. *She should come with us.*

Dad tossed the shotgun on the back seat. 'The car keys,' he said. 'Where are the fucking car keys?' He fumbled again. They were in his pocket. He dug them out, and the shotgun cartridges fell to the ground. He picked some of them up, but others had rolled under the bakkie. There was no time to get them.

'Right, Rosalind,' he said, clambering into the bakkie. 'Have you got the passports?'

She stared at him blankly. 'I thought *you* were getting the passports.'

'I was getting the farm documents! I don't have our passports!'

They were always forgetting things. It took them forever to get going on a holiday or a simple trip to town.

'I don't have them!'

'Who had them last?'

They had to think back to their last trip out of the country. Was it to Mozambique for fuel or to South Africa for food? Suddenly they remembered: Mom had managed to get an emergency travel document, a temporary replacement for her invalid passport; they had gone to get Mozambique visas three weeks before.

'They're either in your desk drawer or in the bedroom,' she said.

'You check the bedroom, I'll check the study!'

They ran back to the house. Mom looked in the mahogany chest and dresser table in the bedroom. Nothing. Dad searched the safe and his desk drawers. Not there. He saw his old leather briefcase leaning against the wall and opened it. Their passports fell out, along with her travel document.

'Got them!' he shouted.

They were bounding through the living room when Mom saw Mrs John sitting hunched on the veranda steps, her head between her knees, rocking back and forth, mumbling to herself. She ran over to her.

Mrs John, come, you must come with us. We are going into town.'

She didn't look up.

'No, madam, I am to stay. I am to stay.'

'Naomi, please, it's not safe for you. You must come with us.'

'No, madam, you must to leave. I am to stay.'

They stared at each other. What were they to do? Mom tried to grab her by the shoulders, to lift her up. But she resisted. They left her there, rocking on her haunches, humming to herself. In the end it didn't really matter. By the time they had raced through the kitchen back to the car, twenty-five war veterans were striding purposefully through the front gate and up toward them. It was too late. Mom froze by the passenger-side door; Dad did the same next to her.

'This is it,' Dad muttered to her under his breath. 'Let's just try to stay calm.'

He was surprised at how young they were. Except for two or three whom he judged to be in their forties or fifties, quite possibly genuine war veterans, they were mostly youths in their

twenties; a few were even teenagers. One was a tall, good-looking, well-dressed man with long dreadlocks. They recognised
him instantly – the dying horse was alive and well. But mostly
they were a ragged bunch: tatty jeans, dirty T-shirts, rubber sandals, laceless running shoes. None was in uniform, which was
a relief. He had been worried that they were soldiers or militia:
Green Bombers. Several of them carried clubs and sticks, but he
saw no guns.

As they got closer he noticed, walking to the side, purposefully, angrily, John Agoneka and John Muranda. Muranda's shirt
was torn. Agoneka had a slight limp. They looked shaken but
otherwise okay. Dad was glad to see they were alive.

In a few seconds the mob had come to a shifty, nervous halt
around them. It occurred to my father right then that he and
my mother were at a crossroads in life, that rare moment when
the decisions they made over the next seconds might determine
whether they lived or died.

Dad spoke to Dreadlocks, who stood front and centre. It was
like old times.

'Can I help you? What seems to be the problem?'

'In our culture one is first invited inside for discussions,' spat
Dreadlocks. He spoke surprisingly good English and held a notebook and a pen in his hand.

'What is it you would like to discuss?'

'First we must attend inside. We have instructions for you on
the election.'

Dad knew right away he didn't want them inside the house.
That would be a disaster. He knew what would happen. Once inside they would start taking things, knocking things over, breaking stuff. He knew he wouldn't be able to hold himself back if
that happened. He had to keep them away from the house.

Mom looked over at Muranda and Agoneka. They nodded gravely at her in support. She was suddenly aware that the

shotgun was easily visible on the back seat of the car, and that the mob could see it if they looked that way. She lit a cigarette with a shaking hand and took a casual step sideways to block the view. She felt something under her foot as she did so, and looked down. *Oh, God.* It was a shotgun cartridge. She side-kicked it gently under the bakkie and looked up. No one noticed.

My father had heard somewhere that if you could get adversaries to sit down, it would calm them. It's far harder to leap up and attack someone from a sitting position. He pointed to the garden chairs under the giant fig tree.

'Gentlemen, why don't we sit down? Come, let's sit and discuss.'

There were murmurs and finally nodding.

There were only four chairs. Mom and Dad took the two facing the front gate. Dreadlocks and one of the older veterans, a tall man with flecks of grey in his hair and a striped shirt, sat opposite. A couple of others were dispatched to get chairs from the front lawn. Soon there were eight chairs under the fig tree. A few of the men sat on the grass around the tables. Others stood, keeping an eye on the two Johns.

Dad thought: *Shit, why don't they all sit down?*

The older veteran slammed his fist on the table.

'We are here to instruct you. If you are not voting ZANU-PF, there will be war. You will return to Britain. To Blair. You must instruct these workers to vote ZANU-PF.'

He pointed at the two Johns.

Dad thought of saying, *I'm not British, and Blair's no longer even around.* Mom prayed he wouldn't. He bit his tongue.

At least half of them are sitting, he thought. *It's a start.*

Just then a truck appeared in the driveway and moved slowly past the front gate. Poor Dawson Jombe could not have chosen a worse time to arrive home at Cottage 1. There was a commotion among the younger war veterans. It appeared they knew

Dawson, and they didn't like what they knew of him. Dreadlocks stood up, military straight, and dispatched three of them to fetch him. Two minutes later, Dawson was frog-marched through the gate and up to the tree, his skinny legs sticking out of his brown shorts. He smiled weakly at Mom and Dad.

'Hello, Dawson,' Mom said, giving him a smile. Her heart was beating against her blouse. She had taken out another cigarette and offered the box around. Everyone was lighting up her Kingsgates.

Dawson told the war vets that he was a ZANU-PF supporter and there was no reason to drag him here. They were sceptical, and he was instructed to chant the party's slogans.

Every black Zimbabwean knew these slogans. They learned them by heart for when the war vets or militia stopped them or visited their villages at night. Dawson had learnt the slogans, too. The problem was, he had learnt them too well.

'*Pamberi ne ZANU-PF!*' he began, thrusting his fist enthusiastically into the air. Forward with ZANU-PF! '*Pamberi nekushinga Mugabe!*' Forward with consistently supporting Mugabe! '*Zvikaramba Toita Zvehondo!*' If we do not win the election, we go to war!

There was suddenly a stunned silence. For a second, Dawson didn't know what he'd done wrong. This was indeed a ZANU-PF slogan. War veterans used it all the time. But then he realised, as did the two Johns: the slogan was a national joke. Across the country, under their breath, in beer halls and bus stations, ordinary Zimbabweans mocked the war veterans by using the slogan ironically. If there was no bread they joked, 'We're going to war!' When a bus was late they joked, 'We're going to war!'

Anyone who used the slogan who *wasn't* a war veteran was having a laugh.

The war vets erupted. One of them shoved Dawson in the chest. Muranda, a few metres away, muttered something under his breath, and they turned on him, too. Dawson tried to explain himself. They weren't going to listen. The war vets were shouting now. It was about to turn ugly.

Just then my father saw a peculiar sight. A tall, handsome black man in loose-fitting slacks and a fashionable floral shirt was walking calmly through the front gate up to the house, as if he was taking a stroll on the beach. He approached with confidence, as if he didn't have a care in the world. He carried a cellphone in his left hand.

Christ, Dad thought, Tendai. *What the fuck is Tendai doing here? He must have no idea what's happening. Why on earth would he be coming here voluntarily?*

But then his heart sank. After casually strolling up the moss-covered brick steps onto the lawn, Tendai said hello to the war veterans hassling Dawson and the two Johns, and they immediately nodded to him and cleared a path for him to the table.

Fuck me, thought Dad. *Tendai knows these people?*

Tendai stood casually over the table and said in his smooth, relaxed drawl: 'Hello, Mr Rog. Hello, Mrs Rogers.'

Then he clicked his fingers at the war veteran sitting next to Dreadlocks.

'You. Up. Get off my seat.'

The war veteran leapt to his feet and gave him his chair, apologising as he did so. Tendai fell in it, crossed one long leg over the other, nodded politely at my father again, and then turned to Dreadlocks.

'Continue, Guruwe,' he motioned with his hand. 'Continue.'

Now my father's head was spinning. *He knows their names? Are these his men? Is he part of this?*

Muranda and Agoneka were now instructed by Dreadlocks to chant. Agoneka held up his right fist and started moving his feet, marching on the spot, weakly reciting the slogans like some wretched political dissident in a labour camp. Muranda muttered something underneath his breath once more. One of the older veterans started pushing him again, shoving him in the chest, trying to slap his face. Muranda shoved him back and started shouting. Dad had seen Muranda in a rage a few times before, usually arguing with drunks down at the camp who didn't want to pay for a chalet. It was an impressive sight. You didn't mess with a kraal headman from the Honde Valley. His targets usually backed down. But now? Now there was no chance. They were outnumbered twenty-five to four. Or was it twenty-six to four? Whose side was Tendai on?

And then an astonishing thing happened. Tendai's cellphone rang, a loud, shrill blast, sharp as a cockerel crowing at dawn. He had been holding the phone in his left hand all this time, as if he'd been expecting a call, but before he answered it, he raised his hand in the air to command silence. The chanting stopped. The war veterans hushed.

Tendai made a great display of leaning over to Dreadlocks and showing him who the call was coming from.

Then he answered it. 'Brigadier Gatsi,' he said with a smile, and it was suddenly so silent that all you could hear was a paradise flycatcher somewhere in the back of the land.

Tendai continued, 'Everything is calm ... No problems, Brig ... Do you need to send a truckful of soldiers out here to discipline these war veterans? No, I think everything is calm.'

Tendai seemed to be speaking as much to the war veterans around him as to the voice on the other end of the line.

'No, Brig, I think it is going to be fine. I think they are going to apologise soon and be on their way. ... Okay, Brig, see you later.'

Tendai closed his cellphone and turned to Dreadlocks. He addressed him and his men as if he was talking to unruly children.

'Guruwe,' he said, 'that was my friend Brigadier Gatsi. I left a message for him earlier that you and your men were here, threatening us. Now he has called to ask if things are okay. Now this can be a very big problem for you. Understand?'

Dad recognised the name Brigadier Gatsi. He was the commander at the barracks where Walter was based. He had no idea Tendai knew the brigadier at all, but then there was so much to Tendai that he didn't know.

'Guruwe,' Tendai continued, 'in our Shona custom, if you wanted to discuss a problem, you did not have to arrive with lots of people. You should have come on your own or with a friend. If you come with many people, it suggests you are prepared to have a fight. It means you are trying to intimidate the people you are calling on. There will be no understanding of your position. If you intend to intimidate, it will be a problem for you in the end. Do you understand?'

Guruwe nodded and lowered his head. He looked ashamed. The other war veterans shuffled nervously, their eyes darting, looking away.

Tendai spoke with that calm, confident authority my parents had so admired in him.

'I have told you before,' he said softly. 'This is my business. This is my farm. Why would you want to trouble these old people? They are doing nothing. Next time you come to this area here, you ask for me or Mr Muranda. You leave the Rogerses alone.'

Guruwe nodded, and then, amazingly, he apologised. *'Tineurombo, tiregerereiwo, hatidi mirizhonga naBrigadier, hatizvi pamhe zvakare.'* [We are sorry, please forgive us, we do not want any trouble with the brigadier, we don't do it again.]

Sheepish smiles broke out. The situation had been completely defused. There was much nodding and murmuring. Everyone shook hands.

My parents found it strange to be shaking hands with men who only minutes ago had wanted to do them terrible harm. Dad found he had nothing but contempt for them. Mom, too.

Then Dad shook hands with Agoneka and Muranda and patted them on the back. 'Okay, John, thank you, thank you,' he said. He couldn't find the words to tell them what he wanted to say.

He shook Tendai's hand and smiled. 'So, Tendai. Okay. Well done ...' Again, he couldn't find the words.

Mom was shaking. Tendai went up to her.

'It's okay, Mrs Rogers. These people, they are just harassing. I find them boring. How am I expected to run a business with these things going on? What will our customers think?'

Boring? she almost blurted out. *You find them boring?* It wasn't the word she would have used. *Threatening, terrifying.* But not *boring.*

The war vets had now gathered themselves and began to walk away. Tendai, Agoneka and Muranda escorted them to make sure they left. When the mob got to the gate, one of the war veterans turned around and said to my father, 'Do you have any beer?'

Dad was stunned. For people coming to deliver threats they were suddenly very amiable.

'Ask Tendai or Mr Muranda,' he said. 'They look after this place.'

And then they watched them head into the tall grass, over the creek and beyond the avocado trees toward the camp. Tendai had a beautiful walk, the walk of a prince. A man you could trust. Agoneka and Muranda were next to him. Faster steps, urgent, reliable. Diamonds in the rough. Men you could put your house on.

When the gang was out of sight, Dad took the gun out of the car and collected the bags and his documents. He was humming to himself, going over in his head what had happened, still unsure how they had managed to escape.

Mom held his hand and they walked into the house. She was

unsteady on her feet. They didn't say anything to each other, not even when the albino frog hopped onto the kitchen countertop and stared straight at them, silent, unblinking. Naomi was still on the veranda, still in shock, gently rocking back and forth, moaning to herself. Mom sat with her for a while. Then she started sneezing again. She would sneeze all afternoon and most of the next day, some strange nervous reaction.

'I think I am allergic to war vets,' she would say later.

It was twelve-thirty, early afternoon, and they found that they were suddenly utterly exhausted. Mom went into their room and lay down on the bed. Dad locked the gun away, hid the passports and joined her. The sun was high in the sky and birds were singing in the banana tree. Naomi's gentle sobs drifted through from the veranda on a clear, cloudless day.

EPILOGUE

*'Is this the place on the way up,
or down?*

On 22 June 2008, the day after the visit of the war veterans to Drifters, Morgan Tsvangirai pulled out of the runoff election. The death toll was already too high; he did so to avoid a bigger bloodbath. Walter the soldier had been right: only one party was ever going to win an election in Zimbabwe. The party that had a 'history'.

But something else happened during those three terrifying months: for the first time, the entire world saw the regime for what it was. Mugabe could no longer hide behind the patina of 'democracy', or claims that he was fighting a defiant struggle against British imperialism: he had brutalised his own people in full view of the world.

Pressure finally came from even his closest enablers in South Africa, and on 15 September 2008 he signed a power-sharing agreement with the MDC. Five months later, on 5 February 2009, a Government of National Unity, the Gnu, was formed, and Morgan Tsvangirai was sworn in as prime minister. Mugabe was still president, though, and few people gave the Gnu any

chance. They had reason to doubt. MDC activists were still being abducted, beaten and detained, and farm invasions and assaults on white farmers continued remorselessly. 'It's not a Gnu,'
went the local joke, 'it's a *wildebeest*.'

By then, in October 2008, a month after the power-sharing
agreement was signed, the regime had turned its attention to the
Marange diamond field. Bankrupt, desperate for revenue, they
saw easy pickings in the stones buried in Marange's dust. Fatso
and his friends were right in the cross hairs.

It was called Operation Hakudzokwi – No Return. Planned
and carried out by the Joint Operations Command – the same
officials and military commanders who directed the election rampage – tanks, bulldozers and helicopters were sent in to Marange.
Soldiers opened fire on *gwejas* in broad daylight. Some were buried alive in tunnels, other mauled by dogs. More than 200 diggers
were murdered, many of them teenagers machine-gunned from
helicopters as they ran for the hills. Some of those feral kids who
had swarmed my vehicle on that aborted trip to the field in early
2008 would have been among the dead.

Up until that October I had kept in touch with Fatso by intermittent e-mails. He told me No Matter was in jail; the Baron
had been arrested – then released for lack of evidence. But in
November, all communication with him stopped. I presumed he
was dead or in jail. Then, on 8 January 2009, an e-mail popped
up in my inbox:

hie douglas,
it has been quite long when we last communicated and too
much has been happening. soldiers came, i tell you people
were killed like flies. there were choppers, ground force,
commando, riot police name it. its now a no go area. we
were in exile and some are still even myself i am not staying in mutare. actually as i write to you people are at a

funeral of one buyer called Mabota. beaten by the soldiers.
all the same the soldiers are mining with their syndicates.
i have since started scripting for filth way to riches in marange
regard 'Fatso'

I feared for Fatso's life, and when I told him I was writing a magazine article about our adventure together, he asked me not to use his real name.

By now, a cholera epidemic had broken out and spread to South Africa, another headline in the world news. The country was quite literally diseased. Without medicines or money to pay nurses or doctors, hospitals across the country were closing. Word came to me that Dawson Jombe was praying that his wife Patricia, pregnant with their second child, would give birth to their baby prematurely – before the last hospital closed.

In January 2009, some relief: the government, tired of lopping zeroes off the currency, finally legalised the American dollar and the South African rand. In one move, hyperinflation and the currency black market was wiped out. Goods reappeared in the shops, and workers were allowed to be paid in American dollars, which had real value. But the problem was, so few people had jobs, and the price of fuel and utilities – water, electricity, phone lines – was now astronomical.

Then, on 8 March 2009, barely a month after the fractious power-sharing government was formed, another catastrophe: a lorry smashed into Morgan Tsvangirai's vehicle as it sped to Buhera, his rural home district – the area where I had interviewed him after the political rally in 2006, and been terrified a lorry would smash into me. His wife, Susan, was killed instantly, and he was in hospital. Everyone suspected an assassination attempt, and once again the country held its breath. It seemed certain that a civil war was coming.

But Zimbabwe has a penchant for surprise. Tsvangirai did something quite extraordinary at that point. From his hospital bed, grieving the loss of his beloved wife, he calmly announced to the world that it was an accident. And, when he was released from hospital, he calmly went back to work as Prime Minister in the Gnu. Who knows what cataclysm was averted by his extraordinary response to the crash? Indeed, the belief widely persists in Zimbabwe that it *was* an assassination attempt, and that when Tsvangirai referred to it as being an 'accident', he meant the wrong person had been killed – Susan, not him.

And, of course, who knows what cataclysm still awaits Zimbabwe? As I write this from Brooklyn in the summer of 2009, the power-sharing government, though still together, seems as fractious as ever. What will happen when there's another election? Or another 'accident'.

No one can sift the mud and tea leaves of Zimbabwe's past and accurately predict its future, and I am not about to try. But what I can tell you is what has happened at Drifters since that terrifying visit by the war veterans in June 2008; to the people on and around the farm; and, in the end, to my parents. And perhaps in that you might find your portent.

Brian James, still grieving the loss of his own wife, Sheelagh, remains mayor of Mutare, and a member of the MDC executive committee. A white farmer running the third largest city in Zimbabwe is something to behold. The day he was inaugurated at the Mutare Civic Centre was emotional and inspiring: a dozen black city councillors cheering and singing as they carried him aloft to the mayoral chair.

The political fugitives Misheck Kagurabadza and the two Ps, Prosper Mutseyami and Pishai Muchauraya, have finally taken their seats in Parliament. A year ago they were on the run for their lives; today they represent their districts in a Parliament in which the MDC holds a narrow majority.

Another remarkable event.

Miss Moneypenny is still in Mutare, but no longer in the money-dealing game. Legalisation of the US dollar put an end to that. To those who know her, however, her legend is greater than ever. During the aborted election re-run she threw caution to the wind and became a financial facilitator for the MDC's campaign in the east, risking her life to change foreign currency into trunkloads of Zimbabwe dollars for the MDC to use for food, vehicles, fuel and campaign funds. The risk of reprisals were considerable, and in the end it came to nothing. But Moneypenny is a dynamo, and I suspect she'll find a new game. She still has her balloon-making factory and her golf.

Of the tenants at Drifters, Piet and Mienkie de Klerk are still there, as is Hammy Hamilton, who remarried in early 2009. Dawson and Patricia also remain; their baby daughter Natalie, born in a Mutare hospital, will be one in November. Dawson is working for the same NGO, and Patricia is still teaching, now at the Dominican Convent in Mutare. Since the formation of the Gnu, teachers and civil servants are being paid once more, schools are re-opening and she no longer considers herself a 'social worker'.

Stephen, Tsitsi and Donelle Matongo are there, too, but, tragically, Trevor Matongo, Margaret's oldest son, is no longer. Trevor was killed in a car accident in February 2009. His wife, Zondile, and son Romeo remain in the same cottage, though, and Zondile now assists Margaret in running the Matongo butchery, named 'Romeos', after her son. A few months after Trevor died, Zondile produced another baby, a girl.

As I write this, Tendai Simbabure continues to run Drifters, although for how much longer I cannot say. He took a lease on the chalets in early 2009, but with dollarisation prices are high, and business poor. Few people can afford a trip out of town, a drink in the bar or a session on a mattress with a small house.

And, of course, since the military crackdown on Marange, there are no more diamond dealers like Fatso to rely on.

When I got word that Tendai was struggling, I sent him a note. I told him that my book about my parents and the farm was almost finished, and that it would come out in South Africa by the end of the year. I told him that people there might read about him one day, read about what he did here, and maybe they would want to come visit, meet him and stay at the camp. I reminded him of his dreams for the 2010 World Cup, of importing a big-screen TV to show games on the lawns of the lodge, just as they did in Germany in 2006. I said I would even help him import the big screen. But it is three months since I sent that note, and I have not heard back. I hope he manages to get the business going again.

As for the two Johns and Naomi, they're still there, too. But they have new jobs now. They are employed as coffee roasters for a growing family concern in the valley that sells medium-roast Arabica beans to restaurants and hotels in Harare. With the legalising of foreign currency, the owners of the business get paid in American dollars and the Johns earn good money by local standards. I hear that a gleam has returned to Agoneka's smile. He has a new child now, too: a baby brother for Tariro and Confidence named Divine.

And so, what of my parents? Did they come out of darkness, into the light?

Well, hard as it is for me to believe, as I write this, they are indeed still there, still in their home and on their land, holding on as, it seems to me, they've been doing forever.

Their telephone only takes incoming calls these days, but I speak to them regularly, and once a month Grace (now pregnant with our second child), Madeline and I Skype them and get to see them on our computer screen. I sent a laptop computer out to my Dad last year, and he drives around Mutare in his truck, screen open on his lap, looking for an unsecured wireless signal. Usually he gets one in a parking lot opposite an office block on Herbert Chitepo Road, a few blocks north of the Dairy Den.

We last spoke during the nerve-shredding rugby series between the Springboks and the British and Irish Lions. Dad watched the games with Oom Piet, of course. 'Christ,' he told me after the Second Test, 'I haven't shat myself so much since the bloody war vets were here. Piet nearly had a heart attack. Do those players know what they're doing to us?'

My parents don't get to see the two Ps, Pishai and Prosper, much any more, but they receive regular phone and e-mail updates from them on their progress in Parliament, and they remain, according to my mother, heroic optimists.

My father did buy Pishai his first suit in the end, which he now wears to Parliament. Well, Dad didn't really *buy* it. He couldn't afford to *buy* Pishai a suit. But he knew a man at Drifters who he might be able to barter one off: Hammy Hamilton. Hammy was a committee man, after all – all those Commercial Farmers Union meetings he used to attend. Dad went to see him in Cottage 8, and it turned out Hammy did indeed have a new suit: a sober, charcoal grey pinstripe that he was prepared to trade.

'What you want for it?' Dad asked.

Hammy thought about it for a while. 'A six-pack of Windhoek, Lyn.'

'Sounds reasonable, Hammy. You'll have your beer next week.'

And so a black MDC MP attends Parliament in the suit of a white Zimbabwean farmer who lost his land. 'I don't know what that means,' says Dad, 'but I like the sound of it.'

Remarkably, my mother has a passport now, too, and for that she can thank her new Member of Parliament, Misheck Kagurabadza. She told Misheck her problem and he paid a visit with her to the passport office one morning and cracked some heads.

'It was quite impressive,' she recalls. 'He marched in there and asked them who was in charge. Of course, no-one was. They were all just sitting around doing nothing. Well, he told them that if they expected the Gnu to continue paying their fancy salaries, they had better start jumping around and do some work.'

A month later my mother had her document. She is, once again, a Zimbabwean citizen.

Now it is my father who has passport troubles. Not Zimbabwean ones – South African ones. Soon after the Citizenship Act came in, he opted to let go of his Zimbabwe passport and keep his South African one, in case they needed that as a bolt-hole. But now the South African government had declared him a non-resident alien, and when his document expires in November, *he* will be stateless. 'It never rains it pours,' groans Mom.

They are, however, healthy, busy and, in the scheme of things, lucky to be alive. They also have a new game now which is bringing them a little money at last: coffee roasting, the same business that the two Johns are employed in. In 2006, my father bought a second-hand, charcoal-heated coffee roaster and installed it in the outhouse where he had once stashed his marijuana supply. He made a few modifications to the machine, and it can now produce 150 kilos of medium-roast coffee beans a day. Coffee, it turned out, was a much better bet for them than dagga. In fact, according to Mom: 'It's a much better bet than chickens, wine, tourism and every other hairbrained scheme your father has come up with over the years.'

They buy green Arabica beans from friends of theirs in the Vumba Mountains who somehow managed to keep hold of a section of their coffee farm. The Two Johns roast and pack the beans in the outhouse, and Mom and Dad deliver them to Harare twice a month. Incredibly, they are getting new orders all the time. Who could have known when they bought that machine that they would one day have one of only four functioning coffee roasters in the country? In fact, visit a hotel or restaurant in Zim-babwe today, and it's likely the coffee you order has been roasted by the two Johns at Drifters, and supplied by my parents. Even my sister Stephanie has a coffee shop in Harare now, not far from my old school, Prince Edward, selling their Vumba roast.

And yet my parents are under no illusions. They've seen too much in their lives to believe that this is the end of the nightmare, or that what will follow will be paradise.

'What do you reckon, Rosalind,' Dad asks my mother when they walk through the hills on the back of the land and gaze down on the camp, the cottages and the valley. 'Is this place on the way up or down?'

My mother smiles to herself, but she says nothing.

She had a depressing reminder of the unpredictability of it all when she walked into the kitchen a few months ago and found her albino frog spread-eagled on the kitchen floor, perfectly dead, as if he had taken a dive off the egg rack. 'I keep looking out for a relative or his reincarnation to turn up,' she told me, 'but so far, nothing.'

And, for all they've been through together, they still have very different views on tactics, on staying alive and on facing the future. Just the other night the telephone rang and my mother answered it.

'Hello,' said the voice. 'I'm calling from Cape Town. Is that Drifters?' 'What's left of it,' Mom said.

'Do you have a room?'

'It's not what it used to be,' she warned.

'I'm coming up on business next week. Can I make a reserva-tion?'

'Well, as I say, it's a little bit run down…'

Dad heard her from the kitchen.

'Come on, Rosalind!' he bellowed. 'Have some faith here. It's open. Tell him to come.'

Mom rolled her eyes. Then she took the man's booking and gave him directions.

'Drifters ... the Harare Road ... 19 kilometres outside Mutare ... Hopefully we'll still be here.'

GLOSSARY

bakkie: a small pick-up truck or van
chef: chief (slang)
chimurenga: revolutionary struggle
CID: Criminal Investigation Department
CIO: Central Intelligence Organisation
gandanga: guerrilla or soldier (slang)
Green Bombers: youth militia
gweja: diamond digger (slang)
kanjani: hello
mahure: prostitutes
MDC: Movement for Democratic Change
mujiba: young collaborator
ngoda: diamond, diamond dealer (slang)
pungwe: late-night political rally
sadza: maize porridge
sekuru: grandfather
shamwari: friend
UANC: United African National Congress
UDI: Unilateral Declaration of Independence
ZANLA: Zimbabwe African National Liberation Army
ZANU: Zimbabwe African National Union
ZANU-PF: Zimbabwe African National Union – Patriotic Front
ZAPU: Zimbabwe African People's Union
ZESA: Zimbabwe Electricity Supply Authority
zhula: gem diamond (slang)
ZIPRA: Zimbabwe People's Revolutionary Army

ACKNOWLEDGEMENTS

This book would not have been possible without the cooperation of my parents and all of the staff and tenants at Drifters over the years. This is their book, their story, and while I don't expect them to agree with everything in it, I hope I have done them justice.

I'm particularly grateful to my parents, who answered several hundred e-mail, telephone and taped interview questions over the years, and then helped research and edit the book. My beautiful sisters Stephanie, Sandra and Helen were also always there for me. Thanks to Stuart, Holly and Michael Ingram, Marion Cundall, Melanie Hillebrand and Karen and Roland Rogers for family information that still surprises me.

My agent, Heather Schroder, who phoned me within minutes of my daughter, Madeline, being born to say she wanted to represent the book, never let me down. Neither did John Glusman, my editor at Crown, who took a leap of faith in buying it at a time when Zimbabwe was a little-known story. In the UK I would like to thank Vanessa Webb and Rebecca Nicolson, my editor and publishers at Short Books, and Elizabeth Sheinkman and Felicity Blunt, agents at Curtis Brown.

I'm grateful to the gracious Dennis Pinto of Micato Safaris, who arranged a stay for me at Singita Grumeti Reserves in Tanzania, where I honed the idea for the book. Several friends helped me shape the proposal that followed. Thanks to Melanie Thernstrom, David Evanier, Andrew McCarthy, Julie Merson, Vanessa Mobley and Tom Downey.

When the writing began, Karen and Damian Chmelar lent me their home on Shelter Island, New York, where the first chapters slowly came to life. Later, through my sister-in-law, Alison Rice, in Cape Cod, Didi and Mike McKimmey lent me their house in

Barnstable Village, where I completed the final third of the book. In between, my desk at the Writers Room in Manhattan was my second home.

In mining precious details for the story, Jacob Ginsburg of Bard College transcribed some twenty hours of taped interviews – a thankless task that he performed with great dedication. Sydney Saize in Zimbabwe, and Terence Mukupe, Simba Mhungu and Chris Showalter in New York, assisted with Shona translations. Andrew and Gary Pattenden, Eric Cross, John Worswick and Sandawana gave me valuable insight into Zimbabwe's voodoo land and economic policies, as did Geoff Hill, author of *What Happens After Mugabe*, and Professor Ian Taylor. Alistair Ford in London advised me on the illegal diamond trade. And thanks – and *ẓhulas* – to Farai T.

For those who assigned me stories in Africa that allowed me to travel back to Zimbabwe, I am eternally grateful. In London, Tessa Boase, Tim Jepson, Graham Boynton and Jessamy Calkin at the *Telegraph*; and Andy Pietrasik at the *Guardian*; in New York, the classy Heidi Mitchell at *Travel & Leisure* and then *Town & Country*, and the author Kate Sekules at *Culture & Travel*. Kate also commissioned Stefan Ruiz to take photographs. Stefan's extraordinary portraits of the characters who appear in this book can be seen on my website douglasrogers.org, where this story continues. Thanks to the brilliant Karol Nielson at Epiphany for assigning me my first literary non-fiction story on my parents.

Many friends contributed to the editing of various drafts. The author and journalist James Zug at times knew more what this book should be about than I did. I am indebted to him for his guidance and encouragement, and for the invaluable reading list he gave me, most importantly Laurie Lee's *As I Walked Out One Midsummer Morning* – for my money, the most beautiful travel memoir ever written. Gavin Heron spent valuable time he didn't have editing the first draft of the manuscript. Judith Matloff,

Rebecca Kenan, Jonny Steinberg, Michael Soussan and the inspirational Charlie Graeber all gave great advice along the way. Thanks also to two heroic Zimbabwean exiles, Gerry Jackson, of SW Radio Africa in London, and Annabel Hughes in Virginia, for their generosity and wry wit.

At Short Books I would like to thank Emily Fox for her design for the cover.

In New York my close friend and consigliere Tom Coleman was not only an early and consistent cheerleader for the book, but also enlisted the brilliant Ahmer Kalam who designed the frog cover concept for my website and blog. Alex Erasmus, Mike Long, Sandy Stokes, Deon Hug, Hermann Niebuhr, Michael and Kathy Kirvan gave invaluable support, and Sam Erickson took my mug shot.

Finally, I owe my wife, Grace, an enormous debt. Having listened to me *talk* about writing a book for years, she then supported me all the way while doing it. She edited several drafts of the proposal and manuscript, too, and has, without doubt, the finest eye for the structure of a story I have ever seen. She has my respect, admiration and deepest love.

As I write this in the summer of 2009, my parents are still on their land. Their situation remains precarious, however, as it does for all the other remaining white farmers and their workers in Zimbabwe. I would encourage anyone who reads this book to visit Zimbabwe and, if they can, visit Drifters. Pull up a stool, order a beer and tip handsomely.

Douglas Rogers
BROOKLYN
AUGUST 2009

Douglas Rogers is an award-winning journalist and travel writer. He was born and raised in Zimbabwe and now lives in Brooklyn, New York. Visit him at douglasrogers.org or email him at douglas@douglasrogers.org